The Hidden Worlds of Polynesia

Also by Robert C. Suggs

THE ISLAND CIVILIZATIONS OF POLYNESIA
MODERN DISCOVERIES IN ARCHAEOLOGY
LORDS OF THE BLUE PACIFIC

Contents

List of Maps and Illustrations

Prologue

On a black, dismally wet winter evening in 1956, a group of graduate students were gathered in the physical anthropology laboratory of Columbia University's Department of Anthropology. Outside the laboratory windows in the sooty night, muffled bits and snatches of the conversation of passersby mingled with the clamor of engines, brakes, and horns, punctuated by the periodic deep roars of asthmatic buses. Students and traffic hurried along in the bleak neon light of the snack shops and bookstores as the evening's round of classes began.

These graduate students, myself among them, were awaiting the convening of a class in "An Introduction to Methods of Physical Anthropology" taught by Dr. H. L. Shapiro, Chairman of the Anthropology Department of the American Museum of Natural History. For weeks we had absorbed the skillfully presented information on the evolution of the human organism, studying carefully the development of each bone of man's skeleton, comparing it with its cognate bones in the lower primates, and examining the differences in the configuration of this bone among the races of man.

We were examining some mounted skeletons ranged along one wall of the room when Dr. Shapiro entered, carrying the blue cloth sack containing his notes and lecture materials. He drew me aside for a moment, to ask me with a smile what I intended to do that summer. I replied that I had intended to continue with excavations begun the previous summer on prehistoric Indian campsites in coastal Connecticut.

Dr. Shapiro, who was well acquainted with my Connecticut project, smiled broadly as I finished. "How would you like to do some archaeology in the Pacific?" he asked. I could hardly believe that I heard correctly. As in a dream, I heard his voice describe the work that he was planning: we would be going on an American Museum Expedition to the Marquesas Islands of French Polynesia to survey the archaeological remains of that archipelago, a remote but beautiful group of seven inhabited and three currently deserted lofty, volcanic islands situated on the very eastern border of Polynesia, about 9 degrees south of

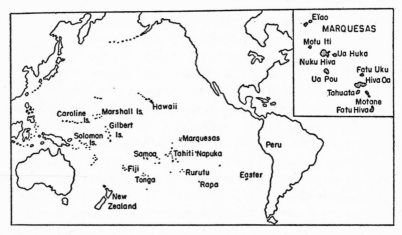

Map of Pacific, showing location of Marquesas and other major Polynesian island groups in relation to Asia and America.

the equator and some four thousand miles due west of the Ecuadorian coast of South America. The expedition was to be made under the patronage of Mr. and Mrs. Cornelius Crane of Ipswich, Massachusetts, who would join us in the Marquesas. I would go before the main party, to reconnoiter the islands for outstanding archaeological sites. Very few intelligible notes went into my notebook during that evening's class as a swirl of mental images, evoked from my anthropological reading on Polynesian cultures, shut out Dr. Shapiro's exposition of the fine points of the construction of the human nasal bones.

The commuter's train could not move fast enough for me that night, but I covered the distance between the station and my house in record time and poured out the whole story to my wife, Rae, even before I took off my coat. We talked long into the night about it, and decided to curb our excitement so that a change in plans would not bring disappointment.

Four months later, still feeling a certain disbelief, I was aboard the schooner *Te Vega*, heading for Tahiti. A few weeks more, and I stood on the wildly heaving deck of a particularly unseaworthy copra boat in the fresh dawn of a tropical winter's morning to see the veined cliffs of the island of Fatu Hiva towering ahead—there were the Marquesas, at last.

The survey was to begin on Nuku Hiva, the main island of the northern Marquesas, where we finally dropped anchor after a long tour of the southern islands. In the months that followed, I visited every part of Nuku Hiva with my capable native companion, Tunui, checking and investigating all the archaeological sites known to the natives. The archaeological opportunities of the Marquesas were fantastic—we were seldom, if ever, out of sight of some relic of the ancient Marquesan culture. Through all the valleys were scattered clusters of ruined house platforms: huge rectangular constructions that had supported the high-gabled wood and thatch houses of the natives of the past. Overgrown with weeds, half tumbled down beneath the weight of toppled trees and the pressure of the inexorable palm roots, these ancient village sites were sources of stone axes, carved stone pestles, skulls, and other sundry curios which the natives sold to the tourists. Among the village sites were the rectangular ceremonial plazas, hundreds of feet long, set on raised terraces. These, with the now ruined house-like temples, had been the pivot points of Marquesan ceremonial life. High up in the cliffs that bordered each deep isolated valley were burial caves containing the remains of the population of centuries past. After death, corpses had been allowed to rot until the bones could be cleaned and collected. They were then wrapped in bundles and placed in caves, which were generally in very dangerous locations, for the protection of the remains from intruders who might desecrate them. In the rolling green hills of the central plateau of Nuku Hiva we traced the lines of ancient fortifications built along strategic ridges. On the ground around the banks and trenches

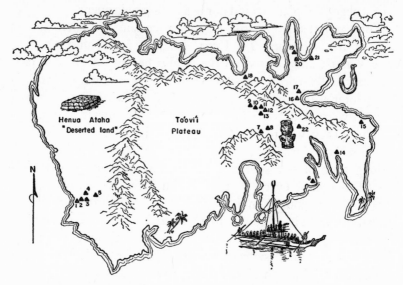

Nuku Hiva. Location of major archaeological sites marked by numbered triangles:

1, 2, 3. Rock shelters in cliffs, Ue'a Valley

4, 5. Small hamlets at the head of Ue'a Valley

6. Cave of the Warrior Band, Hapa'a coast

7, 8. Large fortifications overlooking Taiohae Valley

9. *Tohua* Te'ivi'ohou, Taipi Valley

10. Temple of Peupeu, Taipi Valley

11. *Tohua* Vahangeku'a, Taipi Valley

12. *Tohua* Tepakeho, Taipi Valley

13. *Tohua* Te Uhi'atea, Taipi Valley

14. Ho'oumi beach site

15. Sleeping cave in Ha'a'au'a'i Valley

16, 17. Ha'atuatua beach site (two major locations)

18. *Tohua* Hikoku'a, Hatiheu Valley

19. Adze-factory site, Ha'ata'ive'a

20. Quarry workers' houses, Te A'avehie and Ha'ata'ive'a

21. Red-tuff quarry, Ha'ata'ive'a

22. Ancient hamlet at Ha'i'ie'ia, Taipi Valley

of these imposing military works were found the spent projectiles of another age's "ultimate weapon"—the polished stones for the Marquesan war slings. We collected skulls and ancient stone tools exposed on the surface. Little children often brought their treasured stone adzes to me in return for candy or a yard of cloth. Their elders also engaged in this barter, but drove much harder bargains.

Amid all this wealth of antiquities it was difficult not to be skeptical of the comment on Marquesan archaeological possibilities made by an anthropologist some years ago who, after spending some time in the Marquesas, had decided that nothing was to be gained by attempting excavations, implying that all that was of value was on the surface. It was not long before my contrary ideas about this pronouncement were vindicated; the earth of the Marquesas, in fact, contained a treasure trove. Checking on a native's story that "pig bones" had been found in large quantities on the beach of the depopulated valley of Ha'atuatua, we found an entire village site, opened to our view by a tidal wave that had partially cut away the beach dunes. Human bones, not pig bones, littered a burial area, and hundreds of artifacts were washing out of the face of the bank. On the western end of Nuku Hiva, in the valley of Ue'a, we found three caves with miraculously dry interiors, in which had been preserved not only the usual durable stone and bone tools but also a wide range of wooden objects, hand-braided coconut cords, pieces of loincloth, and even fish scales from fish caught centuries before.

At the end of our field work in 1956, after excavating the Ue'a caves and sampling the extensive village of Ha'atuatua, we packed up countless sacks of carefully labeled artifacts and skeletons, and sailed away on the *Te Vega* to Tahiti and home, leaving a tremendous amount of excavating still to be done. Our digging had given us only a brief glimpse of what was there, but time ruled out any further immediate work.

When the crates containing our finds arrived in New York, we unpacked them eagerly, and the process of preparation and study of the specimens only whetted my appetite for a second opportunity to delve into the Marquesan past.

We had found much that was vitally interesting, but we also needed more data to make a complete picture. There appeared to be little resemblance between the culture represented in the deposits of the Ue'a caves and that uncovered on the Ha'atuatua beach. This difference had to be explained. Did it represent the existence of two separate groups of people or of a great span in the dates of the sites? What was the meaning of some strange un-Polynesian-looking tools found at Ha'atuatua?

Another problem that demanded solution was that of the apparently nonexistent relationship between the huge stone masonry structures and the sites which we dug on which no masonry structures existed, and in which the implements differed from those found around the stone buildings.

With Dr. Shapiro's aid, I re-embarked for the Marquesas in 1957, this time with my wife. What follows is the account of our archaeological investigations, our daily lives with the natives, and—most important—the chronicle of Marquesan society that our work revealed, spanning the years from the second century before Christ to A.D. 1958, through the rise, decline, and near-obliteration of a vital culture.

It is my sincere hope that the lay reader of this book will leave it with an appreciation of the fascinating subject of archaeology: not merely an appreciation of the thrill of making an exciting find, but of the whole method of the science, from the excavations in the field through the analysis of the finds to the final interpretations. There is much more to archaeology than the mere finding of statues, tombs, and temples; the fitting together of the little scraps of evidence is often more fascinating than the actual excavation. No amount of intuition can ever replace the laborious process of interpretation, which enables one to discern the significance of innocuous-looking bits of bone or stone, or the contents of an ancient garbage heap.

My reason for describing, in a popular scientific work, our relations with the modern Marquesans is to indicate the kinds of experience an anthropologist may have who is trying to do his projected task in an alien culture and at the same time maintain good personal relations with a group of people who act, speak, and think in a completely different fashion from himself. This is a very important but seldom discussed aspect of archaeology and field anthropology.

Secondly, I believe that the living natives are fully as interesting as the ancient stone buildings and crumbling tools that I removed from the Marquesan earth. The living Marquesans cannot be separated from their dead ancestors' culture; instead, they represent the culmination of the entire drama of Marquesan prehistory and history.

My attention is given to the modern natives in an attempt to correct the Hollywood-American tourist stereotype of the "carefree, friendly native." This image of an inarticulate, intellectually and emotionally undeveloped, wanton child is not only offensive but also false. Beneath the smiling exteriors are human beings as loaded with cares, tensions, hostilities, and anxieties as any others. The fact that the causes for such tensions and hostilities are different from ours does not make them unworthy of our consideration.

Let us now turn to the subject of Polynesian prehistory, beginning with a brief summary of the scientific evidence thus far accumulated on the general subject, before we turn our attention specifically to Marquesan prehistory.

For millennia, the islands which we know collectively as Polynesia in the central and eastern Pacific remained secure from the effects of the activities of man, that ultimate modifier of natural landscapes. Far from the coast of Asia, broadcast over the surface of the calm sea, these heaps of volcanic rock and coral were visited only by birds and sea creatures.

So it continued until, probably in the second millennium before Christ, the charmed endurance of geologic time was broken, for men arrived from out of the western sea, down the blazing trail of the sunset, in long, low canoes slicing swiftly through the swells, mat sails well filled with breeze. These men, ancestors of the modern Polynesians, had arrived in the vast spaces of the eastern Pacific by virtue of a knowledge of shipbuilding and the sea that was to be unequaled in the world for many centuries thereafter. Their migrations into the nether reaches of the Pacific represent a great step forward in man's struggle to conquer his environment and force it to work for him. The distances covered by these bronzed sailor-explorers in their double canoes of pegged and lashed planks are not to be lightly undertaken today in boats of similar size with far superior equipment. Even within the Polynesian region itself, the distance between some of the islands is more than a thousand miles. This region can be enclosed in a giant triangle inscribed on the surface of the Pacific, with its apex at the Hawaiian chain and its base angles at New Zealand on the southwest and Easter Island on the southeast, the base being some four thousand miles long, and its altitude about six thousand.

Where had the rugged sailors come from who chanced into this area some four thousand years before the arrival of the Europeans? Although precise dates and locations are impossible to give in the current state of our studies in Polynesian prehistory, we can nonetheless make certain statements on the basis of the accumulated years of research that have gone into this problem. In forming our hypothesis as to Polynesian origins, we must draw on evidence from many fields of scientific endeavor in support of the information gleaned by archaeological research. We must draw on the work of linguists who have studied the Polynesian languages; physical anthropologists who have analyzed data on Polynesian physique and genetics; cultural anthropologists and their descriptions of rituals, political organizations, and religion; and a host of others such as botanists, zoologists, bacteriologists, and oceanographers, each for their contributions to the elucidation of this problem. In another volume * much of this evidence has been presented in detail: all that is required here is a brief summary of scientific findings.

* R. C. Suggs: *The Island Civilizations of Polynesia*, Mentor, New York, 1960.

To find the origins of the Polynesians we must go to the coast of what is now South China, about 2200 B.C. Here, a group of tribes were dwelling along the coast and in the river valleys, their existence dependent on livestock raising (pigs), fishing, shell fishing, and garden agriculture. Adaptation to their environment had made them excellent sailors. In the archaeological explorations on sites of ancient villages inhabited by people of these tribes on Hong Kong, Formosa, and in the Hoifeng area of South China, many tools have been found that are reminiscent of those used by the Polynesians up to a century ago. In both areas, stone adzes of similar highly characteristic shapes are most common. Also frequently found are various ornaments, pottery, stone fighting clubs, and more mundane woodworking tools such as stone files and knives which also have counterparts in tools of the Polynesian cultures of four thousand years later.

These people evidently all spoke dialects of a common language, Malayo-Polynesian, which has been partially reconstructed by painstaking scientific study over the years. The languages of the Polynesians are offshoots, many times removed, from this original language community, as are those of the Philippines, the Melanesian islands, Indonesia, the Marianas, and the Micronesian islands. Even today a small remnant population of Malayo-Polynesian speakers exists on Formosa. The Thai and some other languages of southeast Asia are also indirectly related to the Polynesian.

Physically, the ancestors of the modern Polynesians may have been a stabilized racial admixture of old Asian Caucasoid stock (such as that currently visible in the Ainu of Japan) with elements of Mongoloid stock and Oceanic Negro. Of this race that existed on the China coast during the period in question, remnants survived until long afterward. One might hypothesize, according to a well-known anthropological principle, that the true eastern Polynesians of today resemble more closely the original Asian coast population of four thousand years ago; but we are not able to be precise about this without considerably more archaeological evidence in the form of well-preserved, dated skeletons than we now have.

How long this population existed, spread along the coast of China, it is impossible to say, but by 2200 B.C. some changes in the local situation had probably begun to occur. In the North China plain of the Huang Ho, the first Chinese state was rising out of the consolidation of the earth-walled neolithic villages which had thrived there earlier. Under the Hsia and later Shang dynasties this state began to spread its influence in all directions. By dint of a well-organized governmental, religious, and military hierarchy it was able to expand at the expense of its less powerful and often primitive neighbors. To the cultured Shang people with their precious stones, beautiful, strangely ornamented bronze vessels, and newly devised writing system, such people must have seemed barbaric.

The development of the first Chinese state to the north of the early Malayo-Polynesians probably caused widespread disorder as unabsorbed tribes fled from the Shang sphere of influence, displacing other groups in their flight and resettlement. This chaotic condition finally spread to the South China coastal groups, which reacted by moving, although no mass migrations of thousands of canoes at a time took place, as has sometimes been suggested. Primitive population movements seldom involve mass movements or even unidirectional ones. It is quite probable that the departure of the Malayo-Polynesians from South China took place over a number of years with various small social units moving away to offshore islands or down the coast, returning to depart again, but in general gradually vacating their home territory.

The routes of migration followed by the Malayo-Polynesians in their departure from the Asian coast will probably never be precisely known, owing to this haphazard nature of the migration. The archaeology of the western Pacific islands and Southeast Asia can tell us much in general, however, about the pattern of settlement that followed, and the movements of these ancestral Polynesians can be traced by means of the clues they left behind. The characteristic Polynesian-type stone

adzes, ornaments, fighting clubs, etc. are found in the Philippines as well as in Indonesia. It is not clear which area was
settled earlier—perhaps both were settled simultaneously, Indonesia by those who came down the Malay Peninsula, and
the Philippines by voyagers from directly across the inter-
vening sea. Again, the Philippines may have been occupied
first, and served as a springboard for an infiltration south into
the Indonesian islands.

By 1000 B.C., however, there had already been considerable
penetration of the Pacific. The Marianas Islands had already
been occupied, possibly for about a thousand years, by descendants of the South China coast people. Islands of Melanesia—Fiji and New Caledonia—had also been settled by other
branches of the same parent group; the ancestors of the Polynesians were thus brought to the western edge of the Polynesian triangle. From the islands of the Fiji group it is but a
relatively short jump to the Tongan group, so it is quite possible that the western Polynesian islands were discovered quite
early in the first millennium B.C., with settlement following
shortly thereafter. The stage had therefore been set early for
the development of that genus of cultures which the anthropological fraternity today labels Polynesian. The first settlers
in western Polynesia pushed eastward and southward, finding
new islands and implanting settlements which in turn gener-
ated exploring parties to push on farther, thus imparting germs
of the present-day Polynesian cultures. Each of these cultures
is the result of a complex of factors involving the nature of the
island itself as well as the size and relative degree of prepared-
ness of the group. Although the volcanic islands of Polynesia
are broadly similar in terms of soil resources, native flora and
fauna, marine ecology, and weather, each has its own unique
qualities which would necessarily affect the lives of its inhabitants, whether favorably or adversely. The same applies, of
course, to the coral atolls, with their more limited resources.
Thus, each island offered a certain limited range of possibilities for exploitation by the settlers. The settlers themselves, in
turn, could only bring a limited range of abilities to their new

home, since they were not a replica of the parent group. The interplay of these two factors, the island environment and the nature of the settling group, generally determined the subsequent evolutionary direction taken by any given society in Polynesia.

The settlers who beached their canoes on the new-found soil of these islands had some rather difficult and uncertain years before them. There was a great deal of clearing to be done, followed by planting of the slow-maturing coconut and breadfruit trees, establishing the all-important sweet potato and yam patches, planting banana groves, and building terraces for taro. The tasks of building houses and temples simultaneously also faced them. There would have had to be a substantial waiting period before society could be established on a good sound economy, with gardens and groves producing abundantly. Once the adjustments were made and the period of uncertainty was past, however, the growth of the society was in most cases assured. I say "in most cases," for there is some evidence that the settlers of various small marginal islands such as Pitcairn and the tiny Equatorial Islands departed again after residing there for a reasonably long time. The reasons for such departures are not evident, but they may be connected with crop failures or other environmental problems.

By the time the Europeans arrived in the Pacific, the island cultures of Polynesia had developed considerably. The people who greeted Cook, Porter, and others were members of sound, self-sufficient societies numbering into the hundreds of thousands, ruled by an aristocracy of hereditary chiefs (many of whom were considered divine), powerful priests, and warriors, in various combinations.

Their brilliant ceremonials, often featuring overt sexuality of all types, coupled with extremes of pomp and circumstance and numerous human sacrifices, bespoke the power and importance of the priesthood. When they aroused the hostility of the Polynesians, the Europeans often faced hails of polished sling stones and barbed spears released by massed formations of tattooed, paint-smeared warriors advancing to do battle with their feathered plumes and war ornaments of shell and ivory bright against their brown skins.

Evidence of an unusual development of artistic talents, as well as of social structure, was everywhere visible, in the carved shell ornaments, huge wooden figures on temple altars, intricately carved houseposts and canoe prows, handsome feather cloaks and headdresses, and finely decorated utilitarian objects of every variety. The strangely beautiful styles of the various Polynesian cultures have never lost their appeal for Western collectors.

All these things, combined with the overpowering beauty of the islands and the sea, can easily account for the glowing descriptions of the early navigators who set Europe aflame with their tales of the South Seas, thus establishing a series of stereotypes that have endured (with much elaboration, to be sure) to the present day.

But what of the background of these societies that the Europeans of the eighteenth century were fortunate enough to have observed? Until recently, very little was known of their development, even though the general direction of the Polynesian migration had been known for some time and many researchers had indicated Asia as its point of origin. Anthropologists, however, occupied themselves with studying the characteristics of the living societies rather than past ones. As a result, a considerable body of knowledge was accumulated about the social organization, religion, economy, and technology of most of the major existent cultures of Polynesia. These data were all the more valuable because the cultures under study were undergoing more or less rapid changes as a result of the influence of their colonial overlords.

Another reason for the relative lack of information about Polynesian prehistory was that Polynesians abhorred intruders who might attempt to make excavations around the ancient temples, villages, and burial caves of their ancestors. Gruesome supernatural punishments were invoked upon those who meddled with the bones of the dead.

Because of the lack of impressive ruins like those in the

Near East, many archaeologists believed that there was little reason to excavate. In any case, the historical traditions and long genealogies of the Polynesians gave some detailed accounts of their own past, and it was easier to question the older natives who knew these legends than to spend sweaty days rummaging through ruins and incurring the wrath of the local populace. Examinations of the legends and the genealogies convinced some scholars that the Polynesians had arrived in their island homes relatively recently—within the last thousand years at the most. It was assumed that since occupation of these islands was so recent, there would be little for the archaeological excavator to uncover, an assumption astounding in its naïveté.

During the years between the world wars, some studies were made of the ruined temples and house foundations in Tahiti, the Hawaiian Islands, Easter Island, and the Marquesas. More digging was done in New Zealand, but without benefit of the standard scientific controls necessary for reliable reconstruction of long-dead societies.

It was not until after World War II that archaeology in the modern sense arrived in Polynesia and adjacent islands, with scientists probing into the past in Fiji, New Caledonia, New Zealand, and Hawaii. By "archaeology in the modern sense" I mean the scientific methods of recovering from the earth all possible evidences of the human past and reconstructing, as completely as possible, the life of ancient man. Modern archaeology entails careful excavation of village sites, temples, and graves to obtain a full view of the culture. It entails the laborious preservation of all the traces of ancient man, whether they be simple tools of stone, shell, or bone, fragments of rotting cord plaited by long-dead hands, or bits of shellfish exhumed from an ancient garbage dump. The archaeologist wants to know how the members of all classes of the society lived, what grew in their gardens, what their pastimes and religious ideas were.

The first results of the postwar archaeological boom in the Pacific were some rather drastic alterations of many of the old preconceptions about the age of the Polynesian migrations. Rich archaeological deposits were uncovered in the caves and on the beaches of the Hawaiian Islands, indicating that men had been there for a longer period than had been assumed. The myth of Polynesian archaeological sites that are non-existent dies quietly, especially when the new technique of radioactive carbon dating was applied to charcoal scooped from ancient campfires in Polynesia and Melanesia. Anthropologists began to realize the potentialities of a long-neglected area for original research as well as for testing many hypotheses that stood in need of validation.

The archaeological work in the Marquesas described in the following pages was one result of the increased interest in Polynesian prehistory. Since its completion, the archaeologists' spades have broken ground on other hitherto untouched islands. Tahiti and Mangareva were most recently the goals of two separate expeditions, and Tonga has received further attention after initial excavations made there in 1956. Within a decade our knowledge of Polynesian prehistory will have advanced so far as to be overwhelming to a newcomer in the field, and our now dim view of the lengthy saga of Polynesian prehistory will be illuminated by the bright light of scientific fact.

1 / *Nuku Hiva Landfall*

The *Tiare Taporo* rolled and pitched on a choppy gray-black sea. My wife, Rae, and I stumbled about on cramped, aching legs, trying to shake off the chill of a night spent on the quarterdeck in deck chairs, wedged against the ship's rail within reach of the helmsman and the sound of the ship's bell. Although we had huddled under raincoats against the heavy spray and the incessant downpour, our legs and feet had been soaked and morning was a mixed blessing bringing relief from the cold and damp but making further sleep impossible.

The *Tiare* had departed from Tahiti five days previously for the Marquesas Islands, setting a course through the Tuamotu Archipelago of French Polynesia. After five weeks of frustrating delays in Tahiti the departure had become a major goal in our plans and we had settled down aboard, hopeful of a pleasant trip. The *Tiare* herself was a ship that any real canvas sailor would have enjoyed. Built in 1911, this 113-foot two-master had carried copra in the Cook Islands and Samoa under a series of famous captains, among them the well-known Andy Carlson. Her original deck timbers bore the scars of five typhoons. She rode the waves and carried cargo better than any other schooner of the fleet based in Tahiti. It was not unusual to see the *Tiare* riding nose down, with a full hold and her midships loaded solid between the fore and aft deckhouses, with goats and chickens clambering around the forecastle, pigs bobbing and squealing in the davited whaleboats, and about thirty native passengers and their belongings festooned around the roof of the stern deckhouse and the quarterdeck.

The captain of the *Tiare* had no less remarkable a history than the ship. Forty years of storms and calms, landfalls and farewells were engraved on Captain Louis Tapoto's brown face. He had sailed at the age of fourteen as a cabin boy on a large sailing ship and won his master's papers by nineteen, acquiring in the process a fine regard for the pure science of mathematics which he had never lost. In moving from post to post in the hierarchy of command he had accumulated a variety of experience on ships of all types and nationalities, skippering an administration boat for the French government, running rum to Baja California during Prohibition days, and carrying merchandise to isolated islands of the Polynesian triangle. Behind his heavy brow and deep-set eyes reposed a wealth of information that would not be recorded in any pilot book for years to come, if ever, for Louis had learned the pathways of the Pacific by heart rather than by chart, as charts of much of his operating area were generally inaccurate if not absolutely erroneous. In Polynesia, safety depends on knowing a host of data concerning the location of reefs and shoals in the innocent-appearing channels between the low coral atolls of the Tuamotu group, for example, and the appearances of the different islands from various directions. The innumerable correction factors for compass bearings taken on the charts were also a necessary part of this knowledge, for an error of a few degrees in course in some areas would be enough to bring a ship to a grinding halt on the broken-bottle edges of a coral reef. Louis's presence was most reassuring, for he had complete control over a devoted, able crew. Professional attributes aside, Louis had the fine style of a polished raconteur, regaling us at the table with stories from his great range of experience and stimulating discussions on religion, politics, mathematics, women, and literature. He even dabbled in water colors, painting his favorite land- and seascapes as well as other vessels in a unique style which displayed an unusual sensitivity to the atmosphere of the islands.

We passengers aboard the *Tiare* made up a rather random group consisting of the Bishop of the Marquesas, a French gendarme being "out-posted," two Territorial Assembly delegates from the Marquesas, both of whom were French colo-

nels, and a flock of twenty school children of both sexes, returning to the Marquesas for vacation from mission-sponsored
Tahitian boarding schools. My wife and I, accompanied by
John Belmont, a Harvard anthropology student who was to
assist in our work in the Marquesas, had booked first-class
passage through the Tahitian representatives of the *Tiare*'s
owners. "First class" aboard the *Tiare* meant that one had a
bunk—of which there were four aboard, all in the after deckhouse in the room which also served as the dining room. As we
had no mattresses we could not sleep on the roof with the school
children, and as we were burdened with suitcases and cameras
we threw in our lot with the bishop and the gendarme, who
occupied the other two bunks, and we planned to rotate among
the three of us the occupancy of the two bunks that we had
been able to obtain. The decision proved to be a poor one.
We had no sooner got out of placid Pape'ete harbor than all
of our juvenile passengers were afflicted with *mal de mer* almost simultaneously. The bishop, a chronic sufferer from
motion sickness, had wisely gone straight to bed upon coming
aboard, and the messboy was kept busy carrying a large stain-
less steel basin to and from his silent curtained bunk. I experienced a little queasiness myself amid all this indisposition, and
I was glad to see night fall, hoping that a good night's sleep
would refresh everyone. When we entered the cabin, we
found a number of sick children who had decided to spend
the night there, accompanied by the two messboys (who had
pre-empted the benches for the dining table). A few other
passengers had requisitioned the remaining floor space, including that beneath the table, and as I passed the "vater closse"
(as a hopefully bilingual Tahitian friend called the sanitary
facilities) I fully expected to find a few sleepers curled up
even in that snug haven. The "facilities" were an impressive
bit of engineering, formidable to the uninitiated. An array of
pipes, valves, and levers covered one wall of the tiny chamber,
prompting one to contemplate what might be the drastic con-
sequences of using the wrong controls. A small washbasin
and mirror stood in the opposite corner with a recessed rack

above them which held a standard enameled chamber pot. This provision was puzzling until we learned that this was the shower. One undressed, filled the chamber pot with water, and dumped it onto one's head, soaping and rinsing merrily.

We hoisted ourselves into the bunks and tried to settle down for the night with our eleven new roommates, who were already slumbering peacefully. The atmosphere in that fifteen-foot by ten-foot room soon became somewhat oppressive, however; the temperature rose and the distinctive odors of copra and diesel oil which permeate all auxiliary schooners, combined with the odor of unwashed sick children, began to work their subtle witchcraft. Soon we had flung open the ports and opened the bunk curtains, but to no avail; the temperature rose while the atmosphere got worse. Finally, dragging blankets and raincoats, we fled to the deck, where we settled down in beach chairs and spent the rest of that night and every other night during the voyage.

The remainder of the trip passed without incident. With few utensils but a maximum of ingenuity, the short, heavy-set Tahitian cook prepared excellent meat dishes and casseroles, which he himself served, balancing loaded platters in each hand, nonchalantly and nimbly climbing over the canvas-covered mound of cargo amidships to our cabin.

The steerage class, including our school children, did not fare quite so well: three times a day they lined up at the galley entrance, picking up tin plates into which they spooned large helpings of rice and heated canned bully beef, a favorite of the Polynesians—this, topped off with a few chunks of bread and bowls of native coffee served as breakfast, lunch, and supper. They seemed to thrive on this diet, displaying a great amount of excess energy (when not bent over the rail) which they used up in all sorts of pastimes: chasing each other over the ship, watching for islands or sea birds, helping the sailors, or leaning against the filled sails and swaying with the boom.

For a group whose average age was about twelve, the children evidenced a degree of independence and self-reliance not commonly found among children of similar age in our own country. They had no overseers and slept without any safety precautions under a tarpaulin pitched on the deckhouse roof. Such maturity is a direct result of the child-rearing techniques of their culture, which emphasizes the gradual easing of children into adult responsibilities.

After five days of sailing we watched for the landfall that would indicate the end of our voyage and the beginning of a season of intriguing explorations into the Marquesan past. We clambered around the ship waiting for breakfast while the tantalizing vapor of Tahitian coffee drifted up from the galley. The schoolboys sat on the roof of the deckhouse carefully scanning the mist for the first sight of home in a year. Suddenly an arm shot out against the billowing gray sky, followed by more arms and shouts. Looking toward the east, we saw the black shape of the island of Ua Pou rising like a medieval castle above the heavy layer of fog close to the sea, its volcanic spires poking four thousand feet straight up. We were not stopping at Ua Pou, however, but going straight on to Nuku Hiva, the main island of the northern group and seat of the French administration, about twenty miles north. We then began to search the sea ahead for the island that would be our home for nearly a year, joining the boys on their rooftop perch, accompanied by the French gendarme, who was interrogating me in a last hasty effort to compile a vocabulary in the native dialect.

Gradually, we saw the long, serrated outline of Nuku Hiva materialize out of the gray dead ahead, looking like a huge reptilian sea monster sprawled on the surface of the sea with its backbone sharply sculpturing the mist and clouds. As we drew closer the sun began to push through feebly, casting its light on the tumbling dark green mountainsides covered with grass and ferns and streaked with the huge wounds of erosion in the clayey red volcanic soil. The precipitous, rock-bound coastal cliffs of Nuku Hiva repulsed the tireless sea in a line of white foam along the perimeter of the island as far as the eye could see. To the west in the Ue'a Valley was the flat-topped spire of Akipou—the Pillar of the Sky—at the base of which was located the large rock shelter so rich in archaeological specimens where we had broken ground in 1956. On the south coast an abrupt break in the rock ramparts of the island opened into what was apparently a narrow fjord. This was in reality a large hidden bay which in 1914 had accommodated ships of the German naval squadron on their way through the Pacific to their heroic end in the Falkland Islands.

Up the coast, the "Sentinels," small rocky islets at each side of the entrance to Taiohae Bay, stood out clearly.

Escorted by a school of leaping, diving porpoises, we rounded the west Sentinel and entered the calm bay. A few curls of smoke rose from houses scattered along the shore and deep in the acacia and coconut groves of the valley floor. Two fishermen in a solitary outrigger canoe hailed us as we rode past. A few figures appeared on the beach, running and walking, converging on the dock from both sides of the valley.

After what seemed to us an eternity, Louis finally dropped the anchor and the whaleboat. We piled happily into the boat, already heaped high with baggage and crates, heading for shore on the strokes of six hefty oarsmen. The crowd on the dock, consisting mostly of children who had run out of the nearby school to see the new arrivals, had swelled considerably. They stood in a tight group, whispering and peering at our boat and us, as we alighted on the wharf ramp. One phrase was repeated over and over: *"A'a Rope me te vehine"*— There's Robert and his wife!

As we left the dock a familiar figure in denims, a white undershirt, and an Afrika Korps cap appeared on the road. I recognized the familiar walk of my old friend and helper, Tunui, moving up the road at a rapid pace, his face radiant with a smile. He embraced us in greeting, tears running down into the gray stubble of his cheeks. Partings and meetings are times of great emotion for the Polynesians; even a departure for a short routine trip is an occasion for the preparation of flowered wreaths and a great deal of sobbing, embracing, and paternal kissing *en façon française*. The emotional atmosphere of the departure of an individual for a long trip, however, is not far removed from that of a funeral. Tunui, overwhelmed at my departure in 1956, was equally overwhelmed to see me once more, and in displaying his feelings in what Americans consider to be an effeminate fashion he was also showing his prestige in the community, for he alone was privileged to be able to display such emotion. Its dividends were my friendship, the added prestige, and the material gain derived from working with me.

Tunui had worked, as a young man, for the Pacific Entomological Survey sponsored by the Bishop Museum, collecting insects and specimens of the plants in which the insects dwelt. The results of this work, by the British scientists A. M. Adamson and L. Mumford, were published in a series of volumes which are still considered classic studies of the relationships of insects to their environment.

Following his introduction to entomology and botany, Tunui worked for a movie maker, capturing giant rays, sharks, and octopuses for the screen. Subsequently, an opportunity arose for a surveyor's helper who knew the interior of Nuku Hiva, and Tunui got the job, thus beginning the long series of surveying jobs which had made him as knowledgeable about field procedure as the surveyors. During World War II he had talked to Admiral Byrd, who had landed at Taiohae seeking suitable sites for the establishment of American air bases in the Marquesas. Byrd had arranged to have Tunui serve as guide until the time when the Pétainist French governor of the islands flatly refused to allow any Americans ashore. Tunui's offer of co-operation with the United States Navy nearly landed him in the local prison.

Between his scientific project stints, Tunui led the same kind of life as his fellow Marquesans, raising vegetables and livestock, cutting a little copra and making contraband alcohol. Tunui was a man of action. On a horse, he seemed to have grown from the saddle, and he rode with perfect confidence over the most dangerous of the Marquesas' muddy miles of narrow, rock-cluttered paths. In the water, although past fifty, he could dive easily to twenty-five feet, and more than once, when we dove together for fish, he had me at the point of exhaustion. It was Tunui's marksmanship that I found most impressive, however, for despite slight cataracts he made kills over very respectable distances with good regularity. Once he returned from a hunting trip complaining that he had failed to break the neck of a cow with a single shot—at a distance of six hundred meters. He had killed her but failed to hit the vertebral column. When embarking on a trip for some wild beef, he never took more than two cartridges for my Winchester 70. "Why take more?" he would say. "You can only kill one animal on each trip!"

When he came to work for me in 1956, I did not realize the extent and depth of his experience, but I soon came to respect his very considerable accomplishments. Before long he was adept at stratigraphic excavation techniques and had learned to act independently in many aspects of excavation work, such as surveying, stripping levels, preparing excavations for photographs, etc. In any independent traveling that he did, Tunui kept a close lookout for all archaeological sites, often returning from a weekend jaunt with important information.

Although we had made plans to remain for a few days with one of our friends, an elderly Englishman named Bob McKittrick, who ran a store in Taiohae, it was obvious from the beginning that Tunui had no intention of allowing us to stay with anyone but himself. Before we knew it, we were slogging up the muddy path to Tunui's house about a half mile inland, while our baggage was rushed on ahead of us to ensure that we would not escape. The house was situated on a slope dropping away from the main valley road. It consisted of two stilt-supported separate houses built side by side in which the family slept, with a small dining house adjacent and a cook shed open on three sides built off the dining house. Pigs were tied beneath the sleeping houses as well as in the yard. A horse grazed placidly by the line on which some clothes dried, while a flock of chickens jerked and flapped to and fro in search of tidbits. Three vicious-looking dogs lounged about the house; these were Tunui's hunters—Mua (Forward), Mui

(Backward), and Bismarck. Tunui's wife, Tahia, ran out of the cook shed followed by several children and grandchildren. After a round of embracing and shaking hands we were ushered up onto the porch of the main house, which was to be ours. The conversation was rapid-fire; Tahia alternated between complimenting me on my selection of a wife and telling me of her innumerable personal problems which I was to relay to my wife.

News in Polynesia travels with absolutely astounding speed from ear to ear with expectable exaggeration plus some additional ornamentation peculiar to the Marquesan character. It was therefore no surprise that even before we could get rid of our sea legs, a number of people just "happened by," first probably to see if what they had heard was *really* true, but mainly to see how they might fit into the plan of the work that they quite correctly assumed I would be doing. Thus, we soon had a number of offers of horses for sale and hire, on terms easily arranged to fit my needs.

Our plans called for us to proceed from Taiohae Bay to Hatiheu on the north coast of Nuku Hiva. There we were to set up a base of operations from which we would work the rich site in Ha'atuatua, several miles away, and investigate other promising sites on the north coast. We wished to obtain additional information from this site, and were quite prepared to spend a rather long period probing the secrets of this large area. The very unusual character of many of the ancient artifacts which we had found made me believe that we were dealing here with the remains of a very ancient society.

As soon as we could get Tunui alone for a while we discussed our plans, our requirements for horses and personnel, shelter in Hatiheu, and the all-important topic of Tunui's pay. Our projected timetable was subjected to some alterations at once, however, when Tunui stated that no one would be available before the Bastille Day celebration. None of his compatriots would leave their home valleys so soon before an event of this magnitude; the contraband alcohol had to be made, and the workmen would want to enter the competition for the most decorative drinking stand. This hotly contested event was quite close to the hearts of everyone, especially since the prizes, donated by the administrator, could be taken either in cash or in demijohns of wine. Needless to say, little cash ever changed hands. Tunui himself was willing to follow me wherever I went. He sincerely hoped, however, that I would stay, for he felt the need to lift a glass or two (no more!) with friends, and anyway my wife would certainly not want to miss the festivities.

It would have provoked a major rift to depart under such conditions, so we remained in Taiohae. Determined to make the best of the lost time, we went out in the rain every morning, climbing up into the valley to investigate reported burial caves in the rugged talus deposit at the base of the huge basalt cliff that formed the valley head, and examined the numerous stone masonry ruins that filled the valley. These impressive platforms and terraces were built by the Marquesans for a variety of purposes, some of which are not yet clear. Some of the stones used in construction weigh several tons each, which is astonishing when one reflects that the stone moving was done over the rugged Marquesan terrain without the aid of wheels or domesticated animals.

The annual bacchanal of Bastille Day drew close and the valley was vibrant, the anticipation being heightened in certain quarters by the news that a French frigate and a gunboat would be present for the period.

Evenings, the pressure lamps burned late and bright in the thatched shed by the wharf. There, seated around the carved roof posts, the musicians of Taiohae rehearsed for their stint in the dancing and singing competitions, and much effort was expended on the construction of bigger and better drinking stands; now that everyone knew the French Navy would assist at the celebration, profits were insured. Every inhabited house in the valley was filled to capacity as relatives of varying degrees of kinship moved in to enjoy the prerogatives that strongly kinship-oriented social organization can give. Two warships floated at anchor in the bay, while their crews came ashore for the solemn inauguration ceremony at the monument to French military personnel fallen during the occupation and colonization of the islands. During the speeches and flag raising, the sailors stood by, under arms, while the natives scrutinized them, making sundry observations, in Marquesan, of a highly personal nature about their individual hygienic practices, their sexual behavior, and the general appearance of their ships.

After this sober beginning, the party erupted. Wine demijohns poured out an endless stream, and the booths were jammed. Before long, some uncertainty was noticeable in the gaits of both natives and sailors as they toddled from one booth to another quaffing wine and beer alternately. By noon, the whole affair had gathered so much momentum that all the athletic events were called off—the contestants almost universally declaring themselves incapacitated. The sailors, less unfit, had obtained several horses, which they took turns riding up and down the damp road around the wharf until they exhausted them; they hung from the horses singly and in pairs, their boats and "white undress" uniforms covered with mud and purple stains. By sundown a number of weaker individuals of both the French and Marquesan contingents had left this plane of consciousness, and lay scattered here and there on the dewy grass in various unlikely poses. The hard core of survivors had settled down to a steady consumption rate, while others who had yet to participate in the dancing and singing recruited their strength.

The dances commenced with the arrival of the administrator and the ships' officers, who took seats of honor in the center of one end of the dance area, while the audience stood around the perimeter. Each large valley on Nuku Hiva had entered a team of young men and women in the competition, and teams from Ua Huka and Ua Pou, two neighboring islands, had also arrived. The Taiohae team began, appearing in grass skirts and head wreaths, the girls all sporting new bras from the Chinese trader's store. Some of the dancers looked shaky; others showed signs, in the form of puffed lips and bruised cheeks, of having engaged in violent behavior. Despite these embarrassments, the group lined up and began their dances, all of which were accompanied by group singing of Tahitian or Tuamotuan hit tunes popular throughout French Polynesia. As the mission had long ago banned native singing and dancing in the Marquesas, most of the dances were not holdovers from the pagan past but revised versions of Samoan and Tahitian dances, and some Yankee sailors' hornpipes. The words of the accompanying songs were relatively unchanged from the Tahitian originals, except in some minor stock phrases that were altered to fit the present circumstances and wish the governor and his principal guests a happy Bastille Day. At one point, however, a few glimpses of the old Marquesan appeared, when the ancient *ru'u* chants and the *maha'u* or pig dance were presented. The words of the *ru'u* are very ambiguous, seeming almost nonsensical at times, but the average Marquesan knows their implications well enough. They are largely obscene or derogatory (or both) in nature and they exist by the thousands, for *ru'u* are made up for many occasions, or just for fun. The meaning, hidden by elaborate symbolism or circumlocution, is further camouflaged by the use of a set of linguistic conventions, involving sound changes and alterations of grammatical structure. The Taiohae dance team stood that night before their French guests and performed a beautiful series of these chants, with camouflaged obscene hand motions which were often directed at the administrator himself. He smiled indulgently at it all as his native interpreter whispered the literal, innocuous, at times inane translations into his ear. The dancers depended on the interpreter to help them with their little bit of clean fun, which he did. These bawdy chants were sung slowly and monotonously in a minor key and with absolutely solemn countenances. They resembled passages from Gregorian liturgy, and served admirably the purpose of poking fun at the Marquesans' masters. When the singers launched into the *maha'u*, in which the male singers imitate the sounds of rutting wild boars, the dance leader moved to within a few yards of the administrator, flashed a pleasant smile, and danced a short solo, graced with very graphic and unmistakable little movements.

When all the performances were finished, the dancers and the audience intermingled. The red wine flowed inexhaustibly. We stood for a while, watching the drinking and the dancing in the big copra warehouse, where pompoms adorned nearly all the other heads, then decided to call it an evening.

The next morning, the zest of the first day had dissipated, but the drinkers were still there. As the French naval detachment, clad in shorts, T-shirts, huaraches, and the inevitable pompoms, marched up the hill to the flagpole to raise the tricolor, the besotted and bruised onlookers made comments that were far more vitriolic than those of the previous day. Rumors were flying: someone's wife had been approached by a stray male, there had been a terrible fight—he had beaten her and gone off to get drunk; a French officer had been cruising around the house of a married beauty, and it was rumored that he would meet a violent end if he persisted. And thus it continued for three days, each day and each night, with more and more signs of combat appearing on both male and female faces; some participants vanished completely from the fun. The dirt floors of the drinking sheds were a soggy mass of mud, trampled grass and leaves, broken glass, and discarded food. Bad tempers exploded into open violence between the natives and the military visitors. The wine supply, finally depleted, had been replaced by beer which, despite the fact that it was also in perilously low supply, with no other replenishing schooner due for several weeks, was consumed in tremendous quantities. Finally, the sun rose one morning on a filthy, reeling, incoherent group of natives, singing and staggering about amidst the shattered remains of the drinking stands. The beer, like the wine, was gone, and so were the French ships. Wives had been beaten, husbands deserted, families split. Symptoms of various social diseases had already appeared. The revelers tottered off to their homes to fling themselves on their sleeping mats. The Bastille Day celebration was over.

Gratefully, we began to collect our things in the Tunui

household, in which we had blended well in the past days.
Tahia was already talking hopefully of John Belmont and his
excellent qualifications as a husband for her daughter, Paha-
kua, the shy object of many sidelong glances from the local
rowdies. Tunui had shown admirable restraint during the festivities but had finally given in to temptation and got pleas-
antly soused on the final night. Horses had been brought down
from grazing areas in the plateau, and typical Marquesan one-
piece hand-carved wooden saddles had been collected to fit
our needs. Amidst a great bustle and excitement we loaded up
the pack train early on a promising bright morning, said
good-by to the Tunui family, and started off on the steep
winding road that would ultimately lead us, by a grueling
climb, into the high grasslands of the Nuku Hiva central
plateau. For an hour the horses skidded in the mud of the trail,
slipping and lurching over the smooth basalt boulders in the
way. Finally, we stood at the notch in the crest of the cliff
that formed the back wall of Taiohae Valley, looking down
into the calm bay with its fine fringe of white where the surf
broke rhythmically against the rock-shelved sides of the bay.
The valley looked peaceful in the slanting early morning light
with the smoke columns of breakfast fires rising and drifting
here and there, as the white phaeton-birds wheeled and soared
above the valley walls.

We turned and struck off into the plateau, shivering slightly
at the freshness of the breeze that had greeted us at the end of
our climb. The clouds moved by seemingly at arm's length,
throwing their shadows across the rippling grass and ferns.
An auspicious beginning for our work, we thought, as the
horses carried us closer to our goal—the north coast valley of
Hatiheu and the ruins of an ancient village on the deserted
shore of Ha'atuatua.

2 / Marquesans of History

When the Spanish conquistadors had consolidated their holdings on the west coast of South America, they searched for
new lands to conquer. In 1596 an expedition under the leadership of Alvaro de Mendaña y Castro set sail from Callao, carrying aboard four ships a diversified human cargo of noblemen,
priests, and soldiers, as well as male and female dregs of the
waterfront of that Peruvian seaport. Their intentions, besides
those which were standard motivating factors for Spanish colonization, were to rediscover and colonize the Solomon Islands, which had been discovered twenty-eight years earlier,
in an on the whole unsuccessful exploration by Mendaña and
another Spanish adventurer, Sarmiento de Gamboa.

After several tedious weeks at sea, the ships came in sight
of a group of high volcanic islands on the western horizon,
and slid into a deep bay, surrounded by lofty peaks and pin-
nacles of dark volcanic stone, towering above a green fertile
valley. The native inhabitants paddled out from the shore in
outrigger canoes to examine the fourfold apparition.

They shouted at the Spaniards, and though their tongue was
incomprehensible, their manner was not unfriendly. The word
which seemed to recur most frequently in their shouts was
recorded by a Spanish historian as sounding like *"atalut"* or
"atakut." Today we know that the natives were trying to tell
Mendaña's pilot to anchor in closer to shore, for the word
"atalut" or *"atakut"* is an approximation of the Marquesan
phrase *Katau uta*—"anchor closer to land"—a friendly bit of
advice from one group of navigators to another.

It at once became obvious to the Spaniards that the blessed
landfall was not the sought-for Solomon Islands at all. The

tall, light-skinned inhabitants of this beautiful bay and island
in no way resembled the short, black, and wiry cannibals who
had so rudely greeted Mendaña's first debarkation in the Solo-
mons.

Before long the curious natives, swarming about the ships
in their canoes, were given a demonstration of European musketry, the Spaniards needing little provocation to open fire on
a crowd of pagans. The slaughter of the "Indians," as the
Spanish chronicler disdainfully called the Polynesians, was
presumably begun to revenge some innocent act of pilfering
by the jabbering natives. After suffering several casualties,
the natives withdrew to the shore, not to return. The Spaniards, however, going ashore to say their first Mass in this
newest territory to feel the weight of Spanish culture, came
directly to the heart of a native village, and soon found cause
for further punishment of "outrage."

Mendaña's group remained for two weeks on this and another island in the immediate vicinity, where similar carnage
resulted. As soon as it became obvious that the all-important
gold and jewels were not to be found in these pretty, but
clearly useless, islands, the little fleet weighed anchor and departed.

For the natives, the only remembrances of this fortunately
short-lived visitation were the bloated putrefying corpses of
relatives and friends, filling the pleasant valley with the stench
of the charnel house. For Europeans, the site of this first contact between whites and Polynesians was marked on maritime
charts with the cumbersome but wisely chosen name of Las
Islas Marquesas de Don Garcia Hurtado de Mendoza de Ca-
ñete—the name of the current viceroy of Peru; Mendaña knew
how to curry favor. The islands which had received the Spanish onslaught were piously named Magdalene, Dominica, and
Santa Christina, and the bay in which the native population
had been so scrupulously decimated became known as the
Bay of the Mother of God.

So it was that the Marquesas Islands received their name

and their baptism of fire and were catapulted onto the pages of history from the silence of the unexplored Pacific.

Mendaña had come upon a Polynesian society at a point near its peak of development in a period long before any other European was to have a similar opportunity. The terse, spotty comments of Pedro Quiros, the pilot and chronicler of Mendaña's expedition, cause anthropologists to experience a galling sense of frustration at not being able to wring more from the few disinterested pages devoted to this historic contact. Mendaña, however, was followed by a succession of navigators who had better powers of observation and description as well as the invaluable blessing of interest and in some cases a certain degree of empathy for the native culture. Besides the accounts of the maritime visitors to the Marquesas, there are the records and diaries of missionaries and soldiers and a number of precise monographs written by anthropologists who during the years around the turn of this century studied the Marquesan native culture. Putting all the evidence together, we can obtain a picture of the native life as it was when the first Europeans arrived in Polynesia. Naturally, there are many details of Marquesan culture that are lost forever through various combinations of historical accidents. It is unfortunate that knowledge of religious lore was restricted to high priests alone, that the ancient chants and songs were stamped out by missionaries or simply forgotten, and that knowledge of the techniques of navigation perished because no one troubled to inquire about them. The main outlines of the society—its social and political organization, warfare, religion, architecture, handicrafts, food production, etc.—are well documented, however.

The civilization of the brown, tattooed canoemen who met Mendaña's fleet was a far more complicated affair than that Spaniard realized. The deep, high-walled valleys of the Marquesan Islands were well isolated from each other by all routes except the sea, for the absence of coral reefs along the coast had prevented coastal flatlands from forming and the precipitous peaks surrounding most of the valleys on three sides made overland journeys very difficult. Therefore, the inhabitants of each Marquesan valley almost perforce formed largely self-sufficient, politically independent tribal groups. The tribes were generally named after some mythical ancestor of the tribal chief or some totem-like animal representing an apparition of a tribal deity. Thus, the tribe of Taiohae Bay on Nuku Hiva was called Te'i'i after its mythical founder, Teiki nui ahaku (Te'i'i=Teiki), who, according to legend, had divided the island between himself and his brother, Taipi'nui'-avaku. Teiki or Te'i'i settled in one half, the central valley of which was Taiohae, and Taipi in the other half, the central of which was long, well-watered Taipivai. On Nuku Hiva, this legendary division into halves was honored by military alliances, for tribes related to the Te'i'i would join forces to fight any of the Taipi descendants, although they fought among themselves at other times, as did the Taipi.

At the head of each valley tribe stood the chief, the first-born male of the direct male descent-line of the tribal ancestor or god.

The certificate of a chief's high position was his genealogy, going back in history to the time when no men yet existed and the great gods of Polynesian mythology, Tu, Tangaroa, Tiki, and others, roamed among the islands of the blue sea, or even beyond this period into the time—or nontime—of the primeval void when all was emptiness.

The Marquesan chiefs did not rule with the iron-fisted tyranny displayed by the nobility of Tonga and Samoa; however, the chief held all the tribal lands, parceling them out to families in return for a share of their produce—chickens, poi, fish, etc. —which was to be gathered at specified times of the year. With this produce the chief could support workmen to build and repair the tribal temples and the larger rectangular tribal ceremonial plazas on which all major ceremonies were held. The chief also supported himself and the high-ranking priests and craftsmen from this income. In many instances the chief made his decisions on the advice of a council composed of the ranking warriors and priests of the tribe, but on other occasions he would drop his paternalistic role to act in an extremely autocratic fashion, decreeing death for someone who overtly flouted his commands or ejecting an unruly tenant from his lands. The Marquesan chiefs might perhaps be distinguished from their subjects by their dignified bearing or certain elements of personal dress or adornment, such as feather headdresses, complete body tattooing, or whaletooth necklaces.

A very impressive symbol of chiefly rank was the size of the chief's house and his household. Marquesan houses were elevated on rectangular stone platforms, called *paepae*, the height and size of the platform increasing with the prestige of the owner. The surface of the platform was divided into two parts, the largest area being a paved veranda. Across the back of the platform was a dais on which the high-roofed house itself stood. The dais was usually about seven feet wide, as the house was intended for sleeping and hence only had to be wide enough for a man to sleep stretched out across its short dimension. In chiefs' houses, the face of the dais was made of cut and fitted slabs of sacred red *ke'etu* stone, a soft, volcanic tuff. A chief's quarters consisted of a main house of this type, an elevated house for men only, several houses for servants and family members, and cooking sheds.

It was important for a chief to have a large household group to help in his plans and care for him. Chiefs selected beautiful wives who were renowned for their sexuality, lending them out to promising warriors to entice them to join the household. Thus, chiefly households often were composed of a good proportion of tough, able warriors, capable of backing up the chief's words with muscle and war club.

Next to the chief, and often his younger brother, stood what for all purposes was the real power behind the throne—the *tau'a*, or inspirational priest. While the chief controlled tribal lands and productivity, the *tau'a* ruled the all-pervasive domain of religion. The *tau'a* was the mouthpiece of the tribal gods, transmitting their orders to the chief and his subjects. While the priest prayed and entered a trance state, his god descended from Hawaiki, the Polynesian spirit world, and, entering the priest's stomach, spoke through his mouth in weird falsetto, demanding human sacrifices, informing the people of the existence of undiscovered lands far over the sea, and commanding them to go and settle them, or telling of secret war preparations of another tribe.

In the chiefly council, the word of the *tau'a* carried much weight, even more than the chief's on many occasions, leading an early French missionary to remark that Marquesan government was a theocracy.

Below these two figures at the pinnacle of a Marquesan tribe stood the lesser-ranking people of the chiefly descent line and the collateral lines which formed large clans—social units based on descent through often-mythical male ancestors. Several clans might be found in each tribe, their individual size often being so great that one might refer to them as "subtribes." Each of these subtribes inhabited a defined area of land within the tribal territory. Each subtribe observed ceremonies of its own under its own subchiefs and priests, propitiated its own gods, built and maintained its own ceremonial plazas and temples, and in some instances its own fortifications as well. Relations between subtribes in any given valley were not always good, and occasionally deteriorated to the point of open warfare. When the missionaries first arrived in the Marquesas in force, they found one church to a valley to be woefully insufficient, for whenever people from more than one subtribe attended, the inevitable result would be fights, bloodshed, and all too frequently fatalities. Therefore, the sage missionaries built little chapels for each subtribe, usually on or near the group's ceremonial plaza.

There were no sharply defined social classes in the Marquesas, as in Hawaii and elsewhere—only a long continuum of different ranks based on the ever-important genealogies. The mass of the population had no pretensions to status but spent their lives working their gardens, fishing, fighting, and laboring on the chief's tribal projects.

There were no real villages in the Marquesas in the sense of organized groups of houses with streets systematically laid out. The Marquesan population was spread over the landscape

in small, haphazard clusters of houses built on massive platforms, each cluster usually being the home of one large family
—a patriarch, his wife, and his sons and their wives. These
family hamlets were most highly concentrated along the little
brooks and streams that tortuously weave their way down
the sloping floors of most Marquesan valleys. Around the
stone house platforms and their narrow palm-thatched houses
were the cooking houses and storage huts of the families' food
supply. A number of large, deep holes dug into the earth
contained stores of fermenting breadfruit paste, a Marquesan
staple. In these pits, sealed with leaves and stones, the slimy
brown contents remained nutritious and edible for years.
Another pit, long and shallow, was filled with porous lava
boulders; this was the earth oven or *umu*, a form of primitive
steam cooker. The boulders were heated on a fierce wood fire
and covered with a layer of fresh leaves, upon which the pigs,
breadfruit, taro, sweet potatoes, and fruits would be placed,
and covered with another layer of leaves. Lean dogs hung
around the hamlet; these, together with pigs and chickens,
constituted the Marquesans' only terrestrial sources of protein, besides human flesh. The pigs fed on food leftovers and
other garbage, spending their days in stone-walled pens or
tied to trees by long bark tethers. The dogs foraged for themselves; the chickens, tethered in hutches, were fed grated
coconut meat, seeds, and other rations. Various kinds of taro
grew in terraced mud patches fed by water carried from
streams in reed pipes. In nearby garden patches, sweet potato
vines crept from the little mounds of dirt concealing the
golden tubers, and mingled with the blue-belled yam vines.
Several coconut trees were planted around each house, and a
grove of breadfruit trees produced quantities of the crinkle-
skinned green globes that formed the solid foundation of
Marquesan diet. Bananas grew in straight rows in the garden
patches.

Each family might possess extra lands in addition to those
in the immediate vicinity of the hamlet upon which food
crops could also be planted. Besides food crops, a large variety

of useful trees and plants were cultivated, such as pandanus, several inedible palm species, and a variety of spice-yielding and medicinal plants.

The Marquesans depended greatly on the sea for the protein in their diet. Women clambered over the rocky shelves along the bay sides, prying off chitons and picking up cowries and other shellfish, occasionally finding eels or small lobsters. The men in their long bird-prowed canoes combed the bay with net and line for fish, working in fleets or singly, depending on their quarry. Often the fishermen went far outside the bay to cut swaths through schools of bonito or tuna. Again, they might dive for octopuses and large lobsters, or swim with trolling lines clenched in their teeth. Sharks were lured with bleeding chickens, lassoed, and dragged home alive; the giant manta rays, whose quick-rotting flesh served as a prized condiment when infested with maggots, were harpooned.

There were many tasks and services in Marquesan society that required specialized knowledge that the ordinary individual did not possess. To fill these needs, the services of craftsmen, known as *tuhuka,* who were specially trained, were acquired by payment in kind or in reciprocal services. One of the most important groups of specialists was that of the *tuhuka avaika,* or fishing masters, who organized and led major fishing expeditions involving large numbers of canoes and huge, complicated net systems. Another very important class were the tattoo artists, who deftly worked their beautifully balanced designs into yielding human hide amid a welter of blood and sweat, while the client, often in a state of repentance for his decision, was held spread-eagled by four stalwart friends. The tattooers were hired for the duration of their task, and fed and housed throughout this time. Their virtuosity was occasionally tested in contests between tattooers to see who could finish a design element most quickly and cleanly.

The canoe builders formed another very select class of workmen whose product was in great demand. They could and did impose stiff fees on their clients. From the felling of the breadfruit and tamanu trees to the final assembling of hull, strakes, and prow, and the launching, these men toiled away with stone adzes, coral polishing stones, shell and bone punches, and fathoms of coconut fiber cord. Most famous today are the wood carvers, whose bowls, war clubs, and statues decorate the museums of the world. The expert handling of the media and tools in the execution of the grinning tiki-faces, animals, and mazelike designs that cover the work of these departed artists rank the Marquesans among the masters of primitive wood carving.

Another group within Marquesan society were the warriors, who were not as a rule considered as part-time professionals like the *tuhuka* groups. Some high-ranking warriors, such as the tribal war chief, devoted much of their time to duties associated with warfare, such as planning and maintaining fortifications and lookout posts or formulating strategy for raiding other tribes. Most men, however, simply bore arms in times of danger only, keeping their blunt-tipped clubs, barbed spears, and slings in readiness. "War" was seldom total for the Marquesans, but consisted of constant raids and counter-raids for sacrificial victims, revenge, or just for the purpose of stirring up trouble. The shock troops of the Marquesan tribal forces were the young males who had been only partially tattooed. These rowdies, led by chiefs' elder sons, roamed the mountain trails and the waters of enemy bays when victims were needed for sacrifice, and fought hard in open conflict to prove their extreme bravery. They would smear their war clubs with the brains or blood of an enemy hero, thought to impart to the weapon the strength of its victim. If no heroes were available, an old woman or even a child would do to help elevate them above the common warrior.

Ritual cannibalism was quite common. It has been claimed, furthermore, that the Marquesans really valued human flesh as a food, although this is not certain. During warfare, cannibalism was practiced to partake of the dead's strength and prowess. Eyes were often eaten raw if time did not allow for cooking; otherwise the victim was roasted like a pig or cubed and eaten with a minimum of searing. In cases where a victim was taken alive, parts of his body would often be carved, cooked, and eaten before his eyes.

On key ridges above Marquesan valleys, fortification systems were erected for protection against overland attack and to serve as places of refuge during an attack by sea. A wide part of a ridge or a peak was selected and flat areas for houses were created by skillful terracing. Possible routes of attack were made impassable by trenching through the ridge on both sides of the strong point. Enemy attackers advancing along the ridges would have to descend into the deep, wide trenches and be exposed to pelting by stones from defenders on the other side of the trench. All slopes around the fort were so dug away that they were practically vertical. Finally, the fort with its terraces was ringed with wooden palisades upon which firing platforms were constructed. Storage pits for breadfruit and other food supplies were also dug, and a rotating group of observers moved in to watch for raiding parties.

Religious customs and observances permeated much of daily life in the Marquesas, and played a large part in all decisions in the top levels of government. Below the *tau'a* were a series of priestly orders in decreasing ranks of importance, the tribal sacred historian, the *tuhuka 'o'oko*, coming next in line, and below him a large group of priests who operated on a private basis, perhaps officiating part time at lesser temples and divining or working magical spells for individuals in the tribe. Religious and magical practices spread down to the lowest level of the society, with everyone carrying out personal devotional practices and being capable of some magical work for either good or ill.

A particularly common practice in Marquesan sorcery was that known as *nanikaha*, or "binding the bait," a method of enlisting supernatural help to obtain the demise of an adversary. Using a scrap of hair, a fingernail paring, the earth of a footprint, or even cast-off food or feces of the intended victim, a magical package was assembled, wrapped in leaves, and tied tightly. Within a short time the victim would be made to see that he was the object of someone's evil wishes, by means of a hint or a rumor carefully spread. Psychology took care of the rest, for unless the victim availed himself of supernatural protection quickly, his own anxiety at being the object of *nanikaha* was sufficient to kill him in a week or so, the general symptoms being a rapid "withdrawal" into a semialert state, refusal of food and drink, swelling of the lips and stomach, and, in the final stages, fever.

The Marquesan pantheon, insofar as it is known, was enormous and complex. Within Marquesan religious organization there were several levels of participation according to the rank of the individual. A number of very remote, impersonal gods were routinely propitiated by tribal priests and chiefs in a routine and unemotional fashion. The worship of the well-known Polynesian deities—Tangaroa, the creator and sea god, Tiki, creator of man and god of artists, Tu, god of war, and many others— was also rather impersonal, but involved the participation of the common people. There were offerings and ceremonies for these gods, most of whom figure prominently in Marquesan folklore. In many respects, however, these pan-Polynesian gods, so mighty elsewhere, lost much of their appeal in the Marquesas, appearing as colorless figures who had once played a part in the creation and population of the Marquesas but had since withdrawn from human affairs to a large extent.

The gods who played the greatest role of all in Marquesan religion were the local tribal gods and deified ancestors of chiefs and priests. The Marquesans would elevate outstanding priests and chiefs to the rank of gods after their death. In fact, they called the high priest *atua*, "god," while he was still alive. If a priest had done many miraculous deeds and prophesied with accuracy, within several months of his death a series of orgiastic ceremonies would be held for his "beatification," and he would forthwith move into the world of the gods. It was to gods such as these, and the older but equally personal tribal deities, that the Marquesans reared their greatest temples, erected the most important statues, and made their most elaborate offerings. If an anthropologist, for instance, were to question an old Marquesan to determine to which god a temple was dedicated, the answer, if forthcoming, would very likely be such a name as Tau'a Vahiaki or Peahei—strange names, known only in that particular valley on that island, and nowhere else in Polynesia.

Marquesan temples were built like ordinary dwelling houses, but of finer materials and with more care. They were actually intended to be houses—houses for the god or gods to whom they were raised. During ceremonies, the gods were believed to descend from the sky world and enter the images which stood in the house or on the paved platform before it. Offerings of pigs, fish, human victims, fruit, and vegetables were placed before the images, and remained there until they rotted. If they were dedicated to particularly important gods or goddesses, the temples were declared "off limits" during most of the year, only the priests and their assistants being permitted to approach them. In such cases, the boundaries of the sacred ground around the temple were marked with white bark cloth streamers tied to bamboo poles, the sight of which would send an ordinary native post-haste in the opposite direction. Besides the temples there were many small altars and shrines scattered throughout the hamlets in the valley floors. These sometimes took the form of crude wooden tables or platforms or miniature houses. Private families made offerings to numerous local spirits at these points. There was an astronomical number of local spirits, each possessed of certain limited powers. Everyone who died by enemy action or in childbirth or in any number of other untimely ways usually attained some sort of semidivinity, and his spirit inhabited the place of his death. These spirits were particularly annoying, as they inflicted such ills on their victims as boils, skin diseases, and temporary insanity.

The hub of ceremonial life in any tribe was the expansive *tohua*, or ceremonial plaza, consisting of an oblong terrace several hundred feet long and over a hundred feet wide, on which a rectangular court was laid out. Around the perimeter of the court were temples, shrines, and long, shedlike structures to house spectators at the tribal ceremonies. Often, at one end of the dance floor, a low platform of red tuff slabs would serve to display the maggot-ridden corpses and heads of the most recent victims, usually members of neighboring tribes. During the ordinary day, much social activity took place on the *tohua* grounds. People met there before going off in co-operative work groups, others went there to relax and amuse themselves, children played among the sheds and stone walls.

During ceremonies, the sheds were packed with painted, plumed onlookers, and the whole court vibrated to the deep booming of the ceremonial drums and the fast pounding staccato of broad, brown dancing feet. Groups of singers ranged about the court provided a background to solo leaders in the minor-key Marquesan chants intoned with power and dignity. Troops of naked girls whirled and postured through the intricate, seemingly endless sequence of dances, boldly displaying themselves and their charms to the audience and participants. The most beautiful and talented girls danced atop elevated flat boulders, going through the same motions as their friends on the plaza floor. Most of the tribal ceremonies were affairs of several days' duration, featuring continuous singing, feasting, and drinking, culminating in an orgy that would have compared favorably with the best that pagan Rome would offer at the nadir of its decadence. With passions aroused by several days of erotic songs and dances and public ritual intercourse, the population could scarcely be restrained from joining in the festive mood. As a result, most ceremonies ended in a fury of drunkenness, overeating, and prodigious sexuality in every form known to mankind, so shocking and outraging the tender sensibilities of the early missionaries that they could bring themselves to refer to them only in the vaguest terms.

Life in the Marquesas before the advent of the European was no idyl, as many may have wished to envision it. Fruit did not fall ripe from the trees among the prostrate forms of soft, lazy natives, groggy from overindulgence in love and festivals. A Marquesan child had precious few years to enjoy the irresponsibility of infancy at the breasts of its mother and her female relatives. As soon as possible, children were drawn into the adult world, very gradually, with little tasks and commissions appropriate to their capacities. Among the first of these services was the care of younger brothers and sisters; the mothers were thus released for other work. Children nevertheless had plenty of free time, during which they ran together in groups composed of both sexes of similar age. In these juvenile groups they played at stilt fighting, learned singing and dancing, played at being adults, and indulged in hundreds of games such as cat's cradle and tag. Such groups never escaped far from either parental authority or the growing burdens of responsibility.

The social relations of the Marquesan child were actually structured and channeled by the society. He quickly learned how to pay respect to a chief and how to joke and indulge in horseplay with his grandparents. He found out with which girls he could have sexual relations and which uncles would stand in his stead during ceremonies. He discovered the complexities of the native religious practices: how to propitiate gods and spirits, how to obtain supernatural aid. He learned which lines of endeavor were open to him as a man and how far he might go in the ones he chose. In war, he knew how he must fight and what would happen if he were to be taken prisoner. The traditional enemies of his tribe, as well as its allies, were clearly defined. A stranger could be precisely placed in this structured world in a few minutes by comparing genealogies until a common ancestor was discovered. In short, the world of the Marquesan was predictable and quite solid: a world in which maturation, both physical and social, was not a problem.

Puberty was marked by circumcision for the boys and genital inspection for the girls. This was the beginning of a period of full indulgence of the sex drive, within the wide limits established by Marquesan society. Boys and girls began spending their evenings away from home in dormitories where, among their age mates, they learned the refinements of physical love. With the Marquesan disregard for domestic privacy, the public sexual exhibitions, and the near-nudity of adults of both sexes, it is little wonder that young Marquesans were quite sophisticated by the time puberty wrought its changes in their bodies. Homosexuality and other sex play among younger juveniles was considered normal, but after puberty, heterosexual relations dominated the scene. Parents carefully schooled their daughters in all the subtleties of sexual technique, taking every precaution to see that the girls would in no way offend or disappoint their future lovers.

Throughout this prolonged period of nocturnal license, both boys and girls spent the days preparing for their full adult roles. Amid the washing and careful grooming for the tender adventures with their numerous lovers, girls learned cooking, clothmaking, the medicinal arts, mat weaving, and basketmaking. Boys were initiated into crafts associations, learned fishing skills, canoeing, navigation, and the very important lessons of native horticulture in order to keep the yams, taro, breadfruit, and coconuts flourishing.

After many trial unions of a passing nature, a Marquesan male would finally select a girl for his wife, sealing the bargain with a series of gift exchanges with her parents. The new-formed family, often blessed with children before the marriage, would take up residence on the land of the husband's family, inheriting coconut trees, garden plots, shares in breadfruit and banana groves, and fishing rights along the shore. The work of maintaining these holdings and all the necessary equipment and tools consumed much time for the adults and the children, but there were always the great festivals to look forward to, breaking up the native year into easily tolerable sections of work. In these festivals, the food which for months had been accumulated by the whole population would be devoured, but the community returned to the tasks of everyday life feeling renewed and relieved.

The seasons, with their recurrent duties in the fishing canoes, groves, and gardens, and the complex cycle of re-

ligious and tribal ceremonies or festivals, formed a backdrop
against which the personal contacts of everyday life were en-
acted. Men grew to maturity and died, tribes rose and fell,
but the cycles of plants, animals, sea, and stars were irreversi-
ble and immutable. A Marquesan could see, on the platform
of his family shrine, the skulls of his ancestors extending back
centuries into the past. He knew that one day his own skull
would bleach and gather moss beside those of his forebears,
and that the same sun that had shone so long ago for them
would shine on his children's children and their children to
come.

It was this society that Mendaña's men fell upon in that far-
distant day in 1596, when the bay of Vaitahu received its
Spanish name of Madre de Dios, and Marquesans first faced
Spanish flintlocks. The contempt of the Spanish for those
lowly "savages" could hardly have been more misplaced, but
the Spanish nobles and soldiers of that day were not given to
excessive humility.

Fortunately, two centuries went by before a European sail
again appeared on the horizon. This time the famous Captain
Cook in his well-equipped exploration vessel, the *Endeavour*,
brought a group of scientists to the Marquesas on their way
to Tahiti for the purpose of making astronomical observations
of the planet Venus. Neither Cook's mission nor his personnel
bore any resemblance to those of his illustrious predecessor,
Mendaña.

The observations of these scientists, Cook and his junior
officers, and the sketches of the expedition artists, in sharp
contrast to the bare comments of Mendaña's chronicler, give
us a first fascinating picture of the Marquesan culture of 1768.
The engravings accompanying Cook's journals show us tattooed Marquesan warriors with long-plumed headdresses drifting on a calm bay in long, spritsailed canoes with upturned
prows. Other portraits of Marquesan nobility show us details
of the facial tattoo designs and headdress construction, as well
as the facial characteristics of the natives. The Forsters, a

father-son team of naturalists in the Cook party, collected words in the Marquesan language to compare with words collected in other islands of Polynesia, in order to demonstrate relationships between the dialects spoken in these islands. They also collected native plants and recorded many useful facts about the productivity of the islands, the fortifications, temples, and villages that they saw, and the dress, behavior, and appearance of the native population.

Despite the caliber of Cook's personnel, it was not long before some violence marred the visit and natives again paid the price of their curiosity with their lives. The entire population of the valley in which Cook had anchored, the Mother of God Bay of the Spaniards, finally withdrew to a high fortified position on the mountains above, and Cook departed.

Shortly after Cook, the French explorer Étienne Marchand passed through the archipelago, making an entirely different impression on the native population from his predecessors. Taking a tolerant view of the natives' casual theft of things that caught their eye, Marchand neither attempted to punish the offenders nor to retrieve the goods thus lost. On one occasion a native snatched the ramrod from a French musket and made off at top speed with his trophy into the bush. Some time later, Marchand noted, he saw the thief wearing the ramrod as an ear pendant in place of the beautifully carved ivory and shell ear plugs usually inserted into the pierced lobes. Marchand himself was not free from peril at the nimble hands of his native hosts, who several times tried to remove sundry articles from his pockets. The French captain was equally permissive with his crew, who quickly discovered the tokens of love in Polynesia, and turned the *Solide* into a floating bagnio wherein the native girls sold themselves for nails, metal tools, beads, and trinkets. The commerce between the French sailors and their native lovers assumed such proportions that the commander was often forced to eject the girls, who appeared in such numbers that routine duties could not be performed on the overcrowded ship. During periods when the girls were allowed aboard, there were so many of them that some of the normally more or less private aspects of this traffic were carried out in the ship's rigging, in full view of observers.

When Marchand arrived in the Marquesas, the only islands known to Europeans were those visited by Mendaña two hundred years previously. Little had been known concerning the possibility of other islands existing in the vicinity. When Marchand departed, however, he sailed slightly to the northwest and came upon a group of large volcanic islands about one hundred and twenty miles away from the site of Mendaña's discovery; he took possession of these in the name of the king of France, not knowing that they had already been discovered by Captain Ingraham of Boston, who had passed that way some months earlier on the good ship *Nancy*, bound for the western Pacific. These islands, which were gradually drawn under the blanket term of "Marquesas," extended from Mendaña's discoveries to cover the two discrete groups of islands, as it later became obvious that the two groups were inhabited by people of a single culture.

Ingraham was in the vanguard of a wave of Yankee sailors who began to slip around the Horn and into the Pacific after 1790, entering into the whaling and sailing business and the China trade. The traders and whalers picked up the southeast trade winds off the tip of Argentina, angling northward and westward through the eastern islands of the Polynesian triangle. Among these islands, ships stopped wherever they could to refill empty, fouled water kegs, stock salt pork barrels, or obtain fresh fruit. In many instances the goods given the Polynesians in repayment for their vital food supplies were worthless nails, needles, or cheap cloth. Just as often, the supplies were stolen without the formality of trading, and natives were kidnaped along with the supplies to fill vacancies in the crews' rosters. The losses were not completely unilateral, however, for many sailors departed from their lives of hardship to cast their lots with the native populations.

As the eighteenth century drew to a close, many islands of Polynesia were being visited by vessels from Marblehead and

Nantucket as well as their European counterparts in the mad race for spermaceti and whalebone.

The sperm whalers sought their quarry along a broad band extending across the Pacific on the equator and to either side of it. Here, as the catches recorded in whalers' logbooks demonstrate, the greatest number of sperm whales were to be found. It was only natural, then, that the Marquesas Islands, situated only 9 degrees south of the equator, should have been a handy source of provisions for whalers working in the eastern Pacific, or passing through to the west. The islands possessed excellent harbors, deep and well protected from sudden storms. Furthermore, the natives were able to supply the ships with pigs, vegetables, and fruits in large quantities. Last, but not least, the sexuality of the Marquesan women could not be overlooked by men whose existence contained so few pleasures. For these reasons, the Marquesas became a regular port of call for whalers going both east and west. The northern group of islands—Nuku Hiva, Ua Pou, and Ua Huka—received more visits than the southern islands, simply by virtue of being closer to the whalers' hunting grounds, and the bay of Taiohae on Nuku Hiva was the favorite anchorage of all.

When a Russian expedition arrived at Nuku Hiva in 1803, sailing from the Baltic Sea to reach the eastern marches of Mother Russia, they found two white deserters already well installed in Taiohae Bay, both having been there and elsewhere in the southern islands for some time. The deserters, a Frenchman and an Englishman, detested each other, as might have been expected, but they joined forces in trying to profit from the leader of the Russian expedition, Captain Krusenstern. The English sailor had acquired a native house, land, and wife in addition to a position in the advisory council of the Taiohae chief. The Frenchman, on the other hand, lived the life of a wild young warrior. One of Krusenstern's artists sketched him, standing with legs braced and a war sling tight above his shoulders, his dark tattoo designs contrasting sharply with his light skin.

The Russians had a complement of natural scientists and draftsmen aboard, to whom we are indebted for a fine, detailed account of their unfortunately short visit to the Marquesas, with maps and numerous sketches. Krusenstern left to continue his voyage to Siberia but his observations on native political structures, child raising, sexual behavior, population, religion, and a hundred other subjects can still yield data of value to the modern researcher.

In 1813 Captain David Porter, U.S.N., commanding the *Essex* and accompanied by the *Essex Junior*, sailed into the Pacific on a mission to cut British shipping in that ocean down to a minimum. Porter made a rendezvous with whaling captains in the Galapagos Islands, off the coast of Ecuador, from whom he requested information on islands that would be suitable as bases to shelter his ships. Within a few weeks the long black hulls of the American warships slid between Taiohae's twin sentinel islets and dropped anchor. For about fifteen months they patrolled the shipping lanes, capturing or sinking all the British merchantmen in sight.

For the Te'i'i, the tribe inhabiting Taiohae, Porter's arrival was nothing short of miraculous. Aside from the purely commercial prospects of trading pigs and produce for the tools and trinkets carried by the American visitors, the heavily armed warships and their trained crews became a factor in Marquesan politics, materially strengthening the position of the Te'i'i against their mortal enemies, the Taipi tribe, from an adjacent valley.

The Te'i'i chief, Keatanui, cemented relations with Porter quickly, informing him of the political situation and asking his aid. On their first meeting, Porter presented the chief with several sperm whale teeth, a symbol of high rank among the Marquesans, thus earning the elderly leader's gratitude and admiration.

The business of establishing a shore base for the American fleet was begun immediately with the aid of native labor obtained through Keatanui's co-operation. It was not long before Taipi raiding parties descended into Taiohae to destroy groves of breadfruit trees and menace the inhabitants of the area in which his fort was being built. Insults of this kind, coupled with the Taipi tribe's refusal to co-operate in provisioning the Americans, brought the situation quickly to a head. Amid Te'i'i jubilation, Porter decided to attack Taipi in an amphibious assault. Moving down the coast with his marines and sailors, accompanied by a large group of native warriors, Porter disembarked his large, well-armed force on the sandy beach of Taipi Bay, where they struck inland through tangled underbrush. At first, no natives could be seen, but as the force moved inland, it became apparent that the Taipi warriors had definitely *not* been caught by surprise. Operating in small groups, never forming solid fronts of resistance, the Taipi slipped around and through the ranks of the bewildered Americans, who were busy trying to see where they were going. After a battle in which American muskets proved nearly useless, Porter's men were beaten back to the beach amid a shower of rocks and spears, and the protestations of disbelief of their native allies, whose hopes of a victory over the Taipi were destroyed along with their respect and fear of the arms of the white man.

After this bitter defeat, the Taipi raids on Taiohae increased, making a second expedition a virtual necessity—to save face, if for no other reason. Porter made a second attempt to conquer the Taipi in an overland drive. He intended to attack down the trail in the middle of the southern valley wall, arriving in Taipivai well above the fort of boulders where his first attempt had met its final inglorious end. After a day on the march, with men dropping on the rugged trails from heat exhaustion, Porter mounted the ridge above Taipi, his riflemen firing a volley to show their intent and allow the enemy to prepare. Descending into Taipi, his troops deployed through the heavily populated, well-cleared heart of the valley. Without good cover, the Marquesans' infiltrations and flank attacks were ineffective, and the American musketry took its toll. When Porter left Taipivai that night, his prestige was restored and the pride of his native allies was assuaged. Laden with family skulls, ornaments, captured weapons, and food liberated from the Taipi, the Taiohae tribes were ready to label the attack a complete success. The dirty smoke curls rising from burning houses and temples in Taipi valley were further proof of the clear superiority of American arms.

Porter's sojourn had a variety of effects on the Marquesan population, besides checking the territorial expansion of the Taipi. During the months that his men were based in Taiohae, the native women formed many liaisons with the Americans and their British prisoners, who later accumulated in large numbers. Of these unions, children were undoubtedly born. The short-term visits of earlier explorers and whalers had also resulted in some racial mixture, but never before had the two races been exposed to each other for so long. Furthermore, venereal disease, if not already present, was certainly well established in Taiohae by the time the Americans left. Aside from the sociological and anthropological results of Porter's visits, the effects on the native economic system must be considered. Earlier, we noted that the natives were selling the food from their larders for useless trinkets of prestige value only. When the whalers' stops in these islands were of short duration, this situation was bad enough and, in fact, may have been a contributing factor to a great famine that apparently occured on Nuku Hiva in 1806 or 1807. The Te'i'i were digging deep for their visitor's victuals at the end of Porter's fifteen months' visit, and signs of definite resistance to his demands for food were quite evident.

Although the Marquesans had seen firearms frequently before Porter's visit, there were few natives who could use them. After his stay, however, the rifle was a familiar and highly valued weapon, even appearing in Marquesan ceremonials. The best currency for obtaining provisions were muskets, each of which could buy as many as five good-sized hogs. Powder, balls, and flints became an integral part of each Marquesan warrior's equipment.

After Porter's departure, the whalers came in increasingly

larger numbers, with deserters landing in most of the major valleys of the archipelago. Desperate antisocial men in many cases, these sailors were knowledgeable about firearms and alcohol distillery; they also carried diseases of all varieties. In many of the more frequented valleys, groups of deserters lived wild lives of debauchery and were disliked by even their Marquesan hosts, who feared their mad-dog fighting and drinking.

Venereal disease became almost endemic, and the birth rate began to decline as these virulent infections ran their courses unchecked.

While there are no reliable figures for the Marquesan population, Cook estimated it to be between 50,000 and 100,000 for the southern group alone, in 1767. This would mean a population for the entire archipelago of between 100,000 and 200,000 people. However, by the 1830's, the population estimates were not nearly so expansive: Dumont d'Urville, a French Naval officer, estimated only 25,000, and Dupetit-Thouars, his compatriot, some five thousand less. Père Mathias Gracia, a French missionary who arrived in 1838, wrote that "because of debauchery conception is rare, and the birth of an infant is considered as an exceedingly happy event in a family." Contact with the white man was beginning to take its toll.

The Marquesan society was by no means dead, however, for when Herman Melville deserted his ship in Tai'oha'e Bay in 1840 as a common sailor, he found a healthy, smooth-functioning culture quite determined to go its own way. His experiences among the Marquesans of Taipivai Valley, so admirably described in his first novel, *Typee,* are still valuable reading for anthropologists working in Polynesia. The society described by Melville is not much different from that seen by Porter in Taiohae fifty-seven years before, and there is little doubt that Marquesan culture would have survived the ill effects of its contact with the whites if certain other incidents had not intervened to bring about the Marquesans' conquest in a strange and paradoxical fashion. The real conquerors of these people did not come with guns and military might—they came clothed in the black robes of the Society of the Sacred Hearts of Picpus, their only armor the Christian spirit of sacrifice and devotion. Protestant missionaries, well established in Tahiti, had attempted to bring the cross to the Marquesans in the early years of the nineteenth century, but had failed miserably. The Marquesans had mistreated them, mocking their every effort to impart the gospel or render assistance. One European pastor was stripped of his belongings and forcibly ejected; houses of the missionaries were wrecked; and those who had brought their wives had to be helpless witnesses while arrogant, brutal Marquesan warriors subjected the women to the coarsest type of treatment and invective. The French priests were a hand-picked lot, described by a naval officer as being in the tradition of St. Francis of Assisi. Well schooled, practical, and possessed of boundless energy, these men were also prepared to suffer all indignities. They went ashore in Vaitahu, Tahuata, in 1838, apparently experiencing much less difficulty than they had expected. Within a short time they had established good relations with a local chief, who entered into a name-exchange relationship with one of their number. The formality of exchanging names made each party proprietor of the other's entire stock of worldly possessions, including house, land, children, and even wife. The wife of one chief, feeling slighted that her new black-robed substitute husband did not exercise his rights under the exchange, determined to find out if the black robe did not perhaps conceal a non-human form beneath. With a group of lady friends, she overcame the sleeping missionary one night by force and held him until an anatomical examination certified that he was not only human but a male.

The missionary group learned the native language thoroughly and compiled a dictionary and a rudimentary phrase book. In letters written to his superior between 1838 and 1843, Père Gracia discoursed learnedly on the Marquesan personality, politics, economy, language, religion, history, houses, etc. Behind the polite and objective descriptions of these letters, one can see the soul of a missionary who felt quite close to the pagans whom he had come to save. The understanding which Gracia and his coreligionists displayed must have played a large role in their success, for they were not plagued by the constant threats and acts of overt force that had caused the departure of their Protestant predecessors. Gaining the respect and awe of the Marquesans by their kindness and generosity as well as the speed with which they acquired a working knowledge of the native language and culture, the missionaries expanded their alliances and friendships to include many antagonistic chiefs. Placing themselves in the center of a broad network of good relations, they began to act as "disinterested parties" in arranging for peace pacts between warring tribes, freeing captives, treating the wounded, and serving as intermediaries and councilors in disputes.

Entrée to the native culture was less hard to obtain than converts to Christianity, however. It was many months before even a few grudging prospects could be interested, and more time elapsed before they could be judged reliable. Finally, a small nucleus of native catechists was established who gradually promulgated the teachings of their French masters. By the time that Admiral Dupetit-Thouars returned in 1842 with a French flotilla to take the islands for France, the gospel was achieving a toe hold of sorts in both the northern and southern groups of the archipelago. What was more important, the good example of the missionaries had created a favorable native attitude toward the French, while the escapades of the numerous British and American beachcombers only served to degrade those nations in native eyes.

French military forces gave the missionaries a considerably more solid backing for their work, as a result of which Christianization went ahead more rapidly. But other results of the missionaries' groundwork became apparent: chiefs who were friendly to the missionaries were drawn into the French camp to be used as mercenaries against fellow Marquesans.

Armed with French weapons, they fought and subdued re-
calcitrant elements, indirectly extending French control over
larger areas of the islands. As religion spread, some chiefs
were converted to Catholicism, and found themselves doing
the bidding of the priests on more than one occasion.

The mission team that had labored so hard to lay the foundation for French occupation—for that was their purpose—
was withdrawn, to be replaced by a stricter group that was
to achieve maximal gains against the forces of darkness without heeding the courtesies which had made their earlier coreligionists so welcome among the natives.

The French took advantage of the intense rivalry among
Marquesan chiefs and warriors to extend their power further.
If a pagan valley chief refused to co-operate with the mission
activities, the French searched for malcontents among the
chief's entourage. Their searches were always rewarded by the
finding of a genuinely ambitious young warrior or subchief.
In return for submitting to French rule, and often baptism,
the hopeful would receive French arms with which to over-
throw his chief. Once Christian-influenced chieftains reigned,
the missionaries steered them into schemes of territorial expansion by war and alliances.

The new missionaries began to build chapels everywhere,
while adopting a suddenly uncompromising attitude toward
many aspects of native culture that their predecessors had
suffered with in silence. Nudity was denounced, as were native dances, songs, and musical instruments. Native alcohol
and cosmetics were also brought under this repression. All
activities which were believed to play a large part in Marquesan licentiousness were earmarked for extinction, and the
bayonets of colonial infantry helped enforce the mission
edicts. These prohibitions were enforced gradually, to avoid
a crystallization of sentiment that might provoke real trouble,
but ultimately they became hard, fast rules. Tattooing, a
matter of great pride to both male and female, next fell
under the ban; tattooed adults would not be allowed to take
communion!

Thus began a very systematic destruction of a vital part of the native culture, for the native arts—music, dancing, singing, tattooing—played major roles in the society. Church attendance was a very poor substitute for the richly colored kaleidoscope of Marquesan ceremonial.

In 1867 a terrible epidemic struck after a satanic ship captain marooned sailors dying of smallpox on the beach at Taiohae. According to some reports, two thirds of the population of many valleys were carried away by this plague. As pestilence spread from the decaying corpses scattered over the landscape, the smallpox itself was superseded by a varity of equally fatal ills. The weakened survivors in many areas were too few even to bury their dead. This crippling blow greatly weakened an already tottering culture, completely demoralizing the majority of the survivors. In many valleys all tribal leaders—French-planted or not—had perished, and in the absence of their authority no direction could be found.

In the late nineteenth century the birth rate dropped to an all-time low. Marquesans died like flies, with no offspring to replace them. Amid the deserted, decaying houses, crammed burial caves, overgrown gardens, and tumble-down temples, the Marquesans embarked on a round of debauchery that was calculated to drive off the specter of their own extinction. Life was a constant round of orgies. European alcohol helped fan the flames, and opium and other narcotics contributed to the breakdown. There were no chiefs powerful enough to pull their people together for any purpose but fighting or festivals. Native resentment against the missionaries was high. Murders, looting, and wanton destruction filled the days, while more than once a French military expedition had to put down a marathon debauch that had run for several weeks with indescribable scenes of violence and sensuality.

Marquesan society died a horrible, wasting death. By the early 1920's, only 1500 confused, hostile, and apathetic survivors remained of the possible 100,000 to 120,000 that had inhabited the islands in 1767. With fierce pride, these people clung to the scanty remnants of their lost civilization, maintaining many forbidden practices by subterfuge and passive resistance. But the hour when the Marquesans could be saved had long passed.

Christianity had triumphed, and so had France, but at what a price!

Our picture of Marquesan culture as it was when the Europeans discovered it is essentially two-dimensional—a portrait with no real depth, for all that we know of this fascinating and most tragic of Polynesian societies is from the last few centuries of its existence. Anthropological attention was not turned toward the Marquesas until the process of decay which has been described here was so well advanced as to have greatly distorted the society's structure and functioning. Despite this distortion, shrewd, well-trained anthropologists were able to recover much valuable information on little-known aspects of the native culture in the late nineteenth and early twentieth centuries. A capable French governor of the Marquesas, M. Tautain, published a series of detailed, objective reports on Marquesan architecture, family life, tattooing, and the vexing problem of population decline. In 1897 the great German ethnologist Karl von den Steinen visited the islands; he remained there for a year while carrying out a detailed study of the still-surviving native art, concentrating on wood carving, which was unprohibited, and tattooing. His reports, published in three ponderous and profusely illustrated volumes, are far more than a study of art, for Steinen related the subject of his investigations to all other aspects of the culture and produced a perceptive reconstruction of native culture.

In 1919 Mr. and Mrs. E. S. C. Handy and Ralph Linton spent a year in the Marquesas studying the remnants of the native culture, adding much to what Steinen had accomplished. The Handys' ethnographic studies covered social organization, economy, religion, warfare, children's games, and music. Linton reported on native technology and the ruined house platforms, temples, and ceremonial villages.

Père Simeon Delmas, a missionary to the Marquesas for over

fifty years, has left a volume on Marquesan native religion which has been quite useful, and the renowned Polynesian linguist, S. H. Elbert, made studies of the Marquesan language and songs.

Aside from these major contributions, there is a scattering of published notes and short papers on more or less minor details of Marquesan society, but nothing of great significance. These anthropological reports, added to those of the earlier explorers, have helped to fill in many of the details in our two-dimensional picture of Marquesan society, but they have added little depth to our view. In 1956 we knew a great deal about the Marquesans of the eighteenth and nineteenth centuries but nothing about their past. What little information was available on the prehistory of these islands was derived from the elaborate, highly ambiguous phrases of native legends, and a few supposedly reliable genealogies; but this information was avowed to be unreliable even by the ethnologists who collected it.

When we planned our archaeological work in the Marquesas, therefore, we could only hope that our techniques would be adequate to providing answers to some of the most important queries; anything beyond that would be gratefully accepted as a welcome dividend.

The major problems which I hoped to elucidate were several:

First, what was the geographic origin of the settlers and the date of the Polynesian settlement in the Marquesas? There were many theories concerning these questions: some saw in these islands a combination of Melanesian, Polynesian, and Indonesian influence, while others saw evidence in the native art style and designs of a relationship with the Chou Dynasty of China. Still others claimed that the historic Marquesans could not themselves have built their stone temples and house platforms, but that these must have been the work of a pre-Polynesian race of greater intelligence. The dates which these theories established for the arrival of Polynesians in the Marquesas varied from 1000 plus B.C. to A.D. 1400. Clearly, if ever there was a problem in Marquesan prehistory, this was it.

Another problem of great interest involved the development of Marquesan society, leading up to the culture of the days of Cook and Porter. How could this florescence be explained? Was it a result of a strong, healthy society evolving spontaneously, or did other cultures and races contact the Marquesans and make substantial contributions to their culture? Many strange things turned up in these islands, differentiating them sharply from islands such as Tahiti and the Tuamotus, the closest neighbors. For example, various types of ornaments, rock engravings, religious ceremonies, and songs resembled those found in quite distant cultures. Was there a relationship between these and the Marquesas, or were the resemblances only accidental?

We also wanted to investigate the possibility that Marquesan voyagers might have settled other islands in the general area, such as Mangareva and Easter Island, as anthropologists have supposed. Although our work alone would not establish this, it would provide information and collections to compare with those of other islands, thus permitting some conclusions to be drawn as to what role the Marquesans might actually have played in settling eastern Polynesia. Further, the fascinating stone monuments, temples, and house platforms had to be fitted into the panorama of Marquesan prehistory. There was much investigation to be done to determine the techniques by which natives with ropes, rollers, and muscle power only could have manipulated such massive stones with such skill.

Finally, the population of the islands had always been the subject of much discussion—how correct were early European estimates? How much of a population could the archipelago have supported? How thickly settled were the islands, and where were the population concentrations? Further questions concerned Marquesan physical characteristics. What did the early Marquesans look like? Had they resembled the present population, tall with round broad heads, or had they been a long-narrow-skulled race, as some had suggested?

These were only the most outstanding problems which faced us as we departed for this archaeologically unknown territory in 1956. Our work that year provided no answers, but instead raised a thousand more questions. As we approached the islands again in 1957, it was in eager anticipation of some solutions, but with the knowledge nevertheless that solved problems beget further problems at a furious rate. We fully expected to return home with our share of both; little did we realize that they would exceed all expectations.

3 / Are the Natives Friendly?

We moved along the washboard surface of the Hatiheu trail through the soft-contoured terrain of the Nuku Hiva central plateau. The shaggy horses stumbled along at their shambling gait, sloshing through the puddles of milky water collected in each rut where the whitish clay had been dug away by previous horses' hoofs. After an hour we arrived at the brink of the great Taipivai Valley, the most beautiful and largest of all Nuku Hiva valleys. Like a giant trench, the valley cuts into the heart of the island, splitting at its cliff-bound head into two arms, each of which is crowned by beautiful waterfalls. In the recent heavy rains, even the intermittent watercourses had been swollen; as we paused on the trail before beginning our descent, the stern, layered rocks of the vertical valley walls were streaked with innumerable waterfalls of all sizes, pouring over the precipices into clouds of vapor, oozing down the cliff faces in long foaming tracks. The roar of the big falls could be heard in the distance—the roar of tons of water which each minute emptied from the raging rivers of the plateau and plummeted in a pulsating white column into the green tangle almost a thousand feet below.

Starting down the trail into Taipi, we dismounted, for the overgrown route, carved from the cliff face, was sodden from rain and treacherously narrow in many parts of its zigzag course. The overloaded horses were led and driven, balking, wheezing, and sighing, around the boulder-filled turns where more than one horse and rider had taken a plunge several hundred feet into Taipi. Finally, the trail widened, the steep slopes lengthened, and we were in the dark hibiscus groves of Taipi. The swollen river with its rocky bed presented some problems, but the horses managed it without incident after we had gone in up to our waists to prod them along. The horses, their none-too-solid endurance pushed to the limit, began to tire rapidly as we started the long climb to gain the pass to Hatiheu. Tunui, John, and I took turns dismounting to spare them, but they slowed down, becoming increasingly stubborn and contrary as they grew more fatigued. A momentary lull in their riders' application of heels, toes, sticks, fists, and often the flat of a machete, only resulted in their grinding slowly to a halt.

After a long climb, spent mostly in trudging behind the horses with stick in hand, we arrived dripping wet at the mountain pass into Hatiheu, caked with clay to the knees and dog-tired. From here, at least, it was all downhill.

In Taiohae, during the Bastille Day celebration, we had had great difficulty locating someone who would accept us as tenants in his house or allow us to occupy any of the several vacant houses that we knew existed in Hatiheu. Many natives had offered us what they first described as ideal quarters, but we had to reject all of them, for many involved payment of rents higher than those imposed in much of the United States. When these gestures of magnanimity were rejected, we were as often greeted by a faint sneer as by actual anger. Tiro, one of our workmen in 1956, had finally offered to allow us to use his parents' spare house, high up in the valley, so we had a shelter at least; but I was rather unsure of this arrangement, as the other family members were not renowned for friendliness.

There are many varieties of houses now in use among the Marquesans, for European concepts of construction and the influx of Polynesians from other archipelagoes have caused a general abandonment of the ancient native-style house with its high-gabled roof and open front. Houses are often made of planks with galvanized roofs, while others are of the now standard rectangular eastern Polynesian type—plaited bamboo walls and raised floor with a thatched roof. Tiro's large wooden frame house, standing on an ancient stone platform on a wide terrace in the steep hillside, was quaint and weathered. Across

the house front stretched a rickety veranda. The entire structure sagged heavily from a high point in the middle to both
front and back. Instead of the hoped-for cool, palm thatch
roof, there was a dirty, rusted corrugated iron one to ward
off the rain. On the terrace below the main house were two
smaller buildings, the dining house—a similar, but newer,
structure—and the cookhouse—a shed with a pounded dirt
floor, an open fire pit, and sides on which wooden bars were
nailed horizontally at intervals.

A coconut leaf enclosure with a faucet was intended to
serve as a shower, but no water was available, as the pipe was
out of order. We found later that this house was actually quite
a historic bit of Marquesiana. It had been built for the chief
of Hatiheu in 1870—the first European house to be constructed in that valley. Practically nothing in the house had been
replaced since it was built.

After straightening up the house and bathing in the nearby
stream, we saddled up to ride to the shore, where most of the
Hatiheu settlement was located. Coming out of the coconut
groves onto the shore, with its wide elevated path, we passed a
few natives squatting beside copra-drying racks erected on
the boulder-strewn sand above high-tide line. They glanced
up, then looked at each other and engaged in a bit of rapid-fire,
barely audible conversation. They then looked back at us, displaying only faint traces of hard smiles, and spoke directly
to Tunui and Tiro. The conversation was quite brief: "Who
are they?" "Americans. You remember him—Robert. That's
his wife and his brother-in-law." "What do they want?"
"Looking for old things, same as last year." "Ummm."

Then followed a further exchange of glances and rapid
whispers, after which an old woman nodded at Rae, saying
"Bo-shoo!"—the Marquesan version of *"Bon jour"*—and we
rode on, leaving them to talk openly about us. This scene was
repeated several times that afternoon. Some of the inhabitants
simply avoided us and, when they had to approach within any
reasonable distance, acted as though we were not there.

Although we had our shelter, we had yet to find some food,

for we had brought none with us. We were forced to depend on the bounty of the local people, although our reception indicated that this would hardly be generous. A few more natives came to lounge on the walls and paths, looking at us with sly, knowing grins. Tunui tried to presume on his slight familial connections with a few of them to get some food. When he approached these distant relatives, explaining our situation, he was told, with a cold smile or a glare, that there was no food, despite the very plain evidence of breadfruit on nearby trees, chickens scurrying about in the yards, and taro poking its big heart-shaped leaves above the black mud patches in which it grew so well. The search continued as the sun dove behind the rocky-crested point on the west side of the bay. The obese subchief, Viriamu, perched his rippling hulk on a wall near us, demanding with a smile, "No food tonight?" He had been one who had offered to rent us an almost-collapsed shack for fifty dollars a month. I replied that we had found nothing. "Tsk, tsk, tsk!" was the reply, as the smile grew a bit brighter. Rae was not feeling well, as the result of her six-hour ride on a carved rosewood saddle—an ordeal for which the average American girl is little prepared. Besides, she had many quarter-dollar-sized sores festering on her ankles from the virulent bites of a tiny species of fly called *nono*. Her ankles had swollen to about twice their normal size, and her whole system seemed to be upset. Spotting the ankles, one of the loungers started to laugh, "Ha ha, Madame has elephantiasis!" This started off a whole new train of thought, and we were regaled with stories of the ill effects of that disease, its remedies, and finally a discourse on various types of insecticides to use. We were told precisely how to prepare these native herbal insecticides, and some well-meaning soul even offered to prepare some for us, for a price. But no offers of food were forthcoming.

Finally, one of our chance meetings in Taiohae bore fruit: the Hatiheu wood sculptor, Pauro, had been delighted to find that Rae was a nurse, and promised that he would see us in his home valley. He now appeared, offering us supper, which we gladly accepted. He had hurried home and had been frantically getting together quite a sizable feast: chicken boiled in coconut sauce, breadfruit, *poke*—a gelatinous mixture of arrowroot starch and bananas—and some marinated fresh fish. Even a bottle of wine came out of hiding, much to Tunui's delight. Pauro, having placed an obligation on us, discreetly inquired after the meal as to Rae's knowledge of various female complaints, while his wife listened with intense concentration. When they heard of Rae's background in obstetrical nursing, their joy was hard to conceal. It was not too long before we learned that Pauro's only daughter was pregnant but had several times threatened to abort spontaneously. It was obvious what role Rae, with her nursing experience, was going to play in this community.

By the next day our situation had eased considerably. Some bread, rice, and other staples from Pauro and some fish which Tiro had managed to spear kept us going pretty well. Pauro's wife, who could be depended upon to act as a good transmitter of information, had evidently been able to see nearly everyone in town, because a few curious people showed up to present their problems to the *vehine taote*—the doctor-woman—who had so fortunately descended upon them. Some of these came bearing gifts: a chicken trussed up by its feet, a basket of fruit, some fish. We acquired a housemaid to help Rae learn the highly technical aspects of making a fire, cubing raw fish, and generally keeping house, native style. The maid, Vehine by name, was subsequently dubbed "In a Minute," that phrase being her stock answer to any request. With a care-laden sigh for any situation, fifteen-year-old In a Minute proved to be of more entertainment than domestic value.

At first glance, Hatiheu seemed like any other Marquesan valley in its physical layout. Behind the gently curving arc of brown sand beach, studded with blue basalt boulders, ran an elevated roadway of sorts that extended out along the east shore of the bay to a wharf on a rocky point. On the land side of the road, a raised coastal flat extended eighty to ninety yards inland in some areas, hemmed in at the rear by the steeply rising valley floor that began its long incline to the valley head. On this narrow coastal "plain" stood a number of houses, most of which were clustered around the mouths of two large streams that emptied into the sea at opposite ends of the beach. At the extreme western edge of the beach beyond the end of the road, a little hamlet stood in the shadow of the Te Heu, a vertical volcanic crest about fifteen hundred feet high, standing like the ruins of an ancient wall left by some primordial race of giants. Sculptured by wind and rain, Te Heu's laminated volcanic stone appeared almost paper-thin; in several places erosion had actually worn large holes right through it. Honeycombed with crevices and pocks in which birds and plants found secure homes, this landmark was almost a tribal symbol for the inhabitants of the valley. The house of Tamihau, the stern and impressive chief of Hatiheu, was among those in this little hamlet. Near Tamihau's house stood one of the two trading stores in the valley, operated by a much-maligned Cantonese, Ah Sing. There are Chinese on practically every island in French Polynesia, usually engaged in business enterprises of one kind or another, most often trading stores. The Chinese remain a relatively intact and close-knit ethnic group wherever they settle, generally operating in large family groups that extend over a number of islands. Ah Sing had gone to Tahiti from China many years ago, joining members of his own family or clan who were already well established in French Oceania. He had subsequently moved to the Marquesas with plans to open up a shop in Taiohae. After a few years, when business was well under way and Ah Sing had acquired a large number of debtors and real estate, he had given the Taiohae store to a young relative, Fui Chong, otherwise known as François, himself moving to Hatiheu to start another branch. The inhabitants there were not as receptive as those of Taiohae, however. Neither were they so tolerant of Ah Sing's race and nationality, for they had had relatively little direct contact with Chinese previously, and generally mistrusted these reserved and business-oriented intruders whose language sounded to Marquesan ears like ungodly grunting and cackling. Ah Sing was seldom seen anywhere but in his shop, which was a small, dark, stilted house attached to a compact group of cooking houses and storage huts, surrounded by a stout, high, pole fence. Occasionally he ventured out in European trousers and a bright aloha shirt, his tall, slender frame stooped from years of poring over account books and abacus, his skin waxen from his seclusion in the dimly lit shop. His fragile form was a marked contrast to the muscled brown bodies of his more robust native customers. He had been accused by the natives of all sorts of usurious practices in the running of his little shop. We were told that he often cheated on prices, raising them at whim on unmarked articles; he sold spoiled canned goods knowingly, and refused to give anything to anyone—to him, it appeared, all the world was priceable, and Ah Sing himself determined the value of any goods. Marquesans flocked to him to buy colored, sugared water, frozen into ice cubes called "ice cream"; he also concocted a somewhat more sickening melange of evaporated milk, sugar, and water. He carried a large line of brilliantine, cheap perfumes, and some ridiculous-looking shoes that sold amazingly fast at high prices, and importantly accounted for the dissipation of much hard-earned pocket money.

Native resentment of the Chinese storekeeper was always high, despite the fact that he was continually patronized for his ice cubes, brilliantine, and shoes, as well as for his trade services. Ah Sing's company bought copra at a higher price than the other major company trading in the area.

In the middle of the Hatiheu beach was the churchyard, surrounded by a low stone wall, behind which stood a frame church and the priest's bungalow. Here the native population gathered weekly for services, gossip, and sports that consumed most of Sunday. During the week, native children attended catechism class, and the valley soccer team practiced on the field. The priest, a young Breton farm boy, was im-

mensely proud of his parish, largely rebuilt since the tidal wave
of 1946 which had destroyed the buildings of a church school
for boys run by lay brothers. This school, famed for the beautiful carvings in its chapel, had been visited by Robert Louis
Stevenson during his sojourn in the Marquesas.

Beside a stream next to the church was a second trading
store, run by a pleasant Tahitian and his wife, who represented
Ah Sing's competition in this area, as they worked for a rival
copra company. There were a number of houses on the opposite bank, where the second major hamlet had grown up. At
the extreme east end of the beach stood a few more houses
and the government school, sheltered by a huge tamanu tree.
Here the unwilling youngsters gathered for several months
of the year to learn French, geography, history, and mathematics. Unfortunately, the teaching methods currently in use
encouraged memorization rather than understanding. Because
of this, most of the children could glibly recite stories and
fables, and such useful things as the definitions of an isthmus,
a canal, a continent, etc., in perfect French, with total incom-
prehension of what they had said.

In general, when the average Westerner thinks about existence in the South Seas, an idyllic picture is evoked of soft,
easy living in the midst of an almost shameful superabun-
dance. This romantic Hollywood image could not be further
from the truth. Like all Polynesians, the Marquesans must
work for their existence in this modern world, just as their
ancestors had to work long before a white face ever shone on
the beaches of the Marquesan archipelago. There are basic
differences between the economy of the modern Marquesas
and that of the prehistoric period. First, the modern natives
are being slowly drawn into a cash economy; they need money
for the "capital goods" that have become absolute necessities
to their existence, such as axes, machetes, and knives for copra
production, gardening, and woodworking, sheet metal for copra dryers, ammunition for hunting, various spices and canned
foods, good fishing hooks and line, and dry goods or ready-
made clothing. They also need money for purely prestige

items such as jewelry, perfume, combs, etc. In the past, however, no cash was needed; exchange was in kind, a pig for a pig or something deemed equivalent, or goods in return for labor.

Furthermore, the chiefs no longer levy tribute on their people as in prewhite times. Modern chiefs serve only as low-level administrators, more often than not being mere governmental mouthpieces or figureheads. They organize labor only when the government calls for it, and then the government, not the populace, pays. They are no longer the focal point of ceremonies, because such ceremonies do not exist, nor can they even lead their people in war. Should they exercise enough authority to make them slightly unpopular, they can be sure of not being re-elected at the end of their five-year term.

The introduction of many new kinds of plants and animals to the Marquesas by the Europeans has also made a dramatic difference in the economy. Horses, cattle, sheep, and goats are both domesticated and wild. Pineapples, mango trees, tomatoes, lettuce, melons, and numerous other plants are grown in some quantity, replacing many of the old native plants, while baked bread is growing in use as a substitute for some of the starchy Marquesan staples such as taro, yams, and sweet potatoes.

The main source of income for most Marquesans is copra production. Copra is the dried meat of the coconut, purchased by American and European industrial concerns for processing that will render it into oil which is used in soaps, hair tonics, and various cosmetics. The importance of copra is reflected by the overwhelming preponderance of coconut palms over other varieties of palm trees in any valley. Formerly each family had a few coconut trees, used to provide milk for sauces, husks for cordmaking, and leaves for thatch. Now many families own hundreds of trees, and some properties have thousands.

Each family owns plots of ground of various sizes in its valley, obtained through inheritance, purchase, or loan, upon which coco trees have generally been planted at proper distance intervals to prevent overcrowding and a bad crop. Despite the knowledge that close planting spoils the nut yield, many still attempt it, hoping to beat nature at her own game. Others, less scrupulous, hopefully move stone boundary markers (which are still placed with invocations of the supernatural to destroy trespassers) and expand into their neighbors' plots very gradually, so as not to be noticed. Ultimately, a fight over land develops, necessitating government intervention.

During our stay in Hatiheu I was called upon by a group of natives to act as judge in one such dispute, which threatened at the time to explode into violence. A man claimed that the three parties bordering his triangular plot had cut off some six trees from his patrimony. They knew that I had surveying instruments and had watched me draw maps—would I help them settle this problem? We went to the land in question; they produced French Army maps and deeds for me to examine, some running back to the 1890's, showing their rights through inheritance. Setting up my plane table and alidade, I started checking the maps from a known bench mark—they were incredibly poor; errors of as much as ten meters appeared within a ninety-meter dimension! Careful checking of sides by tape and by triangulation gave similar results. When I checked the angle on one corner of the plaintiff's plot, swinging my alidade to the precise number of degrees shown on the "map," the owner erupted, "Hey, friend! You have just eaten half of my plot! How will I live? The map is wrong! Your eyeglass is wrong! Look again!" His adversaries roared, "Ha, eaten half his plot! Ha, ha, the American eats indeed! Who has eaten who? You see, he is caught!" Tempers were rising rapidly. I tried to explain that I had only been checking and that the map was obviously wrong, but the opposition kept prodding. Then I moved on to their plots and the situation was immediately reversed: someone else's plot was being eaten; someone else's trees were changing hands. By now, all present were in a state of extreme anxiety. The maps were wrong—how would they ever get this straightened out? We talked and talked, circling the plots, checking the number of disputed trees. Finally they decided to split these trees among themselves, forget about the maps, and establish new informal boundaries, which were solemnly marked into immovable bedrock outcrops. We then departed, having successfully postponed trouble until another day.

One of the most successful copra growers in the valley was Tama, who, with his wife, Hina, managed to produce more in a period of a few days than could many of his compatriots in a week. In the prime of his life, Tama had fallen from a coconut tree; one twisted leg was now markedly shorter than the other and he had a pronounced limp. He could not ride a horse or bend over from a standing posture, so he did his copra cutting perched on a box or boulder, using his powerful arms and shoulders. He, his wife, and their oldest adopted son departed early each morning for their copra groves, the wife and boy riding horses loaded down with empty sacks, while Tama hobbled along carrying his ax and a box, with a handmade scabbard holding a machete, a copra knife, and a file clamped to his twisted hip.

Arriving at the grove, they searched out the trees bearing brown coconuts. These were "tree-dried"; the meat inside was hard, oily, and easily removed, therefore of the best quality for copra. The boy climbed up the long, notched trunks after the dried nuts, working hands and feet together like a monkey on a string. Arriving at the treetop, he swung out on one hand, using the other deftly to spin the nuts loose from their stems or to wield a machete if the stem could not be reached. All trees were stripped of their brown nuts; the green nuts with their soft, mushy meat and their effervescent water were left to ripen and age on the tree. The nuts were then collected into one big pile and the copra cutting began. Using an ax, the three split the nuts right through the tough husk, the liquid spilling onto the ground. The whole family usually worked together on this job, Hina swinging a big woodsman's ax with as much accuracy as Tama and their boy. When the nuts were split, each person opened a gunny sack for the meat, set it on the ground, and began to pry the meat from the shell halves, using a blunt-ended knife with an offset pistol-grip handle. The pieces had to be of the proper size; about one third of the meat in the shell in one chunk. The extracted meat in the sack was occasionally shaken down for compact filling. As soon as a sack was filled, its mouth was stitched closed with a narrow bark strip tied to a sharp twig. The sacks, holding about a hundred and fifty pounds of wet copra, were set aside until four or more had accumulated. Then a horse was loaded with these and Hina drove the animal down to the house, where the copra-drying rack was located. The dryer was an elevated platform with low edges about eight feet wide and up to twenty-five feet or more in length. A series of thatched roof segments slid on crude wooden rails over the platform.

When Hina arrived at the dryer with her first horseload of coconut, her youngest adopted son was there to help her lift the sacks from the horse and empty them, one by one, onto the platform floor. There, the boy carefully spread the pieces of meat out to dry, with the side that had been against the coco shell facing downward. As long as the sun shone, the roof sections were drawn off the dryer onto an extension on the rails at one end, exposing the whole floor of the rack to the brilliant, desiccating rays. When rain started, however, the roof sections were pulled along the rails to cover the entire rack, protecting it from harmful moisture that would cause fungus growth, and result in the copra's being rejected. While Hina and the boy worked on the rack, Tama and his helper continued to split nuts and cut out meat, filling enough sacks to burden down two or three more horses; then they too descended. Their working day extended from 5 or 6 A.M. to 3 P.M. When they returned home, they ate lunch and attended to routine household duties.

Once the copra on the dryer was hard and dehydrated, it was raked up, sacked again, weighed and stored in a warehouse, to await the arrival of either of the two copra traders' schooners.

The Marquesans who produce the copra are often paid, when they turn their copra over to him, by the warehouse owner, who is the trading company representative in their valley. The warehouse man then resells it to the schooner for a few sous more than he paid the producers. Some copra cutters are dissatisfied with the almost infinitesimal profit made by this middleman. They build their own warehouses and transport their copra direct to the schooner crew, and thus acquire the profit normally made by the trading store representatives.

The schooner operators collect copra in this fashion from as many ports as they can, returning to Tahiti with an overload more often than not. The copra is sold by the shipload to an entrepreneur in Tahiti, who sends his people aboard the ship to unload it, which they do with much singing, horseplay, and general merriment. Most of the entrepreneurs' laborers are elderly men and women, quite poorly paid, who seem to have a more leisurely approach to their work than is usual even in Tahiti. As the holds are cleared, dancing often breaks out on the planks, and a guitar is always strumming.

The entrepreneur, in turn, takes the unloaded copra to his warehouse, selling it either to the small coconut oil processing works in Tahiti or to French companies who then resell it to other Western countries. Each time the copra changes hands, the price naturally mounts; ultimately it may be bought for manufacturing at about ninety cents or more per pound. When I was last in the Marquesas, the best price that an individual Marquesan copra cutter—like Tama, for instance—could get was six and a half francs (Pacific), or eight cents, for 2.2 pounds of dried coconut meat.

Although copra cutting is most common by far, there are other sources of cash income for Marquesans. Vanilla raising is extremely lucrative, but few care to practice it because of the painstaking work involved: the vanilla vine flowers must be carefully cross-pollinated by hand, or the vanilla beans will not develop.

Other cash-earning lines of endeavor are wood carving, periodic work on copra schooners, hunting and butchering for the government, and guiding the infrequent visitors to the island. Gambling is common despite governmental restrictions, and prostituting wives or daughters to white visitors for relatively enormous fees is a frequent practice. This is most often done when the arrival of foreign ships makes hard liquor available in return for sexual favors. Some of the younger girls receive their sexual initiation at such times, bringing back a bottle of whisky, a discarded American sports jacket, or some ammunition in exchange for their innocence.

Average Marquesan families spend between three and five days a week on copra cutting, depending on the amount of rainfall and the number of people in the family available for work. During the remaining time, gardens and animals must be cared for, meals prepared, fishing parties organized, houses and equipment maintained, and, last but not least, some time set aside for fun.

In addition to gardening for home consumption, fishing and shell fishing are necessary. Tama had a canoe in which he and one or two friends embarked routinely on Thursday or Friday afternoon, fishing all night and most of the following day. Depending on the seasonal variation in fish runs, they might fish several miles off the coast, trolling for tuna and bonito, or bottom-fish in the quietude of a nearby bay, using hand-lines weighted with pebbles. For certain varieties of fish, live bait must be used. A very common type of bait is a small, streamlined, needle-nosed fish which can be speared in large numbers, a light being used to attract them to the canoe. On a cloudless, moonlit night, there is nothing more beautiful than the sight of a silver bay, rimmed with nearly luminescent surf, with the torch- or lantern-lit canoes moving swiftly and silently back and forth collecting these little bait fish for an expedition into the open sea.

Tama knew well the fishing grounds off the northeast corner of Nuku Hiva. As a boy he had learned the locations of the various *toka*, or fishing holes, memorizing the shore bearings by which fishermen triangulated themselves into the correct positions. The *toka* were usually deep submarine pits or rock structures where many kinds of fish congregated to feed on mollusks and algae clinging to the rocks on the bottom. In the *toka* Tama often hooked the incomparable scarlet Midway Jacks, called *haka* by the natives, with flashing gold-and-black eyes, or the brilliantly varied parrot fishes with bony, beaklike mouths.

In trolling, pearl shell lures would often attract the deep blue, projectile-shaped bonito, the long barracudalike *roroa* (wahoo), with its silver striped body, or the *mahimahi* (dolphin), whose body went through the entire spectrum of colors as it gasped out its last in the canoe bilges.

Through the long night hours of these fishing expeditions, Tama would sit patiently with his misshapen pelvis twisted at a crazy angle upon the narrow board seat. Alternately fishing and rowing, he was often obliged to shift painfully to ease his cramped legs and restore their circulation, reduced by the chill of the Pacific night. Often, the humdrum fishing would be enlivened by an encounter with a shark or ray. Bleeding or injured fish bring up the ever-present blue sharks from the depths, in some cases enticing them to attack. Sharks have been known to approach a canoe stealthily, sometimes seizing the fisherman's paddle as it dips into the water, occasionally wrenching at the outrigger in an attempt to overturn the vessel.

When the sea ran high and fishing was impossible, Tama and his companions put in to an uninhabited bay on the extreme northeast tip of Nuku Hiva, beached the canoe at an ancient fisherman's shrine, and, building a fire to warm themselves, bedded down in damp burlap sacks and leaves for the night.

Returning from such a trip, his thin face etched with fatigue beneath a light stubble of beard, Tama set about the task of cleaning and dividing the fish. In the Marquesas, cleaning fish is often done on an assembly line basis; one man scales the fish, another removes heads, fins, and tails, while still another removes the viscera. The latter job is especially sought after, as Marquesans are particularly fond of certain internal organs of the fish, eating them raw, and licking their fingers with relish. Much of the fresh catch is cubed, soaked in lime juice and coco milk, and eaten within an hour or two, without further preparation. Some may be fried whole or sliced, and still other varieties may be boiled. Tuna and bonito are particularly good when salted and dried.

The spoils of fishing expeditions seldom last for more than a few days. In Tama's household, as in many others in the valley, the eldest boy augmented the supply with fish caught in short diving excursions in Hatiheu and nearby bays. Using a homemade sling gun with a handsomely carved rosewood stock fitted with European shock cords and a steel dart, Tama's son Teiki often ventured into the sea from the rock shelves along the bay side.

In the community of Hatiheu there were several individuals who played specialists' roles, performing services that few natives could ordinarily undertake without special training. In some respects, these people occupied the positions of the *tuhuka* craftsmen of pagan days, whose services were so well rewarded by the powerful chiefs. The actual occupational specialties of the old *tuhuka* classes had mostly vanished, however, with the collapse of the ancient culture after the French occupation. The new specialists perform tasks of rather different and often completely modern natures in most cases, but some of the old crafts persist in much-altered form.

A man who spanned the centuries with his considerable talents was Pauro, our host for our first meal in Hatiheu. Heavy, thick muscles rippled and bulged over the robust frame of this middle-aged man. Only the thinning gray hair on his massive skull revealed his age. Pauro was an expert sculptor: working in wood and stone, he displayed an amazing virtuosity that seemed to increase as time went on. On a rainy afternoon you would find him in his work shed, bent over a bowl, on the surface of which his large but agile fingers guided a razor-sharp knife, etching the intricate patterns of the almost forgotten pagan art style. The designs were not the tiresome simplified mazes that the Taiohae carvers engraved on their wares for passing yachtsmen. Far from it. Pauro knew the motifs as they had been taught to the wood-carving and tattooing *tuhuka* in centuries past—each had a name, and often a curious little legend to explain its origin. On his bowls and war clubs appeared turtles, stylized roaches, *tiki* faces, and the now seldom-seen abstractions of human figures characteristic of nineteenth-century native art.

Pauro's carving in stone was even better than that in wood, a fact which he ably demonstrated during our stay. In the process of gardening, a fine old statue had been unearthed. Made of basalt, this little figure stood only about eight inches high, on short stumpy legs, clasping its swollen abdomen with a pair of elongated hands, and glaring at the world through goggled eyes, its tongue protruding through parted lips. It was a prime example of the best of Marquesan art, a masterpiece of a kind seldom found now except in museums or art collectors' shops. Recognizing its worth, Pauro borrowed the figure from its owners, an elderly couple who owned the land where it had been uncovered. He sat down before the little god with chisel in hand and began to chip away at one of the beach stones he had selected. Gradually a figure took shape as he turned the ancient model around and around, checking and copying every possible perspective. In three days the new figure was almost finished, but he was dissatisfied with its proportions. He chose a new stone and began again, this time with a little more success, but with not enough, still, to satisfy his perfectionist ideals. After he had carved five figures, he was elated: the fifth example was so like the original that the two could not be told apart, except for the finish. Burying it in the black ooze of the taro patch, however, gave it a deep antique tone, which was further heightened by several applications of thick coconut oil. When he showed me his completed work, he watched my face intently for any adverse reaction. I told him I thought it excellent, and asked him what he planned to do with it. His broad cheeks ridged in a smile as he rumbled, "Wait until the tourists come—I think it should bring at least thirty dollars, don't you?"

Besides engaging in artistic pursuits, Pauro slaved daily over an old-fashioned oven behind his home, baking French bread, which has become an institution in modern Marquesan culture, and also served the French administration as the district butcher. It was his job to journey to the deserted lands of the west coast of Nuku Hiva every month to kill some wild beef for the inhabitants of Hatiheu. Often he returned with a live wild pig, trussed and muzzled, swinging in a sack next to the bloody beef quarters; or on other occasions, he carried in his arms a snapping wild puppy, deserted by its mother in the rocky grasslands of the west coast. When we became friends, he brought back ancient stone axes and other implements that he stumbled across in his hunting, or news of a burial cave or an archaeological site that he thought might interest me.

While Pauro represented a blend of old and new with his sculpture, his baking and hunting, and most of all his love of cash, the talents of other individuals in the valley lay in different areas entirely—areas well beyond the limits of law and dangerously close to the sulfurous, glowing, lower regions abhorred by the church—the realm of the supernatural.

One of these was a tall, handsome man in his fifties, named Matatupapa'u, or Corpse Eyes, a quiet, retiring fellow whose face always bore a faint trace of a smile. Corpse Eyes had been born and raised in an orthodox Marquesan family, had been instructed in his youth by a native *taua*, or inspirational priest, and had come to be on very good terms with the world beyond the veil.

Blessed with an ability to see spirits even in broad daylight, from which he drew his name, he knew immediately if a man was being dogged by evil forces. He was also endowed with something approximating second sight, being able to predict events as well as report them when they were happening. When he reported that a copra boat had been lost at sea during World War II, his words were taken lightly by some, but when the boat had been officially listed as lost after an exhaustive search, he had then been accused of causing the sinking by supernatural means and had spent six months in jail for his prophecy. Corpse Eyes was an expert card reader and frequently made use of cards to foretell the future or divine the present. In this way he had been instrumental in uncovering one case of malevolent witchcraft, first identifying the person who was bringing to bear the evil power, and then taking supernatural counter-measures to avenge the wrong.

In addition to these rather impressive "professional" accomplishments that resulted in his being held in awe and fear by his fellow Marquesans, Corpse Eyes knew much about the old native culture in general and could be depended on for such things as names and locations of forgotten temples, old sacred chants, ancient tribal boundaries, medicinal lore, and an endless store of legends.

When I got to know him, I found that his renown was based on other things besides his acknowledged supremacy in the occult. Despite his shyness and reserve, he possessed an envied reputation as a gentle but determined seducer of young girls, and a discreet lover of married women. His virility was no less famous than his capacity and love for alcoholic beverages.

Corpse Eyes lived by dint of hard labor for the most part, but was available for consultation at any time, his fees being taken in fish, breadfruit, or, more often, in his beloved wine. He served in much the same capacity as the lower order *taua* priests of old who were only part-time servants of the gods, but the practice of his art, strictly forbidden by both church and government, had deprived him of many of the benefits that he might have derived from it.

From the first, Corpse Eyes evinced a strong interest in my work but he declined the opportunity to join the crew when it was given him. I did not press him but looked forward with hope to a time when he might change his mind and I could enjoy the benefits of his wide knowledge in helping to interpret archaeological finds.

4 / Ha'atuatua—Silent Valley

After the first few days in Hatiheu, spent in organizing our
new home and getting the feel of the valley, we began to
work, even though the *Tiare Taporo* was still cruising around
in the southern Marquesas with four large crates of our vital
supplies.

In a gray-clouded dawn we loaded our horses and started
for Ha'atuatua. The route was uphill; we mounted to the
crest of the thin ridge separating Hatiheu from the neighboring valley, Anaho, beyond which lay Ha'atuatua. In the deep
red-clay-lined notch where the trail cut the crest, a moment's
pause in the refreshing east wind gave us a view of the entire
northeastern corner of the island. To the left, the bottle-
necked bay of Anaho lay below, its coral-grown shallows
gleaming a beautiful aquamarine in the morning sun, edged
with a soft white sand beach and fenced in by volcanic peaks.
To the right was the narrow valley floor of Anaho, with a low
hill separating it from our long-awaited goal—Ha'atuatua—
with its wide, triangular sand flat standing bravely against rank
upon rank of long white breakers which rushed into the wide
bay. Framed between the bay, the sky, and the rocky cliffs
jutting up on the northern and southern margins of the valley
was the triple-peaked island of Ua Huka thirty miles away.

As we gazed down on the breath-taking valley, the memory
of my first view of Ha'atuatua flashed back to me. It had
been from the same spot that Tunui had indicated our goal in
1956 when we were riding to check on the rumors of large
quantities of "pig bones" to be found in the sand flats there.
On that day, we had come out of the hibiscus tangle covering
much of inland Ha'atuatua and gone straight out to the edge

of the broad sand flats where the ravages of the tidal wave had
left a thirty-foot bank about seventy yards back from shore.
Up and down the length of the gently undulating sand deposit,
the wind lifted a plume of light powdery sand from the un-
protected bank, hurling it inland. The wind was piling up a
few small dunes back of the bank. Not a soul was visible on
the beach—only a few herons stalked solemnly to and fro, and
a flock of tiny sea birds skittered frenetically at the water's
edge, advancing and retreating with the surge of the surf.
Swarms of savagely biting *nono* flies assailed us and the horses
at every slack in the wind, swirling before our eyes, and finding their way up trouser legs and into shirts.

When I caught sight of the debris washing down the slope,
I nearly fell out of the saddle. The bones that were scattered
all along the slope and on the beach below were not pig bones
but human bones! Ribs, vertebrae, thigh bones, bits of skull
vault, and innumerable hand and foot bones were everywhere.
At the edge of the bank a bleached female skull rested upside
down, almost entirely exposed. Parts of several complete burials were exposed in the bank, where a dark horizontal bank
of stained sand about twenty inches thick appeared in the
profile beneath a clean layer of the loose surface sand. The
dark color of the sand was a result of charcoal, ashes, rotting
vegetation and garbage. After a period of occupation the site
had then evidently been abandoned, for the thick layer of
clean white sand above the black band did not contain a single
trace of human occupancy. In the dark stained band were
flecks of charcoal, big beds of ash, and sand discolored by
long-dead fires, bits of carved pearl shell, stone and coral
tools, and large stones that appeared to be part of an almost
completely buried pavement of some type. The same dark band
showed all the way up the beach to the north to a point where
the sand disappeared against the boulders and earth washed
from the steep valley sides. To the south the deposit continued
for a short distance, but beyond that a change in beach conformation had altered the effect of the tidal wave and the sand
hill was intact, hiding its archaeological treasures.

We walked up the beach to the north and saw that the heavy black band had been exposed in many areas by wind erosion. In these areas, often many square feet in extent, we got a glimpse of what the surfaces of ancient living areas must have looked like. The wind had removed the overlying sand grain by grain, leaving every bit of stone, bone, or shell, and every broken tool in the place where it had fallen. While I busily took notes, photographed, and collected all sorts of objects or bits of objects that looked as though they might have been artifacts, Tunui looked on in astonishment. He had not realized that this mess could contain anything of such obviously great value, and I believe that in those days he frequently doubted my sanity.

Finally we packed our collections carefully and rode back to Hatiheu, thoroughly pleased, not thinking that our good fortune had really been to hear and heed a native's rumor of an isolated, completely deserted valley.

Breaking the reverie, we descended the breakneck trail into Anaho, galloped along its white beach, and soon were in the stillness of Ha'atuatua. Tiro's family was residing in the valley for their periodic stint of copra cutting and bootlegging in their large plantations on the fertile, well-watered incline below the southern cliffs. A trail of smoke rose and shot off at an angle in the breeze passing above a tiny bamboo hut and a thatched cookhouse in a clearing close to the south beach, indicating that breakfast was not yet finished.

After looking over the site again to reorient myself and introduce Johnny to it, I began to consider where we would profit most with our limited equipment.

One goes about the search for archaeological sites in a rational, systematic way, utilizing various sources of information. First, the obvious archaeological monuments such as house platforms, temples, burial caves, and ceremonial plazas are carefully examined and their locations noted. Also, the ground surface is surveyed whenever possible for tools and accumulations of refuse, signifying a possible habitation site. Road and river-banks are examined for clues in their exposed faces, in

the form of fire pits, partially buried buildings, burials, and
the constantly sought tools and refuse. Old garbage may seem
like a peculiar object of scientific search, but more broken
tools will generally be found in a garbage deposit than anywhere else, and information about diet and economy can be
gleaned from an examination of the refuse.

It is also necessary to observe the location of the modern
natives' dwellings: their distribution in relation to streams,
beaches, ridges, cliffs, etc. In the Marquesas, the modern natives, clustering their houses on beaches, at the mouths of
streams, and along brooks in the interior, provided clues to
possible ancient settlements which when checked immediately
paid off in the location of sites. Marquesan fishermen today
often sleep in caves and rock shelters near their fishing areas,
when long expeditions are in progress; an examination of such
caves showed that they had been also well visited in primitive
times, resulting in rich deposits of ancient tools in their earthen
floors.

It is also profitable to put oneself in the natives' place in the
matter of considering a house site. Obviously, one would want
a house near a fresh water source with sunshine most of the
day, sheltered from possible neighboring tribal attacks and the
forces of nature. Then, if one wanted to find and use a particular type of raw material such as stone for manufacturing
adzes or statues, one might also want to build a temporary
house or at least a workshop near the best deposits of these
natural resources.

Once a site is found, only a limited time can generally be
spent working on it. Therefore, it is best to find out the most
one can about the site and its contents as quickly as possible.
As it is seldom practical (or possible) to excavate a whole site
completely, some selections must be made of the areas most
likely to produce rich archaeological deposits. Much of this
work was done at Ha'atuatua in 1956. We examined the surface
of the site closely, noting the places where the most artifacts could be seen. In addition we dug some test pits sampling

the deposits far back from the bank; there was a possibility of their being richer than those exposed by the tidal wave.

In this way, we soon gained an idea of the structure of the site. In the center of the beach on a rise called Te'oho'au (The Canoe Shed) was an ancient burial ground. There, the heavily stained sand stratum indicated that the area had been much used, but the main concentration of houses on the site appeared to have been at a river mouth called Mouaka, six hundred yards north of the burial area. Here, almost all the artifacts recovered were everyday utilitarian household objects; food remains were quite common, in the form of shells and pig, dog, bird and fish bones. It was interesting that so few of the huge Marquesan house platforms in use when the Europeans first appeared were still in existence. In the area between the house sites and the burial area few artifacts were found, and farther inland from the burial area, even fewer, the deposit gradually thinning out and disappearing.

With this background from our 1956 work, it was a relatively simple matter to decide where to begin. The area selected was inland from the burial area, where our tests had shown little refuse accumulation but a thick black layer of sand indicating much use. Our short-term goal became that of finding out what connection existed between this area, the nearby graveyard, and the pavements. The graves, around and beneath the cobbled flooring, were particularly intriguing. Were they burials of a much greater age than the stone floor or were they of the same period? Had this been a sacred place, despite the fact that it bore no relation to any Marquesan temple that I had ever seen before? To find out about these things it seemed best to cross-section the deposits with long trenches in two directions: roughly north-south and east-west. These trenches would show the extent of any construction hidden in the drifting sands of the centuries beneath our feet, opening up a bigger section of the site than we had ever opened in 1956. One trench was to run to the bank, north of the graveyard, at which point the other was to branch at a right angle cutting across the promontory upon which the pavement was

seen. The trenches were divided up into numbered five-foot
by five-foot squares which were generally excavated sepa-
rately down into the layer of clean sand beneath the dark-
stained stratum. All artifacts from a given square were kept

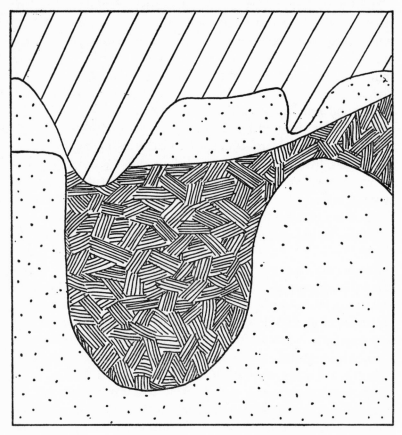

Cross section of a five-foot-wide test excavation at Ha'atuatua,
showing the thin, stained earth layer over a small refuse pit filled
by ancient Marquesans with remains of a fish feast.

in a separate sack or sacks, identified by the number of the
square, inscribed on it in heavy marking crayon. The exact
locations of all important finds were recorded in sketches
and notes, showing depth and distance from any two corners
of the square.

The sides of the trenches were shaved carefully with a trowel as excavation progressed, so that they were perfectly vertical and even. On these clean trench faces could be traced faint outlines of ancient burial or refuse pits, house floors or postholes, which we uncovered and sectioned in our excavating.

We began the trenching with much gusto. In the first few squares we found practically nothing, however, beyond a few fragmentary pearl-shell fishhooks and a coral file or two. A dark blotch appeared in the floor of one of the squares: we had struck the top of a filled-in pit. Although long ago covered and forgotten, the outlines of the pit were still visible in the bottom of our excavation, because the disturbed sand which had been thrown into it was much darker than that of the surrounding deposit. We opened the pit carefully; it might contain a burial—but it held nothing. We continued, uncovering some filled-up postholes, each containing some beach boulders, placed as bracers for posts that had long since decayed.

Proceeding, we moved slightly closer to the beach. I had taken a position near Tiro, watching the fine wire mesh earth-sifter that he held in his hands. The sand was removed from the excavation and dumped into the sifter, through which it was carefully pushed; artifacts were caught in the screen. Tiro, who worked rapidly but with a sharp eye, was already growing a bit impatient at our having found nothing. Suddenly, something among the pebbles in his screen caught my eye. A flat fragment of some brick-red substance had appeared briefly: it looked very much like a tiny bit of broken pottery! This could not be, I told myself, as I carefully sorted through the contents of Tiro's sieve. Pottery had never been known in eastern Polynesia. It had been found in the western Polynesian island of Tonga, where the ceramist's art was believed to have been introduced by the neighboring Fijians, a Melanesian group who had kept up trade relations with the Tongans. Certainly it could not be pottery.

Nevertheless, what lay in the palm of my hand was an ac-

tual potsherd, from the very bottom of the stratum of dark
sand that had been deposited during the Marquesans' habitation of the site. This find had hardly been examined when a
second, larger fragment was uncovered. The big question now
was: Just how did this find alter our ideas and theories concerning the origins of the Marquesan people and the Polynesians in general? We knew comparatively little about Marquesan archaeology, and speculation had to be suppressed until a great deal more evidence had been accumulated from
many more weeks of excavating, both at Ha'atuatua and elsewhere.

One fact was sure: at one point in their history the Marquesans had been in contact with a culture that made pottery
—or they had made pottery themselves. The nearest places
where pottery was known to have been made were several
thousand miles away due west (Tonga) or east (Ecuador).
As all scientific evidence ruled out consideration of South
America as the home of the Polynesians, the source was obviously in the west, but where? Not far beyond Tonga lay
Melanesia, where pots were still being made. We could not
exclude this area as a possible source for the Marquesans without further evidence.

Within two weeks, the trench had reached the edge of the
beach. We had a series of postholes uncovered, running in
lines roughly parallel with the long axis of the trench. Apparently a long shelter had stood in this place at one time,
probably a simple structure of poles with a thatched roof and
walls. It seemed to have some relationship to the pavement
and burial ground, but it was still too early to say. In carefully cleaning out the postholes, we found that they sometimes contained a few artifacts and occasionally some scraps
of human bone, possibly bits of a cannibal feast celebrating
the construction of the long building. In one large posthole
well down in the deposit we discovered still another piece
of broken pottery—this time a fragment of the rim of a pot,
with the rounded, grooved lip quite well preserved, and light
striations on both inside and outside surfaces from the hand

of the potter who had smoothed this vessel in the dim past. Premature enthusiasm over these repeated finds of pottery was difficult to suppress, and I wrote a guarded letter to Dr. Shapiro, trying not to sound too excited. Tiro and Tunui, on the other hand, were very little impressed by these chunks of baked clay, which to them were featureless. The only pottery they had ever seen was the stoneware in which forbidden absinthe and kümmel had once been sold. These fragments certainly did not resemble pieces of a kümmel bottle; therefore my native helpers had nothing to compare them with in their minds. Although they had learned rapidly to recognize all of the tools of the ancient Marquesan technology, and to spot fragments of them with equal facility, these potsherds were completely unacceptable. Tiro looked at me in wonderment as I tried to explain their significance. His wonderment changed slowly to a slightly mocking hint of a smile, and even Tunui, whose prolonged association with scientists had given him a good grasp of scientific method, looked a bit embarrassed, although he declared himself determined to find for me more bits of *hue kea* (stone container), as they were christened, even if he could not understand their possible value. He had never before heard of Marquesans' making pottery, but then, white men often knew surprising things about the old Marquesans!

Striking off from our first test trench at a 90-degree angle, we started to cut across the base of the promontory upon which the pavements and the graves were located. More postholes appeared, and a number of large, empty pits. Then suddenly Tiro shouted, *"A'a! e tupapau!"*—There! A dead man! He pointed to a tiny bit of brown bone protruding from the sand at the base of the sea side of the excavation. Out came brushes, brooms, sacks, cameras, and note pads; the shovels were put aside while all had a closer look. Brushing away the sand, I uncovered the outer ends of a heavy human collarbone and a shoulder blade. In the socket where the heavy knob of the upper armbone should have rested was nothing but sand. A little more sweeping uncovered a series of wide ribs just below the collarbone. Our first burial of the season had appeared! There in the face of the trench were seen the dark outlines of the shallow, bowl-shaped burial pit. Working down on the burial from above, the pit appeared as a blackened oval area in the excavation floor. With all possible obstacles removed, the sand was gently brushed away, revealing a macabre sight: a headless, limbless, human male torso, slumped in a shallow pit. Flecks of charcoal in the surrounding sand and shiny splotches on the bones resulting from cooking suggested that these bones might have been those of the victim of a cannibalistic rite. In and around the solid pelvis we found hand and foot bones dumped haphazardly. The victim's extremities had evidently been disjointed completely and thrown into the grave with the limbless torso.

Just beyond the grave we struck a heavy, coarse gravel deposit in the uppermost several inches of the black stratum. This thick layer of well-smoothed beach pebbles began quite abruptly and continued for approximately forty feet, stopping as suddenly as it had begun. The trench had cut across a rectangular gravel pavement which, as some quick test pits proved, extended out parallel to our first trench. A mental picture of the structure which we were excavating began to form: here were long, low sheds, extending along the side of a gravel-covered hard-packed rectangular court, at the end of which lay a group of pavements and a burial area.

It was to the burials and the stone pavements built over them that we next turned our attention. The *Tiare Taporo* had arrived one happy day and the four bulky boxes of equipment and supplies had come through the surf in the whaleboat. We now set up a little laboratory on the back porch of our house so that we could treat fragile human bones with various chemical preservatives. Film was plentiful, and the surveyor's instruments had survived the rough handling: in short, we were ready for the most difficult archaeological problems, of which the burial hill was obviously going to be an example. The short exploratory excavations of that spot in 1956 had clearly shown the complicated hodgepodge resulting from the burial of a large number of individuals, in a rather limited area. Burials had been made right into or through earlier cadavers, babies by the score had been stuffed into small pits, and large group burials consisting of up to ten people in one entangled mass of fragile brown bones were not uncommon. It was therefore not without some trepidation that I made preparations for working on the burial area. A grid of five-foot squares was laid out over the surface of the hill, stout stakes being set at each grid co-ordinate intersection. The position of any object which was uncovered, its distance from any other object, and its depth, could then be measured precisely. We then recorded this information in the notes and transferred it to a map.

With grid set out, the excavations began on the bone-littered face of the bank, below the crest of the promontory. A long step had been cut into the bank across the entire width of the burial promontory well below the burial level, and on this step we began to slice slowly into the face of the enigmatic hill. Before long we found a deep grave containing three well-preserved female skulls, piled tightly together just above a flattened infant's skull. On the three upper skulls the middle teeth of the upper and lower jaws had been removed, indicating that the skulls might have been ancestral or trophy skulls. Such skulls were cleaned and dried after the decay of the flesh; the lower jaw was attached to the skull by coconut fiber cords passed through the nasal passages, around the lower jaw, and through the gap where the upper front teeth had been removed. The entire skull was then tightly covered with bark cloth to simulate flesh, and facial features were painted on the cloth. A heavy cord was attached to the skull at the rear or passed through holes drilled in the skull vault: the cord was for hanging the grisly relic in the house or carrying it on the person, during important ceremonies.

In excavating the three skulls, it was of course necessary to remove large amounts of sand from above and around the grave so that it could be isolated properly. When we began to clear away the sand, however, it was impossible to excavate in any direction without encountering other graves, some containing several individuals. This condition lasted throughout our entire period of work on the burial hill and stone pavements. Often, in fact, we found it impossible even to isolate a single burial, so closely were the graves placed. As many burials had been disturbed by later graves dug through them or into them, we found human bones scattered throughout the deposits among the graves: teeth, skull fragments, and scores of hand and foot bones wherever the excavations were extended.

The burials contained individuals of all ages and sexes, buried in just about every form of burial known to anthropologists. Among or just beneath the stones of the pavement we found many infant skeletons that had been tucked away hastily with little evidence of the care that had been given to the adult dead. These pitiful little skeletons with tiny, smooth boneshafts, buttonlike vertebral fragments, and paper-thin skulls appeared everywhere, often crushed beyond all hope of preservation by the pressure of the rocks above them and the weight of the living who had passed above their unmarked graves year after year.

It was obvious that the infant mortality among the prehistoric Marquesans had been high, as it is at present, when many babies die during the first two to three years from respiratory infections, dysentery, and the effects of ill-tended insect bites and scratches.

Pig burials were numerous throughout the whole cemetery: most of those uncovered contained complete or partial skeletons of young pigs. Dog bones were common, but only one complete dog burial was found: a very significant discovery, as it was believed that the Marquesans had not had dogs before the coming of the whites.

The adults of the prehistoric village of Ha'atuatua had been better cared for than their children, and from their burials we learned much about the early Marquesan religious customs. A number of large burials were uncovered containing neatly stacked piles of arm and leg bones with groups of foot and hand bones grouped to one side. These are what the archaeological fraternity calls "secondary burials": burials in which the bones of corpses have been reburied, after an initial period in the earth or on a platform bier, during which the flesh has rotted away. After a cleaning and sorting of the remains, the fact that most such burials contained the bones of several individuals was evidenced by the finding of several right or left leg bones in one burial. This indicated that the identity of the owners of the bones was not of great importance. Probably these bundles contained the remains of the dead of one family collected over a long period, and then interred.

The state in which the bones were found in such graves indicated that they had probably been wrapped or tied in a package before being placed in the sand. All this evidence seemed to accord well with what we knew of Marquesan mortuary customs from the eighteenth- and nineteenth-century European visitors, who described the process in which bodies were allowed to desiccate on a platform. The bones were then collected, the skulls placed on the temple platform or prepared for hanging in the house, and the limb bones gathered into a bark cloth bundle to be buried, placed in a cave ossuary, or hung from a sacred banyan tree.

Many of the prehistoric Ha'atuatuans were buried intact and left undisturbed, however. Some were placed in deep pits, flat on their backs with their hands crossed on their pelvises. Others were buried with knees tightly flexed, lying on their backs or on one side, and one burial was made face-downward stretched at full length. Although many male skeletons were found, their skulls were seldom attached. The heads of most male Ha'atuatuans had evidently been carefully removed shortly after death and subjected to a process of cleaning or mummification, and had then become objects of devotion in the family or clan shrine. An examination of the vertebra at the point where the neck was severed showed that the Marquesans had a good knowledge of human anatomy —the head, in nearly every case, had been removed without any mutilation of the vertebra.

The preservation of heads of important people was extremely important to the Marquesans, for the head was the seat of all the individual's supernatural power, or *mana*, and even after death the skull retained its high charge of unearthly power, radiating a protective aura to all those in its proximity.

Females were generally buried intact, with their heads; it appears, therefore, that their supernatural powers were not held in high esteem.

The graves contained further interesting evidence of Marquesan beliefs and customs. Most individuals had been buried with some sort of foodstuffs, the most popular being pig and fish. The massive ridged bone from the rear of the pig skull was found again and again in graves, nearly always placed on the chest of the dead, usually displaying the shiny darkened splotches resulting from cooking. As few other pig bones were found with the skull fragment, the fragment was apparently a token or symbol of a pig that had been sacrificed for the dead and then probably eaten by the mourners or the priests officiating at the burial. In other graves the skeleton lay amidst masses of needlelike fish bones, showing that the deceased had started off on his way to the Polynesian heaven in the west well provided with the fruits of the sea that had sustained him in life.

Besides these food offerings, few objects of any value had been placed with the dead. Most often the grave objects consisted of bits of broken pearl shells or an occasional small stone adze or ornament. A porpoise-tooth ear pendant rested near the gaping earhole of one female skull; another displayed an ivory earplug.

Some burials were provided with unusual belongings for the trip to the sky world, however. One young lady in her early twenties carried a heavy-browed male trophy skull with her; an individual secondary burial was accompanied by a beautiful necklace of forty-eight whale's teeth, each carefully perforated by a fine drill for stringing.

Although most of the deaths had apparently been due to natural causes, there was occasional disquieting evidence of

violence. One pregnant woman had been felled with the proverbial "blunt instrument," for her forehead bore a deeply
depressed fracture over the left eye. The force of the blow
had so compressed the flesh above the fracture that a tiny
brown speck of dehydrated crushed tissue still clung tena-
ciously to the bone at the point of impact. On the south side of
the burial area were a number of large, shallow oven pits in
which charred human bone fragments were found along with
those of pigs and fish. Evidently cannibalism played an important part in ceremonies held at this cemetery.

An examination of the bones of these burials brought out
some facts about Marquesan health, the most interesting of
which was the high incidence of arthritis, as indicated by
twisted sharp growths on the joint surfaces of many bones.
One elderly man was almost bent on himself in his grave: his
upper spine had been fused into a solid, sharply curved column
of bone by overlapping bony growths which locked each
vertebra to the next. Not only adults but many adolescents
showed traces of arthritic growths in the spinal column, while
similar growths also appeared in the knees, arms, and hands of
old and young alike. In this high arthritis incidence, the Marquesans were similar to their Hawaiian cousins twenty-five
hundred miles to the north, for ancient Hawaiian skeletons
also display arthritic growths in large numbers. The appearance of the disease may be related to the cool, damp Marquesan nights, certain as yet unidentifiable diet factors, something in the genetic structure of the Polynesian race, or, what
is more likely, a combination of all of these factors.

The burials of Ha'atuatua told us much about the appearance of the ancient Polynesians, but a detailed analysis of the
collection would be necessary before the precise characteristics of the old Marquesans could be determined and their
resemblances to other Polynesian groups charted definitively.

Some things may, however, be said at this time, on the basis
of our cursory examination. First, the skeletons displayed
distinctive Polynesian traits, distinguishing that race from all

others in the world. These include features of facial and skull conformation and jaw shape.

The old Ha'atuatuans were somewhat shorter than modern Marquesans but extremely muscular, with very heavy, thick bones. The males had rugged skulls with well-developed brows, wide cheeks, and massive, beautiful dental structures, while the females were shorter, of lighter build, with more fragile skulls and smooth brows. They too generally had beautiful teeth. All males and most females were long-headed, in contrast to the round-headed modern inhabitants.

As we worked our way into the heart of the ancient cemetery, we were also systematically dissecting the overlying pavements. These paving stones, large, smooth, blue basalt cobbles from the beach, were at once a source of interest and trouble to us. Their weight, atop the relatively loose sand in which the burials had been made, caused frequent collapses of the sides of our excavations. At various points in the excavation it was necessary to obtain cross sections of the entire hill, or parts of it, along various lines in the grid system that we had established earlier. On a number of occasions a day was spent in carefully cleaning off the excavation face in a twenty- or thirty-foot profile, so that I could photograph and sketch the deposits so revealed, only to have the whole face collapse.

At first, no arrangement was apparent among the stones. Then one day we struck a low curb, some twenty inches high, buried beneath the pavement. This curb, formed of flat stones set on edge, was discovered at the south side of the hill, where a portion had been exposed by wind erosion. We traced it beneath the pavements through the whole deposit to a point where it terminated in a 90-degree corner. At that point, long ago, someone had removed the rest of the curb.

Here was evidence of a building of some kind beneath the obviously ancient pavement. The curb had evidently been part of a low rectangular enclosure, the first structure to stand on the hill. Inside the curb several natural stone pillars had been erected, of which one still stood, rakishly projecting above the present ground surface. The others had long since disappeared, leaving only gaping pits within the enclosure to mark their places. The one remaining pillar that had not been removed had been incorporated into the pavements that had been laid above the little curbed enclosure.

Simple structures such as these have been identified as the earliest known types of temple in eastern Polynesia. Such a temple, however, had never been found in the Marquesas before. Information from other islands in Polynesia indicated that this crude enclosure was an altar, dedicated to a series of gods, each of which was represented by one stone pillar. In many islands it was believed that the stone pillars—or slabs, as they often were—were infused by the spirit of the god descending from the sky world or arising from the depths below, when the proper invocation ceremonies had been performed. The stone uprights had evidently been dedicated to gods of some importance at Ha'atuatua, for beneath the single remaining pillar we found the headless skeleton of a dismembered man, his legs thrown in helter-skelter onto his torso, before the great stone had sealed his grave.

The small altar had probably stood on the hill for some years while the important dead of the Ha'atuatua tribe were buried around it. Some small houses and sheds, possibly for the priests and their equipment, stood near it. Then for some reason the whole area was rebuilt: a series of rectangular pavements was placed over the low altar and houses were built on some of them. On the inland side of the pavements the long, gravel-covered court that we had discovered earlier was laid out and the narrow buildings were erected along its borders. The area in which the little altar had once stood now had become the site of a large and rather formal ceremonial complex, where the tribesmen gathered for both sacred and civil ceremonies—a complex that was probably an earlier version of the great tribal *tohua* or ceremonial plazas that were seen by so many European visitors in the eighteenth and nineteenth centuries.

In the river bed, just south of Te'oho'au, a series of designs had been carved into the surface of a great flat bedrock exposure where they had been covered partially by coraline deposits while the river still flowed, and later by drifting sands. We located this gallery of primitive art in 1956 and removed the sand and coral covering from the designs, exposing a series of beautiful stylizations of a sperm whale, turtles, sharks, men, and dogs. When we relocated the area in 1957, we recleaned and photographed parts of it for a better record.

Here the artists of old Ha'atuatua had sketched some records of their conquests and their strokes of good fortune on the sea. The drawing of the sperm whale may have represented a huge specimen of that animal that drifted ashore there, the great bones of which were found throughout the ceremonial area of the site. I say "drifted" ashore because it is improbable that the Marquesans could have taken such a great creature on wooden or bone harpoons. In another sketch, a stick figure of a man held a long object in its "hand" to which a line was connected that terminated in the shell of a large turtle. This may have represented an actual harpooning.

The figures of dogs, with long curly tails, on the basis of Marquesan ethnographic studies, seemed to be totemic figures of a type very common on the north coast of Nuku Hiva, where one powerful tribe held the dog as a totem.

I often thought that a photograph of Ha'atuatua would give the impression of a veritable paradise. But a photo would never tell what a vest-pocket inferno this valley really was. Each day, we arrived with trousers tied at the ankles, shirts buttoned tightly at the neck and cuffs, and hats to ward off the heat. We anointed ourselves liberally from a bottle of the strongest insect repellent available and went to work. Within minutes, hands and neck began to tingle as the tiny *nono* flies alighted, to bite first and then die. Soon the backs of one's hands were covered with dead, bloody insects. I once counted eighty on both hands, and gave up in disgust without completing the census. Perspiration washed the insect repellent from the forehead into the eyes, which began to burn fiercely, necessitating a halt and a careful mopping of the brow and cheeks followed by another application of the oily liquid, which, of course, was soon coursing into the eyes again in rivers of perspiration. Sand infiltrated cameras, clothes, and food and clung to the oily film of insect repellent.

Whenever things got really bad, Tiro would race down to the beach, get a load of driftwood, and start a roaring fire downwind of us, in a green stand of hibiscus shrubs. The fire, fed by the dead leaves among the plants, gave off clouds of toxic gray smoke that generally stopped the *nono* attack but drove me, at least, choking and near-blind, to a smoke-free area where the bugs could start all over again.

The natural obstacles to scientific progress were compounded by the personnel problems that had begun to arise in the form of a quiet duel for favor between Tiro and Tunui. Tiro should have been submissive to the older man, but he was possessed of an ego that brooked no rivalry, and acknowledged only the rare threat and admonitions of his father. He treated Tunui as an equal and occasionally as a subordinate. The older man naturally had less vitality than Tiro and his eyes were not as sharp for the fine bits of stone and pearl-shell tools that appeared in the earth screens. Tunui had a much better idea of scientific method, however, and a better understanding of the significance of any scientific mission than most Marquesans. As a result of his laborious insect-collecting period, thirty years before, he knew that patience was of the utmost importance in scientific work. Tiro's volatile personality, however, balked at any time-consuming jobs: *his* only desire was to find "pretty things" and get on with the digging.

We moved our focus of activity after completely dissecting the complicated series of burials and the remains of the pavements, stone pillars, gravel court, and pole and thatch buildings that had been constructed around and over them. At the mouth of a dried-up stream that had emptied into the sea at the north end of the beach was the area known as Mouaka. Here, in 1956, we had uncovered parts of what seemed to be the houses and general living area inhabited by the people who were buried in the cemetery beneath the temple. Our test excavations had shown a twenty-inch stratum of black sand, rich with broken hooks, stone adzes, coral files, shell scrapers, and ornaments. Ovens, fire pits, and a litter of animal and fish bones and bits of broken shellfish showed that many meals had been eaten there, and the dark outlines of ancient postholes were profuse.

On a hilltop on the north side of the river mouth we staked out a grid system and began to work systematically, stripping off the few inches of sand and tough grass on the surface to expose the deposits beneath. Artifacts were no longer scarce, as they had been in the burial area: they appeared by the hundreds. As large areas were cleared, the postholes were located on the site map, cleaned and photographed, and their contents carefully excavated, for we had found that artifacts were particularly numerous in the holes around the beach boulders that had evidently served to support the posts inserted in the pits.

Almost immediately, a surprise came to light: at the brow of the hill, two burials were discovered. The skeletons were of two adolescent females, buried on their backs with the legs drawn up tight against their chests. With one had been placed a quarter of a piglet. The graves were extremely shallow, especially for an area that seemed to be well frequented if not truly a hamlet site as we had begun to suppose. A thin layer of broken cooking stones and pebbles had covered both graves, as if to protect them from the rooting of pigs and dogs.

As the excavations proceeded, a faint trace of patterning began to appear among the postholes plotted on the map of the diggings. Sketching idly with a pencil, I tried connecting some of the seemingly related posts into a pattern, obtaining a rough outline of a long oval figure, round at both ends and slightly wider in the middle than at the ends. Connecting a few more posts, I soon realized that these represented the remains of a series of oval house plans, overlapping and intersecting each other to produce the confused jumble that had first shown on the map. Apparently the houses at Mouaka had been between six and eight feet wide, twenty to thirty feet long, built of poles stuck directly into the earth and bent over at the top, to bear a thatch covering. Small pits had been dug around the house floors, possibly to hold valuables or ceremonial objects. Close by were the remains of thin shallow fire beds, filled with light ash, and deeper oven holes, filled with charred bones and charcoal-blackened cooking stones. These were loaf-shaped volcanic rocks, with deep pockmarks where volcanic gases had been trapped in the lava flow that had formed the rock. These spongy stones were ideal for ovens because they could stand tremendous heat without shattering.

From the ovens, charcoal and ash were collected for geophysical tests that could determine with relative precision the age of the fire. This was done by measuring the amount of a radioactive trace element, carbon 14, contained in a given amount of charcoal or ash. Carbon 14 is present in all living things, plant and animal, being inhaled from the air. Upon death the carbon 14 supply in an animal or plant receives no added increments from the air, and soon begins to deteriorate, at a constant rate. By measuring the amount of carbon 14 still present in charcoal from an ancient wood fire or an old wooden implement and comparing it with the amount that would be present if the wood were still alive, we know how much of the element has deteriorated, and hence how much time has elapsed since the fire or the implement was made. Carbon 14 tests can also be done on shell and bone objects but with less reliability than on samples of wood in natural or charred state. The age of a sample is always given as some number of years, with a margin of error, stated in terms of "plus or minus" a small number of years, meaning that the chances are that the sample's age falls within the range of the "plus or minus" value, added to and subtracted from the date. Carbon 14 tests are excellent for archaeological sites dating back fifty thousand years in age, but no further, for the radioactive element has so deteriorated by then that even the finest instruments cannot detect it.

The tools which were unearthed daily at Mouaka were fascinating, both to myself and to the workers. Tiro, as a very adept wood carver, had a "professional" interest in hand tools of all types. The uses of many of the artifacts which we found were no mystery to me, for I had been able to examine the extensive Hawaiian archaeological collections excavated in ancient sites in that archipelago since 1950 by K. P. Emory of the Bernice Bishop Museum in Honolulu.

We found hundreds of flat, bladelike objects of fine-grained coral that were used as files in the shaping of shell and wood objects and resembled their Hawaiian counterparts quite closely. Other smaller and more delicate files were made of the spines of a species of sea urchin which grew among the rocks of Marquesan bays.

We came to see quite clearly the manner in which the coral files had been used, in examining the numerous complete and fragmentary mother-of-pearl hooks that were recovered from the Mouaka sands. Many of these iridescent hooks had been discarded before being finished for reasons that were seldom obvious to us. When a large number of hooks in various stages of manufacture had been assembled after several weeks of digging, it was possible partially to reconstruct the process of manufacture in which the coral files had played such an important part.

First, a big mother-of-pearl shell was selected, and rough pieces were cut from various parts of it with crude basalt-flake knives that were found everywhere on the site. In some cases the pieces were broken and chipped from the shell. Then, with a large coral file, the ancient Marquesan craftsman began to grind the edges of his pearl-shell stock smooth, removing the blemishes of the flake knife or chipping tool, gradually altering the shape of the piece until it resembled that of the hook desired. Then, the rough, barklike skin of the shell piece was ground down and polished away, to show the rosy-hued layer beneath. During this process, only the

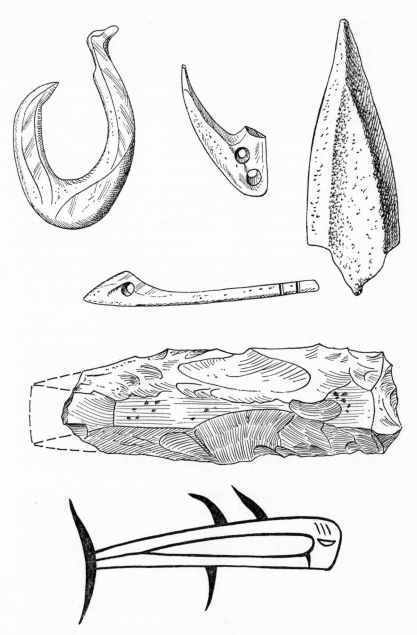

Finds at Ha'atuatua. Top, left to right: one-piece pearl shell fish-hook; point and shank of pearl shell bonito hook; coral file. Middle: stone adze of Melanesian type. Bottom: petroglyph incised in riverbed stone near Ha'atuatua temple.

flat surfaces of the file were used. Then a rotary drill, tipped with a bit of sharpened urchin spine, drilled away at the center of the hook-to-be, opening the hole that would soon be enlarged to form the interior of the hook curve. Once the inside was opened, the sharp end of the triangular file was introduced; gradually the inside contour was smoothed down and rounded and both sides of the now nearly complete hook were polished, while the edges were sharpened and the tip honed to a point. Then, with a smaller file, the craftsman put the finishing touches on his work, until the hook was ready to receive the finely twined cord leader that would hold it to the stout coconut fiber line.

A limited number of basic hook patterns or types appeared over and over. One type was almost circular, describing a beautiful arc from the knobbed shank where the fishline had been attached, around to the point, which curved inward, almost touching the interior of the shank just below the knob end. Another variety, also frequently found, was angular. Both of these were of a type called the "rotating hooks," known far and wide throughout Polynesia and Melanesia. The curved or angular outline of the hook is such that when a fish impales himself on the almost hidden point and begins to pull against it, the natural shape of the point will cause it to rotate in the fish's mouth, so that the fish is entrapped more securely.

Although it was obvious that the various kinds of hooks were intended for different species of fish, there was little that we could determine about the specific purpose of any particular type. Even the multitudinous fishbones which we recovered failed to give us any clues, for most of them were small rib or backbone fragments and quite unidentifiable. Fishbones are difficult to identify except from the skull or jaw remains, which were rare in the digging.

One interesting kind of hook, however, was of a kind still being used by the Marquesans. This is the bonito lure, or *pa:* a shining pearl shell lure, shaped like a minnow or silversides, with a cruel shell or bone hook lashed to one end, and a tuft of pig bristles tied to it to simulate small tail fins.

There were also some very unusual kinds of lures and points that could only be components of other varieties of *pa* that had long since been discarded and forgotten by the Marquesans. Some of these were obviously intended for very large tuna and bonito, yet I could never suppress my wonder that some pieces of brittle shell, held together with a fiber cord, could withstand the shearing force of a big tuna, hooked while cruising along at twenty or thirty knots. Although many broken hooks of all types bore witness to the fact that shell did not always stand the strain, there were the piles of fishbones to convince us that it nevertheless fairly consistently delivered the goods.

Some of the most interesting tools discovered in the little hamlet site were those clearly connected with food preparation, for these told us what varieties of plants the Ha'atuatuans depended upon for their existence. Narrow saw-toothed coconut-grater blades of nacreous pearl shell were quite common. These blades were attached to the end of a long projection extending out from a small bench, upon which the person grating the coconut meat sat, scraping the inside of half a coconut shell against the firmly held blade and removing long shreds of meat which were then squeezed for the nourishing milk.

Many knives were found, made of pieces of pearl shell sharpened on one edge or more, with a thick area remaining for a handle. Such knives were used by Marquesans until relatively recent years to scrape banyan, terminalia, or paper mulberry tree bark in preparation for making bark cloth, or *tapa*. Therefore, we could be certain that the Ha'atuatuans were well provided with the plants to produce bark cloth and actually produced large quantities of it for loincloths and cloaks.

Another common food tool, although a strange one, was made from a handy-sized snail shell, in the side of which a hole had been punched. The edges of the hole were ground sharp, to form a circular knife blade, which would cut a strip of skin from the side of a taro root or breadfruit, allowing it to pass out of the natural mouth of the snail shell. These little parers told us that root crops and breadfruit were grown by the Ha'atuatuans, but they also raised some interesting questions, for they were not at all like the peelers made of cowrie shells which are used today and were in use when the white men first arrived. These were, on the contrary, identical with shell peelers found in the Melanesian islands of New Caledonia and the Fiji archipelago thousands of miles to the west. One solitary example of this tool was known from western Polynesia.

Here was something else to go with the potsherds found around the cemetery that seemed to point decidedly past the western border of Polynesia into the islands beyond. But pottery and scrapers were not the only things that seemed to say, "Look to Melanesia. . . ." Some very peculiar stone adzes appeared, with shapes that put them out of the normal range of Polynesian tools: they were circular in cross section, or planoconvex, and were generally heavily polished on most surfaces, in contrast to the predominantly rectangular or triangular true Polynesian adzes, rarely polished by the Marquesan adze makers, who carefully chipped them out of billets of gray-blue basalt.

Most surprising of all unusual finds were large disks of pearl shell, with notched edges and central perforations, and small buttons of the same general design. These disks and buttons were part of a complex kind of headdress called *kapkap* which is characteristically Melanesian and Micronesian. The pearl shell disks are mounted on a coconut fiber headband, and a finely carved disk of tortoise-shell filigree is placed over the pearl shell, the two being secured by a series of alternating buttons of pearl and tortoise shell. These headdresses were highly prized in the Marquesas at the time of the European onslaught, but they are found nowhere else in Polynesia. The nearest point to the Marquesas where natives used these ornaments is Santa Cruz Island in the New Hebrides archipelago, over twenty-five hundred miles to the west.

Here we had some real food for thought: it had been generally assumed that the Melanesians had been relatively distinct from the Polynesians; if that were so, how had this group of decidedly Melanesian tools ended up so far from home, at the very end of Polynesia, in a site of considerable age? There were no answers apparent, nor would there be, for some time to come.

It was not until the final days of our third month at Ha'-atuatua that we left the site of the ancient hamlet. Excavations there had been continued until it was certain that we had a good sampling of the various kinds of tools and we had had an opportunity to expose a large area of posthole patterns to check on our tentative house plan reconstructions. After that the focus of attention had shifted to a wide, flat area well back on the dune from the cemetery. This had evidently been the Mouaka town dump, for the area was honeycombed with deep, narrow pits packed with ashes, fish and animal bones, and broken food shells.

After sampling these refuse pits, we spent a few days of testing to make sure we had not overlooked any potentially rich areas, a few more days of mapping, and then we left Ha'atuatua. At the house in Hatiheu, bags and crates containing human skeletons were piled high in our storage room, and even overflowed into the bedroom, terrorizing the maid so that she refused to sweep there without considerable prodding.

We certainly knew a great deal more than we had previously known about the settlement at Ha'atuatua, the way of life of its people, and the actual appearance of the people themselves; and when it was possible to make a detailed scientific study of the collections back in the American Museum of Natural History much more could be learned about the Ha'atuatuans. We had provided grist for the archaeological mill but in doing so had raised a large number of new and disturbing questions, foremost of which was: What did the presence of Melanesian tools and ornaments mean to Marquesan prehistory and the prehistory of Polynesia?

The most important question of all which we had been asking since 1956 concerning the relationship between the Ha'atuatua settlement and the culture of the nineteenth-century Marquesas was still unanswered.

We had traveled an unknown distance into the past and caught a glimpse of a little hamlet of thatched houses on the shores of a great blue bay, inhabited by sturdy fishermen whose canoes had probably rested on the sand near the water's edge.

Here, on this now silent beach, naked children had cavorted with their dogs and pet birds among the huts and raced each other to the stream that ran close by. Lovers had met in the shadow of these huts. Men had given their lives to protect this hamlet from outsiders. Down the beach from the houses the tribal temple had risen, decorated with white sacred streamers, ancestral skulls, and fierce images. There, before the long huts bordering the gravel-covered court, spectators had gathered in the torchlight to watch the dancers sinuously weaving to the sound of their ceremonial drums. On other occasions they had come to invoke the powerful gods of the Polynesian spirit world, such as Tangaroa, Lord of the Sea, or Tiki, the Creator. When their lives were done, they joined their ancestors beneath the sands of the hill of Te'oho'au to look down forever on the granite-rimmed bay that had once been their world.

These people had long since vanished from the face of the earth, but the techniques of modern science had enabled us partially to reconstruct their lost way of life, and restore the period to its rightful place in history.

5 / Of the Flesh and the Spirit

A short time after we began our excavations on the beach of
Ha'atuatua, the *Tiare Taporo* called in at Hatiheu to put
ashore our equipment and take aboard my assistant, John
Belmont. My "brother-in-law," as the natives insisted he was,
unfortunately had to leave in order to reach Cambridge for
the start of the fall semester at Harvard.

Thus isolated in the midst of an alien society, one either
adjusts to the local way of life rapidly or accepts a very lonely,
cheerless existence. Naturally, we chose to participate as much
as possible in the native way of life, not only in the hope of
turning up something of anthropological interest, but also for
the experience of living in the completely different universe
of the Marquesans.

A stranger arriving in a Marquesan valley today might
have some difficulty in finding any traces of the wild night
life traditionally attributed to the Polynesians. After sunset,
a few kerosene lamps burn here and there in isolated huts,
going out one by one until by eight o'clock the hamlets are
silent and dark and the only signs of life are the omnipresent
mongrel dogs, skulking in packs, or the young males, odorous
with brilliantine, flowers, and scented coconut oil, squatting
in the shadows at a convenient spot on a trail, teasing soft
muted sounds from a battered guitar as they work up a plan
of action for the evening's *affaires d'amour*.

The Marquesans say relatively little to strange whites about
many of their more cherished leisure-time activities. This is
especially true if the stranger is in a close relationship with any
of the local French officials or missionaries.

One of the reasons for our acceptance was the medical

work carried on by Rae. She treated as many as ten individuals during the course of a day, not only in the "cookhouse clinic" but on house calls. We were frequently awakened before sunrise by someone pounding on the porch and demanding Rae's presence immediately. Young and old, with real and imagined ailments, came to see the white "doctor-lady" and talk about their problems, the weather, that far-off fairyland of *Menike* (America), and, in general, to pass the time of day.

Another reason for our acceptance was the fact that I was rapidly learning the native language; it was therefore becoming increasingly difficult to hide anything from me. Previously all censored topics had been discussed in Marquesan, while that which was meant for my consumption was phrased in somewhat abused French. This practice was no longer possible, however, and both Tunui and Tiro began to show some signs of anxiety over what was to them the unusual speed with which I acquired their tongue.

The Marquesans use their strangely intoned, liquid language as a very effective weapon against all whites and even against Polynesians from islands speaking different dialects. Few white residents have ever learned the language, apart from missionaries, who are required to learn it for their service, but their knowledge of the language represents little danger to the natives, for they are socially isolated, and any dangerous news can be kept from them by a tacit agreement among the natives themselves.

With his language, the native is free to mock a white, insult him gravely, cheat him outrageously, and trick him in any way he sees fit. The white man can seldom see the malice in the carefully controlled voices and expressions of his tormentors. There he stands, a product of many years of formal education, a man of what seems to be boundless wealth, one who knows about airplanes, great ocean vessels, atomic bombs, and a host of other things completely foreign to the native. Yet he is completely at their mercy, because he is too stupid to know their language. After all the indignities suffered by the natives at the hands of the whites, here is a nice handy everyday situation in which the tables are completely turned. The Marquesans call the shots with a vengeance.

To have a white man show detailed interest in their tongue frightens most Marquesans. Characteristically, they react by giving the inquirer completely erroneous information. I once met a poor fellow who had a long vocabulary list of what he considered essential words such as "bread," "egg," "water," etc. The list was actually one of obscenities—his informants had given him the word for penis in place of bread, testicle in place of egg, semen for water, etc.

In my case such trickery was not possible, for I had a Marquesan dictionary to check all words given to me, and I arrived with a vocabulary of about a hundred essential words. As work at Ha'atuatua continued, my vocabulary and knowledge of grammar increased rapidly. Tiro and Tunui doggedly refused to talk to me in their language; all conversation with them was in French, which Tiro spoke abominably. My questions in Marquesan would be greeted with French replies and a smile, but Tiro could not forbear correcting my grammatical mistakes with a great deal of sarcasm. All his corrections were carefully noted for my improvement. Evenings and weekends I found excuses to go visiting people who I knew spoke no French, talking with them as long as possible. Before three months had passed, Tunui and Tiro were quite worried— they knew they would have to watch their remarks, as I could understand just about all they said. Tiro then switched to Tahitian when he did not want me to understand, but neither he nor Tunui would concede and speak to me in their native tongue. They now pretended they did not understand, a practice subsequently adopted by our new maid, who won the title of "I Don't Know" for her remarkable evasiveness, after In a Minute, her giggling predecessor, had departed our service for saying "In a minute" several hundred times too often.

With knowledge of the language, it was easy to learn about all phases of native life. All one had to do was listen attentively; understanding increased by leaps and bounds. Using this method, we soon realized that Hatiheu differed in many respects from a port valley like Taiohae, especially in respect to the leisure-time pursuits of the native population. In Taiohae were to be found the French administrator, his secretary, the gendarme, the French Army doctor, and all their families, plus a large missionary establishment. The presence of so much authority in one place kept the normal carousing down to a reasonable level. Hatiheu, however, was a long horse ride away from Taiohae, separated by a plateau, a mountain chain, and the deep chasm of Taipivai Valley, and therefore was seldom visited by French officials, except from the sea, and as a result large parts of the interior of the valley were completely unknown to them. Here, then, was a little haven where one could cast off inhibitions and unleash the straining forces of innumerable passions. And that is precisely what the populace of Hatiheu was doing and had been doing since the missionaries had arrived on Nuku Hiva.

Every Thursday or Friday we would arrive home to hear raucous laughter and snatches of tuneless song floating up from the steep slope below our cookhouse. Someone was striking chords on a guitar, someone else banging a tin can in time to the so-called music, and wavering hoarse voices were raised toward never-attained high notes in some well-fractured Tahitian air of current popularity. A chorus, when finished, was greeted with a gale of applause and hoots that ended only when the encore was well under way.

From their start, near the end of the week, these gala events lasted until the following Monday or Tuesday in many cases, the noise becoming quite irritating after several weeks' repetition. The prevailing wind carried the sound with admirable clarity, much to our dismay. There was no longer any attempt to obscure the source of the merriment; we were frankly told who was making the racket and why. Every week the men of Hatiheu (with the women and children, too) labored hard at their copra preparation and gardening but also spent more or less time in the manufacture of illicit alcoholic beverages for their own consumption. The remoteness of Hatiheu made it quite easy to maintain a distillery or a brewery as a side line without any elaborate precautions. As the chief was a renowned tippler, he could be depended upon not to inform the government as long as the men appeared for compulsory government labor on the trails and dock in a clean and sober condition twenty-two days of the year. Each week the fresh supply of homemade pop-skull moonshine would be rounded up and a party begun.

We were invited to attend a number of fairly decorous parties, given in honor of a departing Tahitian schoolteacher, acquiring at these a first-hand knowledge of the qualities of Marquesan moonshine. Such parties usually started off rather well, with a few rounds of Cinzano, Cap Corse, or some other mild alcoholic drink. Then followed a formidable meal of about eight or ten courses, washed down with heavy Algerian *vin ordinaire*. The wine never lasted long, however, as the French have imposed strict rationing on native consumption. Therefore, the natives relied on their own produce to carry them through. After the wine gave out, the cans and bottles of moonshine appeared as if from nowhere, and we had to comply with the host's wishes or risk offending.

Most moonshine in Hatiheu was of two types, orange beer (*taimoa*) and coconut toddy (*hi'inoke*). At a party soon after our arrival, we encountered orange beer, a weak, bubbly, orange-colored liquid resembling nothing more dangerous than orange pop. It was sweet and syrupy to the taste, with the faintest trace of what turned out to be a surprisingly stiff alcoholic content, but if the alcohol did not register on the taste buds it certainly made its mark on the central nervous system.

The toddy was made from the drippings of the heart of a mature coconut tree. The firm spike of the palm heart in the center of the leaves at the very top of the tree is gradually bent over during a period of days, by a process of tying and twisting it twice a day. When the elongated spike is bent parallel to the ground some cuts are made in it with a sharp knife and a bit of the heart is removed at one point of the incisions. The heart immediately begins to bleed into a large gourd hung beneath it to catch the drippings, the gourd being emptied twice a day.

After we had attended a few minor parties, invitations arrived to some of the more exclusive kind which had cost us so many sleepless nights, but I usually begged off, preferring to stay out of situations conducive to trouble. Tunui, ever popular, and free from the guiding hand of Tahia, had become a regular participant in these drinking bouts that lasted from Saturday until Sunday night, nearly every week. As a result, he shuffled around on Mondays with swollen lids and blood-red eyes, looking like a rewarmed cadaver. Despite the ghastly aftermath of coco juice and orange beer, Tunui's reputation soared among the people of Hatiheu as a result of his effervescence during the phases of the orgies in which anyone was still sober enough to notice. This state of happiness lasted only a very short time, for Tahia heard of her man's escapades and arrived one day from Taiohae to keep him company. After that, Tunui could no longer drink himself into oblivion: Tahia came to our house when she felt it was time for him to quit and I had to go down to the party and drag him away.

My first visit to one of these affairs was quite memorable, for I have seen nothing before or since to equal the scene that greeted me as I descended a back trail from Tama's into this Pacific grove of Bacchus of which I had heard so much. On the veranda of a large, ramshackle house and on the ground before it were some thirty people grouped around a couple of great wooden bowls of thin orange beer. In among them were the grotesquely sprawled forms of a number of brave imbibers who had already been overwhelmed by the pace. Many of the still-conscious drinkers were only barely so, sitting slumped forward, with torsos weaving from side to side, held upright only by natural balance and the sheer resistance of bone and muscle. Arms, legs, and heads projected at various angles from the veranda, where a completely off-key guitarist planged unmusically at his instrument with as much finesse as though he were wearing gloves and using a Stillson wrench for a pick. A couple of die-hards staggered about on the ground, "dancing" to this accompaniment while the rest joined voices in the unrecognizable refrain. Around the swaying, shouting, snoring mass of humanity were dogs by the score, standing gloomy watch beside the bodies of a fallen master or mistress, or looking as though they had come to watch the people do tricks.

Picking my way among the bodies and debris, I approached the house. One of the group, noticing my arrival, bellowed a hoarse *"Ka'oha nui Rope!"* and tried to get up to meet me—unsuccessfully. His alerted companions slowly turned, grinning, and regarded me with glassy, unco-ordinated eyes. Everyone tried to talk at once, incomprehensibly. I spotted Tunui sitting on the veranda, bent almost double, his head nodding loosely. Peering through eyelids open only a tiny slit, he looked long and hard in my direction, without any visible reaction. Then suddenly he stiffened and tried to pull himself up to an erect sitting posture. *"Ka'oha nui, Monsieur Robert"* came forth in a garbled fashion from the slack lips as he reached for his neighbors to try to get up. Two of the less advanced drinkers rose on shaky legs and grabbed him by the arms, hauling him to his feet. With his legs bending like those of a rag doll, Tunui was dragged to the faucet behind the house for a freshening up, all the while declaiming his fierce and undying loyalty to me, our cause, and anthropology in general.

In twenty minutes Tunui reappeared, still supported by his bearers, still talking about our work, how important it was and how valuable he was to me. They transferred his arms to my shoulders and we started up the long hill to the house, stumbling over the steppingstones into the brook and nearly falling at every third step on the rocky, root-crossed paths. Once we were safely home, I set my cargo down on the grass, where he promptly passed out. Tahia covered him with a mat and some clothing and there he remained, much against my protests, until the next day.

During the periodic drinking bouts, the usual standards of sexual conduct dropped to even more casual levels. Often, as I made my Sunday afternoon pilgrimage to retrieve Tunui, bold proposals would be made by some of the women present without evoking any wrath from their husbands. On the fringes of these parties I frequently saw groups of young boys of Tiro's age, not drinking or drinking very lightly, carefully watching the states of drunkenness of the various participants, male and female. A woman whose husband had passed out could be assured of getting a large number of propositions from the young bucks, and any woman stepping into the bush to relieve herself or take a quick bath in the stream was throwing down a gauntlet that would without exception be taken up.

Much of the really heavy drinking done by the adults was done in the spirit of a contest to see who could manage to drink under the table the husbands of the most accessible females and still remain conscious enough to possess the victor's prize. Many such contests soon became sexual orgies, with discretion and custom thrown completely to the winds; wives took lovers right beside their dead-drunk husbands, young boys lured women of their mothers' generation into the bush, and even incest prohibitions were transgressed. The results of these flights of passion are varied: often nothing happens at all because the people involved care little about the deeds committed by their mates as long as they were committed with friends who might normally request some sort of sexual favors. On other occasions, however, erring wives may suffer physically, or, though more rarely, a husband may himself suffer a certain amount of bodily abuse from his wife. The families may then dissolve, or one male may leave and another come quickly in his place.

Much has been written in tourists' and yachtsmen's books or in the "men's magazines" about the sex life of the Polynesian. It is true that white visitors to these islands can find sexual companions with relative ease, but the behavior of native girls in such circumstances is scarcely typical of their behavior among their own kind. To try to judge Polynesians in general on the basis of such contacts with Europeans is like trying to estimate the sexual behavior of American woman- hood from a study of the brothel inmates in a seaport. Never- theless, these popular images of Polynesia seem to have oc- casionally spilled over, even into the scientific world.

Our interest in this topic grew as we came to see the great separation between popular myths of native sexuality and the actual behavior of the Marquesans. Rae was making a study of matters directly related to sexual behavior for Dr. Shapiro: that of collecting the life histories of her native lady friends, and all possible information about childbirth. The proverbial infertility of Marquesan women in the early decades of this century had prompted many to predict that soon the Mar- quesans would become extinct. Since that low point in the birth statistics, however, the population had nearly tripled, and Rae was engaged in collecting information that might indicate what had brought about the sudden increase in births. She brought back a wealth of interesting information from her interviews with the women. I, for my part, kept my eyes and ears open at all times for statements and incidents that would illuminate and extend Rae's data. As much of the con- versation among my native workmen revolved around sexual topics, it was possible to gain a lot of first-hand information without anyone's being the wiser: I simply jotted down what I heard as I made my archaeological notes. Eavesdropping of this sort was mandatory for the sake of research, for, sur- prisingly enough, sex was one topic on which a Marquesan would not answer direct questions. Tiro, the undying source of lascivious information, even by native standards, shut his wagging jaws with a grim look whenever he thought I was asking him a question "for the record."

In our associations in the valley of Hatiheu we had an ideal situation in which to study behavior of this kind, for we could observe a normal, functioning community, typical of most Marquesan valleys, consisting of people in every stage of life from the newborn to the very aged, whose personalities covered a span from ultraconservatives to complete deviants. Thus our information, based on a typical group, would most likely be typical of Marquesan culture in general, whereas if we had only questioned a few adolescents and adults or a group of elderly people, our information would have been biased, rather than representative.

We found that many Marquesan sexual practices had actually been changed relatively little by contact with Europeans. Our information tallied quite closely with that recorded by the early navigators such as Porter, Marchand, and Cook, and by some later anthropologists such as von den Steinen and Handy.

Marquesan children are likely to surprise Europeans with their sophistication in sexual matters—if they can be induced to talk at all. This is a direct result of the matter-of-fact treatment that such matters receive in daily life and the fact that in most families parents and children sleep in one room. The children begin experimenting rather early; little boys begin masturbating at two or three years of age, engaging in group activities of this type by the age of five or six, and having casual homosexual contacts as well. Little girls are carefully prepared for their roles as future mates by parents and grandparents. At the age of a few weeks a course of medication is begun with a view to making them more satisfactory sexual partners later in life. Astringents, concocted from a number of herbs and bushes, are employed for this purpose, with daily dosages continuing to the age of about twelve. Little girls also engage in "the solitary vice" and begin homosexual contacts at an early age, which continue from the years before to shortly after puberty.

At the age of twelve or fourteen, a boy passes a great milestone in his life—the circumcision rite. This rite marks the beginning of his manhood more or less, for it is considered to be the public seal of approval for his first venture into heterosexual relations; until circumcision such relations are considered unseemly. The rite has, during the last fifty years, been stripped of its pagan religious significance, but it is still of great importance, for a man who has not undergone it is considered to be odd and generally unclean.

Tunui, a popular circumciser in Taiohae, described to me how the operation is performed. As in the aboriginal past, a group of boys go through the ceremony together, each having made a separate contract with the circumciser, who is usually related in some way to him. Circumcision performed by an uncle, for instance, is thought to be especially "proper." The frightened boys are lined up: each has a bit of bamboo inserted beneath his foreskin and a male relative to help him withstand the pain. As Tunui steps before each boy, he stretches the skin tight over the bamboo sliver and deftly slices through it in one longitudinal cut with an old razor blade. In a few weeks, thanks to careful application of native medicines, the wound has healed and the boy has embarked on a whole new phase of life, beginning the pursuit of female sexual partners that will consume a good part of his energies for many years to come.

A boy usually has his first sexual experience with a much older woman, who instructs him in his first bungling attempts. Many of my older Marquesan friends looked back upon this initiation with fond memories and much amusement at their own ineptitude. The boys generally join a small informal group of comrades of similar age, who spend their evenings wandering about the dark valleys attempting to enter the homes of receptive women of all ages and conditions of life. These boys possess an astounding body of information about the internal design of all likely houses in the valley as well of the customs of the inhabitants.

For girls, adult sex life begins somewhat earlier than for boys, usually with defloration by an older male, after a chance encounter in the bush or a surreptitious invasion of the family home. Girls are usually, therefore, far more experienced than boys of their own age and may have been indulging in normal sexual relations for some months before the onset of menstruation.

While riding to and from work with native workmen, we

occasionally passed young girls minding their parents' houses
or working with copra-cutting parties. If we were returning
from work, the group would often break up as soon as we
had passed out of sight of the girls, with two or three men
galloping off into the bush to approach the desired ones from
a different angle with more foliage for cover, to see if they
could not entice them to dalliance on the spot, or at least make
some tentative plans for the evening. Since it is considered a
feat to deflower a virgin, a great deal of attention is devoted
to girls in this category. Men like Corpse Eyes, in their mid-
fifties, were most successful with virgins because of their
refined "line" and sense of appropriateness, whereas the
abrupt, fiery, younger males could seldom succeed, except
through repeated attempts.

During adolescence it is considered normal for boys and
girls to have frequent sexual relations. Parents do not permit
complete openness in these matters, however, except in rare
cases, for it is believed that the settling down of young people
will only lead to a complete split later in life. Therefore, boys
are constantly entering houses at night, skulking around girls'
houses to catch them alone, following them or ambushing
them in the woods, sending messages through "trusted" em-
issaries (who tell every soul in sight), or exchanging looks
and signals in church. The resources of boys and girls in these
situations are fantastic: one enterprising young fellow waited
for his love in the latrine each night, this being the only place
to which she could go freely after dark. Another effected sexual connections through a hole in the side of a house.

When a couple is caught *in flagrante* the uproar is frightening to the uninformed European bystander. The father, if he
did not catch the sinners personally, is informed immediately:
he bellows; he strikes out at animals, furniture, or any in-
animate objects in his way as he heads for the trusty rifle
which most natives own. Brandishing the weapon, he ostentatiously loads it and goes off toward the house of the offending
male, whose passions are by now ice-cold with fear. The wife
screams, cries, clings to his legs, begging him not to kill the

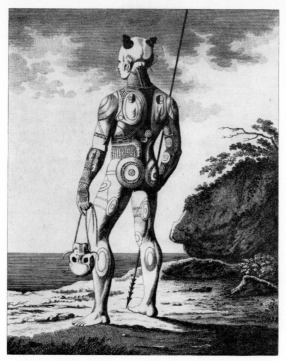

A young warrior of Nuku Hiva with barbed spear and trophy head, as seen by members of the Krusenstern expedition, 1803. The ear pendants and the hornlike twisted locks of hair on the shaven head were characteristic of the period. *Courtesy of the American Museum of Natural History*

RESOLUTION BAY IN THE MARQUESAS.

Plumed Marquesans in graceful outrigger canoes as they greeted Captain Cook's *Endeavour* in Vaitahu Bay, Tahuata, 1768. *Courtesy of the American Museum of Natural History*

Nineteenth-century Nuku Hiva domestic scene. A well-decorated tattoo expert works on an attractive client while children look on and husband enters with a pig's head for payment. This vignette was done by an artist with the Krusenstern expedition, 1803. *Courtesy of the American Museum of Natural History*

One of Krusenstern's artists pictures a Russian officer visiting a temple and burial place in Taiohae in the company of tattooed warriors, 1803. *Courtesy of the American Museum of Natural History*

The business end of an exquisitely carved *u'u* (war club), highly prized weapon of the pre-European period. Note the use of small *tiki* heads and *tiki* eyes in the design. *Courtesy of the American Museum of Natural History*

Stalwart reminder of a vanished era, a large stone *tiki* stands with ten companions amid the overgrown ruins at Vaitaviri in Taipi Valley, the major image site of Nuku Hiva. *Courtesy of the American Museum of Natural History*

A new house rises beside a garden plot in Taiohae Valley. *Courtesy of the American Museum of Natural History*

Ureo, a descendant of Hapa'a chiefs, prepares breadfruit poi for Bastille Day festivities. *Courtesy of the American Museum of Natural History*

Marquesan mélange. The boys in this photo are descendants of unions of Marquesans with Annamites, American Negroes, Chinese, and several European nationalities.

"All your money cannot buy my respect, white man!" An aged Marquesan of royal descent displays her feelings toward Europeans.

Ha'atuatua. A trench bisects an ancient native fire pit in the temple area. The dark-stained layer deposited during native habitation of the site shows clearly between the clean, undisturbed sand deposits below and above.

A "bundle burial," containing the arm and leg bones of several individuals, found beneath the temple floor, Ha'atuatua.

Dawn on the Ho'oumi River.

The great *paepae* at Vahangeku'a, Taipivai.

Charlie and Heiku'a Clark, our unforgettable hosts in Taipivai.

boy or cause trouble. But the enraged father is determined to see justice done. First, he will shoot the boy. Then, he will return and kill the daughter, that filthy rotting sow who sprawls with her legs apart in the middle of the trail, for all comers! The daughter wails; huge tears flow over her face and breasts; she dare not speak to her father for fear that this whirlwind of fury will suddenly crush her. Meanwhile a small crowd of neighbors gather; word of what has happened spreads through the crowd. "Caught in the stream bed, this morning?" "Both naked?" "Tsk, tsk, what a shame!" "Did you say she was supposed to be doing the laundry?" "Ahhh, yes! I know the boy! A bad, bad head he is! Scared him away from my daughter with an ax just last week, serve him right if her father shoots him!" "Go on, Papa Ha'aka'u, kill him, he's no good."

The father, however, is still standing with gun in hand, his wife draped about him, apparently restraining him from the deed of violence. He is uttering frightful, enormous curses, swearing horrible vengeance, on earth and from heaven, and promising now to take the miscreant before the administrator, force him to marry his daughter, pay him thousands of francs for his anguish, and force his family to sell all their goods and chattels. Suddenly, he takes notice of his wife: "and *you!* What were *you* doing while she was fornicating on the pile of laundry this morning? Don't you watch *your* daughter?" Now the gun is put aside, while the wife begins to cower as her husband begins to slap, kick, and strike her with his fists. Falling to the ground, she escapes, and it is now Daughter's turn. When her face looks like a sack of walnuts, with some-times one or two teeth loosened or removed, Father feels satisfied. He unloads the rifle, puts it away, and goes off to get roaring drunk, having provided the neighbors with many days' worth of gossip as well as a view of an entertaining beat-ing. When next he sees the guilty boy, the father may possibly mention the misdeed to him!

This pattern of surreptitious courting and sexual relation-ships is considered normal. No affection is shown openly;

lovers often insult and physically abuse each other in public to divert the attention of possibly suspicious parents and friends. Courtships and affairs of this type continue throughout youth until a boy and girl find each other especially attractive and, after asking the parents' permission, settle down permanently. By this time the girl may have already borne a child or two to her present mate or other lovers, but children are considered an asset and a treasure, and their paternity is of no great importance. Once the union has received recognition from the girl's father, the couple is "married" and may cohabit openly. Only after extreme pressure by the missionaries can couples be brought to church marriage, for they know about the sanctions against divorce, and regard them as highly unfair and restrictive.

There are also patterns of sexual behavior for those who wish to deviate from these cultural norms. The promiscuous girl, or *vehine mako*, for instance, is a very important person in Marquesan society. Each valley has a number of such girls or women, ready to have sexual relations with anyone, young or old, usually in return for favors of some sort. These girls have generally left their families to travel in groups of two or three, living in abandoned houses or with young married friends. They care for the sexual needs of the young men who cannot find partners, aid the older men whose wives have grown unresponsive, and, perhaps most importantly, protect the "good" girls of the community by cohabiting with all strangers, including whites, and keeping them from seeking sexual partners among the marriageable and married women and thus upsetting the equilibrium of the community. These girls are sexually talented and their favors are highly sought after. They are, however, seldom if ever taken in marriage, for no one wishes to own a woman whose relations have been indiscriminate. Therefore, as they grow older and lose their charm, they are gradually abandoned to shift for themselves. I once met an old woman, living alone in a ramshackle hut in a remote corner of Taiohae, who seemed to radiate bitterness, and I questioned Tunui about the cause of this. "Once, everyone wanted to copulate with her, as she was very beautiful. All the white men slept with her. When she grew older, she could not find a husband. Now she has no food, no money, and no property. She is starving and nobody will help her."

Other deviants are habitual homosexuals, known as *mahu*. These are relatively rare. These men are often transvestites, as was the one I had met in A'akapa on a journey to the west coast of Nuku Hiva. Tunui had called a halt to water the horses in a small hamlet in that valley, when a strange-looking person appeared in front of one of the houses, his hair cut like a man's, but wearing a woman's blouse, a wrap-around skirt, and a shell necklace. He was a slim, wide-hipped man, who walked with a mincing gait, swinging his buttocks like a woman. He spoke to Tunui in a high-pitched, lisping voice, accompanied by very feminine hand motions. After he had left Tunui explained that this *mahu* was known as an excellent seamstress and laundress, and specialized in all kinds of woman's work. Although capable of sexual relations with women, the *mahu* preferred the companionship of men, finding most of his lovers among the young boys, who used him as casually as they might a promiscuous girl.

Marquesan married life is seldom smooth, as both mates indulge in considerable surreptitious extramarital relations, the wife taking lovers from among the young boys and her husband's friends and relatives, while the husband may call upon his sisters-in-law, the young girls, or the valley's loose women. Certain extramarital relations, such as sexual hospitality and wife exchange, are sanctioned. Within three months of our arrival we had been discreetly approached three times to participate in wife exchanges. One hopeful fifteen-year-old lad offered his sweetheart of equal age in return for Rae, who was not at all flattered by the intended honor.

The Hatiheu missionaries were naïvely unaware of most of what was transpiring about them. By their refusal to tell the truth in confession, the Marquesans have eliminated the best source of information that any Catholic clergyman has at his disposal. The unspoken agreement to refrain from informing to the priest on matters dealing with sex and alcohol further limits the missionary's awareness.

The mere act of church attendance is considered to be of high religious value. Before and after the service the inhabitants of Hatiheu gossiped, courted, and occasionally even fought over fancied slights in church, or elsewhere during the week.

Invariably, all missionary efforts at uplift are both misinterpreted and brought to nought with incredible skill by the natives. To help consume the energy of the adolescents, and thus divert it from the usual highly carnal activities of Marquesan youths, the Hatiheu priest encourages soccer games in the churchyard. As they are coeducational, the games soon decline into organized sessions of sexual pinching, groping, and rubbing. The resulting "game," with most of the male participants obviously in a state of sexual arousal, defies description.

Desirous of improving the prestige of his congregation, the earnest priest had initiated a program of rehearsals for singing at a coming church festival. These rehearsals were held seven nights a week for four hours a night, and were also designed to keep the sexes apart until they were too tired for mischief. The first night, a few boys came, but after that only girls and adults were present: the boys gathered in the dark fringes of the churchyard, waited the four hours until the singing broke up, and then struck off for various ambush points along the valley trails where they could meet their loves without the usual fear of parental intervention and enjoy a few moments together.

When the priest chose favorites among the congregation he almost invariably backed the worst of the lot. In Hatiheu his trusted housekeeper, a married woman, boasted incessantly of the propositions she received from the poor innocent cleric, while his favorite female aide in the congregation, the organist, had been personally responsible for a number of venereal disease epidemics in the valley and, although married, had acquired a foul reputation for promiscuity throughout the island.

In time it became obvious that this situation, with variations, obtained for all missionaries in the Marquesas; our Hatiheu friends were not being any more devious and brutal than any other population in the archipelago in their dealings with the priest who labored among them.

To many whites, the orgies of drinking and sex, the lack of responsibility, the seemingly complete anarchy of Marquesan society, are aspects of the general devil-may-care attitude of the "happy, friendly native" of travelers' tales. Ritual orgies played an important part in Marquesan society before the coming of the Europeans, but at that time they were generally a part of important religious ceremonies, as they were in all the islands of Polynesia. Licentiousness did not then disrupt the society; the role it played in organized religious activities further cemented social solidarity.

Now native social and political organization is gone, and with it the elaborate and colorful pagan religion. There is no longer any propitiatory significance to drunkenness and sexuality, for the gods of Polynesia have withdrawn to their home in the sunset.

These festivities are hardly of value now for the society; they cause continual animosity, friction, and heap loads of guilt upon the shoulders of the nominally Christian natives, who have managed to absorb only the negative aspects of Christianity.

What purpose does this endless debauchery serve—this immense waste of time and effort that might be better used to obtain an easier living from the fertile soil of the verdant valleys? The purpose is one that perhaps the Marquesans themselves would have difficulty articulating: it is to resist, with the only weapons left, the white tide that has very nearly engulfed their way of life. The missionaries and soldiers forced the natives to yield their arms, surrender their right to self-government, and expose themselves to Christian teachings, which involved mute acceptance of many prohibitions on cherished cultural institutions. What was forced upon them, they accepted, but in a superficial way only, and by not one iota more than necessary. Then, to show their contempt for the civilization being foisted upon them, they adopted as a way of life the formerly patterned sensuality so repugnant to their conquerors, centering their interest upon it alone. Who cared for France and her culture while the coco juice ran free and the orange beer bubbled quietly in the great bowls? Who cared what the black-robed priests shouted from the pulpit when men could burn their lust in mad, wonderful orgies with giggling soft-bodied girls? Only one thing remained to be done: to drain life of the last drop of sensation and go sated to the grave, the quicker the better. Within the span of a normal lifetime, the Marquesan culture had disappeared. Now with the old chiefs dead and all social control dead with them, the temples decaying, the harmless dances and music forbidden, and the children being taught to hate the ways of their parents, what reason existed for living according to any rules?

Perhaps some may be moved to feel pity for the Marquesans in their predicament—a people living a hollow meaningless life, without roots in the past and possessing no hopes or concepts of the future; but there are others more worthy of pity perhaps than the natives—the missionaries.

They, who played the greatest role in destroying the nineteenth-century native society, are now forced to live a life of renunciation and diligent labor in a kind of hell of their own creation: a distorted, hopelessly confused dream in which reality is always inaccessible. This is a world in which they have no means of finding out what the natives really require; a tragicomedy of errors in which their good works are misinterpreted and turned against them only to culminate in evil. I have read the bitter chronicle of this life in the worn face of an insane priest, reduced to babbling idiocy by thirty-eight years of toil among his unrepentant, resentful flock, and I can say that it is these unfortunate dedicated men who are most in need of pity.

6 / Sculptors of the Living Stone

After the excavations at Ha'atuatua, our attention turned to a different sort of archaeological site—a great *tohua*, or ceremonial plaza, located but a short distance from our house in Hatiheu Valley. There are many *tohua* in most Marquesan valleys, often large and quite elaborate in their construction; but this particular site, called in the native tongue *Tohua Hikoku'a*—The Ceremonial Plaza of the Wonderful Banyan Tree—was even more impressive than most. At the seaside end of the broad, flat dance floor was a large stone platform, in one side of which stood a pair of very interesting stone figures. These were carved in the coarse, dull red volcanic tuff known as *ke'etu*, a stone held sacred by the Marquesans.

The figures, one of which was rather badly weathered, displayed the classic features of the Marquesan image or *tiki*: goggle-rimmed eyes bulging over flaring nostrils and a half-opened mouth through which a tongue tip protrudes. The tiny arms were flexed, while the hands, in a highly stylized form, were clasped over the protruding abdomen. On the better-preserved figure, the ears were indicated by earphone-like projections.

The platform was as unusual as the figures that decorated it, for it was constructed of large, thick slabs of the same rough red stone, neatly hewn into rectangles and butted together at the ends. Around the periphery of the dance floor, about four hundred feet long and eighty feet wide, stood the ruins of many stone platforms constructed of the same red tuff slabs.

The site itself was a terrace about forty feet larger in every dimension than the central dance plaza. The construction of this terrace had necessitated cutting away the entire side of a knoll to obtain earth for fill—quite a feat for primitive peoples without even so much as a shovel or a wheelbarrow.

There was one amazing fact about Hikoku'a: although it was located within a stone's throw of the Taipivai-Hatiheu trail, it had been completely unknown to the anthropological world until I visited it in 1956. Large stone statues are rare enough in the Marquesas to excite curiosity on their own merits, but to find two such figures, completely undisturbed, on an extensive site which was further distinguished by a group of unusual ruins was really a stroke of luck. The reason for the excellent protection given this monument of ancient Marquesan engineering and art was soon obvious from the conversation of my guide, the chief of Hatiheu. According to the chief, the present owners of the land were afraid to allow any visitors near the site who might attempt to remove the figures. Later, it appeared that it was not only the loss of the statues that the owners feared, but the possible supernatural vengeance that would be wreaked upon them by the angry gods represented by the figures. I found that the site had a reputation for being inhabited by the spirits of the dead and a variety of evil apparitions. The huge sacred banyan tree, from which the site derived its name, had stood on the platform where the figures were located, but ghostly jungle cocks kept appearing to one of the owners in the tangled branches and aerial roots of the multitrunked, massive tree. He attempted to destroy the tree, hoping to rid himself of the winged ghosts, but fell deathly ill after every attempt. With great perseverance, he kept on doggedly chopping and firing the heavy trunk system every time his strength returned. Finally the banyan succumbed, and with it vanished the ghostly jungle cocks whose crowing had so terrified him. The illness left the man, but his fear of the supernatural powers with which the site was invested remained. He would certainly not take a chance of having the figures of the ancient gods stolen, and becoming once more an object of the outraged deities' vengeance.

The northern islands of the Marquesas are not noted for an abundance of stone sculpture, but in the southern islands, especially Hiva Oa and Fatu Hiva, many exquisitely carved figures may still be seen beneath the ever-encroaching brush.

Like the Hikoku'a figures, most Marquesan stone sculpture is relatively small, having an average height of about three feet. There are, however, two notable exceptions which have attracted a great deal of attention—temple sites whereon groups of unusually large figures are still standing.

The most impressive of these is a temple called Te I'ipona in the valley of Puama'u, on Hiva Oa, where nine massive figures are still to be seen, the largest, named Taka'i'i, some eight and a half feet high. The natives have removed numbers of smaller figures from this temple, either to protect them from European souvenir collectors or in some cases to sell them to the same collectors. The most spectacular figure next to Taka'i'i was a great stone head weighing about three tons that in 1897 was removed for the Hamburg Museum of Ethnology by the famous German ethnologist Karl von den Steinen. This head represented a heroic chief named Tiu'o'o, who, legend had it, was laid low in a tribal war. It is ironic that his statue too should have been a casualty of war—a much more sophisticated and all-encompassing war; the stone Tiu'o'o was destroyed in the massive air bombardments of Hamburg.

In Taipivai Valley, only a few miles from the plaza of Hikoku'a, the second group of ancient monuments is located at a place called Vaitaviri on a sloping ridge, projecting from the wall of the valley. Eleven statues have been built into the walls of a large temple platform and a small subsidiary platform. Little is known of these *tiki* besides the names of a few of them—even the real name of the site and its significance for the Taipi tribe are unknown. Most are standing—"squatting" is a more exact term—but there are also some stone heads of the variety found at the site on Hiva Oa. An unusual figure of this site displays a pair of heads arising from a single neck, a common enough motif in small Marquesan stone sculpture, but quite rare in that of monumental size.

Many theories and hypotheses have been put forward concerning the age of the stone statues, the massive cut-stone masonry and megalithic platforms. Karl von den Steinen spoke with descendants of the chiefs who built the temple at Te I'ipona and decided on the basis of their genealogies that the site was no older than two hundred years (from 1897) at the most. Others have suggested the date of approximately A.D. 400, while still others have attempted to put it back further into the pre-Christian era. Many archaeologists have refused to believe that such monumental sculpture and architecture could have been the work of a Polynesian society, and accordingly many regions of the world have been singled out by theorists as the source for the Marquesan sculpture and architecture, as well as the entirety of the native art in general. These supposed points of origin range all the way from China (in the Bronze Age, some two thousand or more years B.C.) through Melanesia, and even to Peru on the east.

Stone statues, cut-stone masonry, and megalithic architecture in general are found throughout eastern Polynesia. The stone monsters of Easter Island, the largest of which is sixty-three feet long and weighs about forty tons, completely dwarfs the six- to eight-foot Marquesan figures.

In the Society and Hawaiian Islands, large quantities of tuff and softer grades of basalt were shaped and dressed for building temple walls, while only small crude stone figures were carved. However, the Hawaiian masons could equal their Easter Island cousins in their ability to join stone slabs together in a wall. In the Austral Islands, south of Tahiti, large figures as well as great stone slabs were used in temple construction. In the Tonga Islands of western Polynesia, the step-pyramid tombs of ancient high chiefs are faced with great slabs carved from workable coraline rock.

Because of the prevalence of stone statues and megalithic architecture in Polynesia, many theorists had supposed that all such monuments were built at approximately the same time by representatives of a second huge migration of Polynesians who differed markedly from the earlier inhabitants of the islands. This view continued to be espoused despite the fact that the stone monuments in each island differed significantly from those in the other islands: evidence that they could hardly have been made by representatives of a single group of artisans who had arrived practically simultaneously.

It was, therefore, with a great deal of anticipation that I began the final arrangements for us to begin our work at Hikoku'a. Here was an opportunity to throw some light on the problems that had plagued Polynesian prehistorians for so long. We might find, for instance, some indisputable evidence by which to date the stone sculpture on the site and thus to date similar sculpture throughout the archipelago. We might also be able to uncover some evidence that might serve tentatively to date the megalithic platforms on the site. Furthermore, beneath the welter of ruined structures of Hikoku'a we might find some evidence of earlier buildings, obscured by later additions, that would tell us something about the steps in the development of the great stone platforms.

Our work might help to pin down for us the major points in the evolution of the flamboyant society which the Europeans of the eighteenth century saw in action. In this venture, we would also have the help of the work carried out by the Norwegian expedition of 1956 at the famous image sites in Puama'u and Taipivai; in the hope of finding some charcoal from beneath the figures for carbon-14 analyses, personnel of this expedition made some small excavations around the statues at both of these sites.

A conference was held with Meano, the chief, to discuss our plans and clear them with him. With his permission to begin work, we approached the various Marquesans who held real-estate interests in the site. Informed of the chief's support of my project, they readily gave their consent, although several remarked that "it would be nice" if they could join my force of laborers to work on the site, emphasizing their readiness with a show of shiny feather-edged machetes, battered shovels, and pickaxes or mattocks.

As it was indeed necessary to expand the excavation crew to

accomplish a task of this size, I hired several of the petitioners and sent out a call for more, which was quickly answered. I had hoped that Meano would assume control of the group as a foreman, for he was reputed to be a very stern taskmaster. Whether through collusion or by choice, Meano declined the offer of this job but he sent his unofficial second in command, Corpse Eyes, who was by this time an old friend of mine. Corpse Eyes sat in second place on the valley advisory council, for his words carried not only a great deal of earthly wisdom but also the additional force of his supernatural sponsors. The news of Corpse Eyes' appointment was received with some uncertainty by other members of the crew, who probably saw their hopes of pulling a few shady deals vanish completely.

The work began on a steaming morning after some days of almost continual rain. The first task was to clear the site completely of all the brush with which it was overgrown. Corpse Eyes started the group at one end of the site and they moved forward over the soggy ground, the heavy machete blades flashing in the sun. It was wonderful to see the skill with which this rather cumbersome tool was handled by the workmen: they could crop the dew-laden grass so close to the ground with the razorlike blades that one would have sworn a lawn mower had been used. The secret of their skill was soon evident: every fifteen minutes or so, the men withdrew files from the big cowhide scabbards hung on their belts, with which they sharpened the bright edges of the machetes, restoring the feather edge. Then, clamping a hastily hand-rolled cigarette between their lips, they moved on. As they moved over the terraces, house platforms, and walls of the site, occasionally a shout would go up: *"E Rope! E mea!"*—"Hey, Robert! A thing!" This usually meant that someone had found an ancient adze, some human bones, or something of the sort. Scarcely anything escaped the notice of the men, who even managed to spot old musket balls, gunflints, and tiny pieces of broken stone adzes as they cut off the heavy growth of years from the site, scuttling along like crabs on widely placed feet, bent over from the waist.

Soon, thick choking smoke columns rose from many parts of Hikoku'a, where piles of wet brush smoldered. Two of the men who owned part of the site were quite happy to see the work progressing so well. One remarked, "It's a good thing, what the white man is doing! Two weeks ago, I decided to clear off the site on my own for copra cutting, but now I work with a crew of twenty men and get paid to clear my own land!" His naïveté in announcing his pleasure kept me from feeling much animosity at having been hoodwinked a bit.

As the clearing progressed, I set up my plane table and alidade to begin mapping the site. By the time the site was cleared, I had finished the map (with an expenditure of several gallons of midnight oil) and had photographs of the important and unusual buildings, the figures, some rock drawings that appeared on a stone slab, and various general views of the site, to boot.

It would naturally have been impossible for us to have completely excavated and dismantled so huge a terrace, which supported the remains of about twenty buildings, all of them constructed of massive stones. It was necessary, therefore, to be extremely careful in planning our excavations so that each would provide a maximum of information. I examined every inch of the site with great care, looking for unusual features that might have escaped notice.

We were looking for certain specific information: the age of the site and of the statues and the cut-stone buildings, and the changes in the size and form of the buildings, if any, that had been made during the time the site was used. To get this information in a most economical fashion, a series of trenches and small, deep test pits was begun at various strategic points. One of the best ways to find out about the age of the plaza was to find out what was beneath it; Corpse Eyes and his men therefore began cutting a test trench through the eight-foot west wall of the big terrace on which it had been built. If it had been built on the ruins of an earlier Hikoku'a, we would find out as soon as the trench began to deepen. The trench was laid out so that it cut into the *tohua* at a right angle, penetrating the sloping stone wall of the terrace and slicing down through the long, low steps on the west side of the flat plaza. These steps had been built along each side of the plaza to hold the numerous spectators at the tribal ceremonies. Upon them, in ancient times, long sheds had been erected to provide shelter for the onlookers during ceremonies that lasted for several days and nights, as they often did.

Another group of men was set to work systematically dissecting the *tiki* platform. During the clearing of the heavy brush from this strange masterpiece of Marquesan architecture, lines of red slabs, sticking up through the surface of the platform, had appeared. These slab lines at first appeared disconnected, but a little scratching in the grass roots uncovered more slabs and revealed a system of red stone curbs arranged in three rectangular enclosures, one within the other. The outermost rectangle was composed of red slabs alternated with slabs of a rare gray-white tuff. The purpose of these curbs was completely unknown to me and to the workmen as well—including Corpse Eyes, whom I had come to regard as a walking compendium of Marquesan esoterica.

Under Tunui's guidance, the men began trenches into the heart of this big architectural enigma, being careful not to destroy or mar the massive, neatly quarried slabs of red tuff that formed its sides and to avoid disturbing the all-important statues.

Another crew, led by Tiro, began a trench in the extreme southwest corner of the plaza. Here, the stadiumlike steps for the spectators had been interrupted by a wide, shallow depression which filled the floor of the carefully walled-off gap. I supposed that this might be the area where the earth ovens had been dug to cook leaf-wrapped pigs and vegetables for the tribal feasts. A few spadefuls removed in the center of the depression turned up blackened soil containing myriads of tiny, greasy charcoal and ash fragments—my hunch was right. Here was a good source for charcoal for the carbon-14 dates that might give us answers to the question of the age of Hikoku'a and other sites like it. The remaining men I assigned to smaller test excavations on various structures around the plaza. Some of the *paepae*, or house platforms, stood on the ruins of still-visible earlier platforms. Others appeared to have been added to and remodeled a number of times. All of them had to be tested for the secrets that they might be concealing deep among their bulky boulders, earth, and debris.

In digging at Hikoku'a, we adopted a somewhat different technique from that used on the village site on Ha'atuatua beach, where the archaeological deposit had been relatively thin and homogeneous. Only a single layer of debris, about twenty inches thick, remained to attest the ancient occupation of that picturesque locale. We had removed the debris in layers roughly five inches thick, noting the exact depth of the important artifacts, and keeping separate those found in different layers. When studying the collection, we would therefore immediately know at what levels certain tools were to be found.

The choice of five-inch layers was really arbitrary and made for the sake of convenience in digging. At Hikoku'a the situation was somewhat different, for the archaeological deposits were deep and composed of many very different layers caused by successive rebuildings, disturbances, or the methods by which the site was constructed. These earth layers were readily distinguishable by varying colors and textures.

The workmen, therefore, were easily able to peel off the separate layers, the artifacts in each of which were kept apart from those in the other layers, and the position of each of the artifacts in the layer noted. When a trench was finished, one side would be carefully cleaned and straightened to show the exposed layers. Then it would be photographed and precise drawings made. Afterward we could reconstruct the position of all of our finds from the notes, photos, and sketches, relate the artifacts found in the same layers of the various trenches, and thus reconstruct the history of the site.

By the time our excavations drew to a close, after several

absorbing weeks, some very surprising evidence had been uncovered, some that would answer our original questions and—
as usual—some that raised a host of new questions.

We found that Hikoku'a had probably been built on top of

Cross section of excavation through the dance floor of *tohua* Hikoku'a, Hatiheu. The layers of earth of different colors were deposited
during successive periods of rebuilding and enlarging this ceremonial
village.

a very old ceremonial site such as that which we had uncovered at Ha'atuatua. Deep beneath the dance floor there had
been uncovered what seemed to be a low terrace wall and a
pavement that had probably formed a side boundary. When
the plaza had been built and for how long it had been used we

had no way of knowing. However, at some point in the past, the chiefs and priests of the tribe had decided to expand their ceremonial grounds, according to an ambitious plan. What sort of deliberations the tribal council must have gone through we will never know, but one could wager that they were as careful as any modern group of architects or city planners as the plumed chief, the architects, the cold-eyed *tau'a*, and the warriors and family heads gathered in the high-stilted men's house, or *hata'a*, amid the grisly trophy heads and rows of dark glistening spears and war clubs to weigh and discuss the relative merits of various designs, the organization of the working force, and the complicated matter of feeding the workers and their families. Whatever the process in which the plans were evolved, a radical change took place in the appearance of the gently rounded Marquesan hillside on which the crude little dance floor had previously stood. The newly laid stones formed a huge rectangular enclosure, completely enfolding the boundaries of the earlier ceremonial place. Then, at the brow of the hill, crews of workmen began cutting into the clayey soil with heavy-handled stone adzes. The soil was then loaded into long baskets specially prepared for the purpose and borne in a ceaseless parade down the slope to the downhill side of the stone enclosure. As the earth accumulated there, more stones were selected and piled on the original foundation course. Soon a low terrace was building up at the downhill end of the long stone enclosure as the great gash in the hill at the upper end grew deeper and wider and basket after basket was emptied on the growing pile and trampled down.

Daily, other crews brought in loads of food for the workers: big carrying poles hung with leaf packages of poi and the tasty *piahe* pudding; long, bloody coco-leaf baskets bearing the remains of butchered pigs; hundreds of bunches of bananas, green, yellow, and red; clusters of coconuts and long strings of fish. All were cooked in deep steaming earth ovens on white-hot stones and served up to the hungry builders.

As the weeks of labor went by, a huge rectangular terrace grew slowly out of the ground, its sides faced with basalt boulders, its interior filled with earth from the digging in the hillside. Finally, the experts in charge of the building gave the sign to the work group leaders: the terrace had grown to such a height that it was now almost even with the floor of the gaping excavation in what had once been the hillside. The excavation and the terrace were leveled with each other, and the plaza was complete. Now, all that remained was to erect the buildings and sheds around it. At first, only a few pavements were set down—even the long, stadiumlike steps along the sides of the terrace were not added.

Years later, perhaps long after the first builders were dead, another flurry of activity overtook the tribesmen. They dug deep into the red hillside again for more earth, gathered more boulders, and built the long steps along the sides of the terrace surrounding the flat, grassy dance floor. Some low stone platforms were built to house the idols and their priest-servants, and a strange building appeared at the seaside end of the long plaza. Evidence of this building was found beneath the red stone platform, with its wide-eyed figures, by Tunui and his workers. Their test trenches had shown that the mysterious rows of stone slabs on the surface of the platform were not sides of earlier buildings obscured by later additions, but markers for some kind of ceremonial purpose. Beneath the platform, however, were fragmentary low walls and scattered marking slabs of a small platform of the same type made of cut red tuff curbs, alternating with curbs of the rare soft white tuff.

This small altar had been used for some time before its ornate and impressive successor had been built over it and the two ruddy figures had been set in their places to stare down the plaza.

A search through the writings of the early Marquesan missionaries and an examination of the Marquesan dictionary—often an excellent source of information on archaeological matters—revealed that these red tuff platforms, called *tu'u*, were a special kind of altar, used for the purpose of displaying the heads of enemy dead and the bodies of sacrificial victims.

The grisly exhibits were spread out along the edges of the altar and left to rot until they were replaced by new attractions.

At approximately the same time as the big altar with the *tiki* had been built, the megalithic house platforms scattered about the dance floor had evidently also been erected. Some

Native Marquesan house on stone *paepae* platform. Cross section shows arrangement of interior posts and beams. Stairs were a post-European addition. (After von den Steinen, 1928.)

had been raised on the remains of earlier low structures, others started from scratch. In many of these, heavy slabs of red tuff had been used to provide a decorative façade on top of the platform, while in others they formed an integral part of the walls. The house *paepae* at Hikoku'a had been built of some astonishingly large stones, some weighing as much as two or three tons. We could discover no indication of the methods by which these stones were moved into place.

Although some minor reconstruction was carried out on some of the buildings after the megalithic house platforms had been built, the construction of these seemed to mark the last major phase in the evolution of Hikoku'a. Thus, the most impressive house platforms seemed to appear simultaneously with the sculptured figures and their beautiful cut stone altar, a fact which substantiated the truth of the opinions of many previous students of the Polynesian past: the statues and the cut stone buildings were part of the general development of heavy stone construction that also included the use of mammoth unshaped stones, shrewdly selected so as to fit together with surprisingly close tolerances.

But when did all this spectacular development of art and architecture take place? When were the high-gabled native houses lifted on massive rectangular stone platforms above the damp clay of the Marquesan valleys, and when did statues of rough red stone appear on altars of finely cut slabs?

There was no immediate and definite evidence by which to date this florescence of native civilization precisely, but the evidence that did exist was sufficient to give us some idea of the rough span of time within which the site had been used, and it was surprising.

Carbon-14 tests might later be done on charcoal collected in the excavations beneath the plaza and in the bottom of the oven complex that Tiro had found; for the present, we had only a few often-unclear clues to work on.

All over the surface of the site we picked up abundant evidence that Hikoku'a had been used after the coming of the white men: musket balls, gunflints, bits of metal tools, all attesting that the site was occupied sometime within the last century. In the interior of a classic megalithic house platform, we found a crypt made of massive tuff slabs in which an important warrior had been buried. I say "had been," for the grave had been earlier discovered by natives and opened. It had contained many beautiful ornaments, according to eyewitnesses, all of which had been sold to a French antiquarian. All that remained now were a pair of moldering lower leg bones and a rusty cap-and-ball musket of Civil War vintage— but the musket provided an excellent clue for dating that particular grave.

In the trench through the oven area, Tiro and his aides had

also uncovered a series of ovens, one above the other, penetrating some ten feet into the terrace fill. In one of the uppermost ovens was a piece of a French brandy bottle bearing—
appropriately enough—the legend "VIEUX" on a seal impressed
into the glass. The bottle, probably brought in after the French
occupation, supported the evidence of the old musket in the
rifled grave: the site had still been in use and some of the
megalithic platforms were built *after* the arrival of the white
man, perhaps even late in the nineteenth century.

Unfortunately, we found no evidence around the image altar and statues that would allow us to say that these had also
been erected after the advent of the whites. However, the
stratigraphic evidence uncovered in the excavation showed
that all of the massive stone buildings and the image altar had
been built at roughly the same time. Even granting that this
took place over a century, the age of the megalithic buildings
and the statues still did not appear to be more than two and a
half centuries. If our later excavations supported this, it would
mean the quiet death of a flock of theories concerning the age
and origin of Marquesan megalithic architecture.

We wound up our work at Hikoku'a several steps ahead in
many areas of knowledge, but with a lot of the same old questions and some new ones still facing us. We had found out
much about the construction of *tohua,* or ceremonial plazas,
and the house platforms upon them. We even had the first be-
ginnings of the sequence of forms through which the house
platforms had evolved to their final giant stage of development.

But the whole problem of the classic megalithic architecture and, in particular, of stone sculpture and cut stone masonry required something more concrete by way of evidence
than the scanty facts and clues that we had assembled.

Obviously, the best way to find out how old the statues and
cut stone altars were was to find the quarry where the ancient
Marquesans obtained their stone. Once we knew how long
ago the quarry had first been used, we would know how much

of an age, at a maximum, we could assign to any stone building
in which the cut stone had been used.

To this end I questioned Tunui, Corpse Eyes, and others
about the existence of quarries of *ke'etu*. Had they ever seen
any veins of the red stone in cliffs? Had they ever *heard* of
any? The answer was immediately forthcoming: in a barren,
uninhabited valley at the extreme northeastern tip of Nuku
Hiva, one could find some of the red tuff in a cliff beside the
sea.

Apparently the place had been a quarry, for according to
my informant there were still some unfinished slabs of tuff
that had been left lying about by the ancient quarrymen. As
soon as possible, five of us struck out for the valley of Ha'ata'-
ive'a on a Saturday, planning to examine the sites there—if
any—and do a little skin diving to provide a welcome variation
in a sickening diet of rice and canned bully beef. From the top
of the pass we looked down into the still valley where a long,
gently curving beach of white sand separated the turquoise
and darker blue sea from the scrub and brush of the desolate
valley floor. Not a coconut palm or fruit tree of any kind
broke the stunted, gnarled vegetation that covered the rolling
valley like a mangy brown mat. Along the beach, a few twisted
hibiscus bushes and rosewood trees stood in little clumps. At
the far end of the curving beach, however, lay our goal; and I
gasped as I looked, for the huge red band of tuff that was exposed in the cliff was bigger than anything I had been led to
expect. It ran along the face of the cliff for some distance,
varying in width from ten to twenty feet, then disappeared,
only to appear again farther on. Sandwiched in between layers
of the craggy basalt that formed the backbone of Nuku Hiva,
the thick layer of tuff blazed forth in strong contrast with the
brown-black of the surrounding stone. One thing was disap-
pointing, however. The only access to this rock source was
by the narrow rocky shelf along the sea. The waves washed
the base of the *ke'etu* vein at high tide. This meant that broken tools, images, and other objects left by quarriers would
long since have been reduced to shapeless pebbles and rolled

away by the waves. No charcoal-rich campfires would be found in that quarry for the radiocarbon time clock to measure. I hoped that some other site in the valley might give us the much-desired information.

When we examined the old quarry site at close range, we found that on a layer of tuff that projected onto the seaside rock shelf, great rectangular slabs had been outlined by wide, deep trenches. All that remained was for them to be undercut to release them from their rocky bed. In the face of the cliff, several man-shaped niches marked the spots where large *tiki* figures had been removed from the living stone, and in another spot the thick red tuff outcropping had been undercut and overcut to allow the native quarriers to attack their material from above and below, rather than work on the difficult vertical face.

The Marquesans who worked at this quarry had obviously had a number of handicaps to overcome, what with the sea sloshing about their ankles much of the time, and being constantly wet and chilled. There was nevertheless an advantage to the location, as large canoes or rafts could come very close to the quarry face to receive a load of heavy slabs or a statue. This convenience would have made it unnecessary to carry the heavy stones on a grueling overland trail, over steep knife-edge ridges, along slippery sandy beaches, and through incredibly rocky gorges.

The quarry was interesting enough, but it would not tell us all that we wanted to know. If there had been a large quarrying operation going on here, the workmen had had to be sheltered somewhere—but where?

We combed the beach and the valley bottom, but the only traces of habitation were to be found along the low bank behind the glistening beach. Here, an occasional ancient oven pit, crammed with stones and gray-black ash, had been exposed by the waves. Another spot that might have been promising had been eroded by rainfall water that was channeled over it from the cliff face. Only a litter of crumbling fragments of pearl shell and some stone flakes appeared on the scoured ground surface.

At the opposite end of the beach from the quarry, however, the remains of a pair of stone platforms stood in a clump of rosewood trees. This place, a favorite shelter for Tama on his night fishing excursions, had formerly been sacred to the god of fishermen, A'avehie, and was so named in his honor. A quick examination showed that this place possessed some good possibilities as an archaeological site: an unfinished fishhook, some coral files, a stone adze and some flake knives, a bread-fruit skinner, and a number of other artifacts were easily collected in and around these ruins. Here was a distinctly good spot to try to dig—if we could be sure it had been inhabited by the quarrymen. A little further search brought almost immediate support of this hope, for around the ruins we found scattered chunks of the red *ke'etu*, fallen from the labors of the quarrymen who must have taken some work home with them.

Satisfied at having found a good site, we stripped, rubbed down with coconut oil, and went out onto the rock shelf to begin our diving, Tiro chiding me for having feet with soles of cigarette paper as I winced along, barefooted, over the abrasive rocks. Plunging in, Tunui and I pushed along a heavy pole float to which Tiro, Teiki, and a younger boy would string the fish that they hoped to shoot with their homemade spear guns. It was always a revelation to slide beneath the surface of the Pacific and enter that weird, half-lit world of color and movement, although Marquesan waters are not as clear as in the white-bottomed atolls of the Tuamotus or the Tahitian lagoons where I had spent fascinating hours. Fishes darted to and fro; on one side, just out of the range of clear vision, a big familiar silhouette flickered and was gone—a highly prized *pa'ihere*, excellent eating and an uncompromising fighter. A school of black fish with red and white markings near their gills shot by; to my unschooled eyes, these looked like the well-known triggerfish. Down deep among the tumbled basalt blocks sprouting branch coral and marine plants, tiny black-and white-banded fish darted about. Nervously, I kept turning my head and peering over my shoulder, ever watchful for the wolves of the sea—the sharks with which Marquesan waters teem.

Although the natives treat these sharks casually, I could never learn to do so; the sight of a black fin or the character-istic ripples of a cruising shark make me very uneasy indeed. A streak of white flashed in from the corner of my eye—three projectilelike mullet with silver bodies and tiny black gill spots circled me quickly and vanished into the misty distance. As we swam along, Tunui and I occasionally dove deep to get a shell or just examine the fantastic marine life more closely. Soon, I was winded from this exercise and felt a chill creeping up my legs. Tiro and company had long since departed, leav-ing us to tow, somewhat recklessly, a string of bleeding fish through the water. Tunui and I rested on the rocks for a while, carried our float along the rock ledges to where Tiro and the others were diving with whoops and shouts, and re-entered the water in a little side bay.

Diving deep, I was lost in the fantastic world of the sea for some time again. Coming up from a dive with sinuses aching, I was horrified to see a black shadow move through the water off to my right with effortless speed. As I broke the surface, I heard a shout from Teiki, and I half expected to see him afloat in a circle of his own blood.

"*E'aha?*"—"What is it?" I choked.

"*Ha-ha-'ua!*"—"Manta ray!" came back the answer, followed by a boyish horse laugh. It is rather galling for a Westerner to see fifteen-year-old boys armed with wretched little spear guns and flimsy goggles laugh at the so-called terrors of the deep. It was even more exasperating later on when I got a look at what was probably the same ray from a high cliff. Anything with a wingspread of nine feet commands my respect, without question.

Tired and shivering, I finally left the water as the merry fish-ermen continued, emerging on a point at the entrance to one of the many little side bays. The shore in this little bay was of a beautiful white sand with large white slabs of coraline stone jumbled about in the shallows. Behind the miniature strip of beach, a high bank rose, strewn with small chunks of stone. I looked once, then looked again—the stone was a peculiar blue color like that of the basalt used in ancient times for making adzes. I approached the beach over the rough rocks.

In a few moments I had reached it and stood, quite excited, at the base of the bank. The blue chunks of stone were actually hundreds of half-finished stone adzes, and scattered among them were thousands of sharp flat basalt chips, the by-products of the manufacture of the stone carving tools.

What a find! Here, in the valley where the sculptors plied their trade, I had failed to find the necessary archaeological deposits around the wave-washed quarry site, but now the next best thing was at hand—the "factory" in which the sculptors' heavy, sharp-edged adzes had been produced. As the work at the quarry progressed, with *tiki* figures and big rectangular blocks being hewn out of the formless *ke'etu*, this little grassy valley must also have been a scene of great activity, with adzes being turned out in an endless stream to replace those that had been broken at the quarry.

The broken and incomplete tools that remained here represented the mistakes of the adze makers, who, working on the stubborn basalt, often saw their handiwork come to nought as a slightly misdirected blow or the application of too much force shattered a well-shaped stone-cutting tool that they had probably labored over for hours.

The adzes had, I saw at once, sifted out of a very clearly defined archaeological stratum running the length of the bank, only a foot beneath the brown grass of the valley surface. At one point near the center of the beach, the layer of unfinished adzes and flakes was quite thick. Examination of the deposits showed that this was a shallow gully where the artisans had thrown most of their rejects and the sharp basalt flakes that would have posed a problem even to the thick-soled feet of the natives.

Before long, I had collected an armful of very interesting, nearly completed specimens from among the debris that littered the bank, as well as a couple of coral files and a battered stone hammer with which a departed artisan had once shaped the blue stone billets. I was nearly naked and thoroughly chilled in the light rain that had begun to fall, and I had nothing in which to carry my prizes back. Furthermore, I faced several prolonged swimming jaunts before I could return to the place where we had left the horses, so that even if a basket or bag had been available, swimming with ten or fifteen pounds of basalt in one hand would have been impossible. I stacked the adzes beneath a rock and started the long and sore-footed journey home.

The following week we began work in Ha'ata'ive'a quite early on a Monday morning, beginning at the adze factory site in the little side bay and then moving to the ruined platforms where the quarrymen had apparently lived.

The digging in the adze quarry was immensely difficult: as soon as we stripped off the foot of loose earth that covered the layer of shop debris at its thickest point, we were faced with a solid mass of tightly packed stone fragments, bristling with dangerously sharp edges and points. The deep valley was completely protected from any breeze, and the dust raised by our excavations rose up about us in a stifling cloud. The horses, tethered on the steep slopes behind the site, stood immobile in the glaring sun, with eyes shut and necks awkwardly extended. At lunchtime, Tiro would run into the sea with his spear gun, generally returning in a short time with a couple of small fish which we diced in a rock tidal pool and ate raw, as we did not have with us the limes with which the fish were usually marinated.

We recovered several hundred unfinished adzes from the debris of that ancient workshop and also collected for study large samples of the myriad basalt flakes. The adzes were of two types: long and flat with a wide cutting edge, and narrow and thick with a triangular cross section and a very small cutting edge. This was very interesting, as it was precisely these types of adzes that had been designated by earlier ethnographers, on the basis of native statements and traditions, as the main quarry tools. The wide adzes had supposedly been used for heavy cutting and "roughing out" work, and the narrow, fine-bladed ones for undercutting statues and slabs to break them loose from their beds, as well as for putting a semifinish on the piece before it was removed.

None of the adzes showed any trace of the polish that usually appeared on those intended for wood carving. The edges of the best-finished pieces were quite sharp, but without a single trace of abrasion. This was further in keeping with what was known of Polynesian stone-cutting tools—they were seldom, if ever, polished, the edges being chipped sharp whenever they grew dull from cutting through the flinty particles in the soft tuff.

Besides the stone tools, only a few other artifacts were recovered: a fragmentary fishhook, some coral files, and a flat stone disk representing, perhaps, an unfinished drill weight.

The source of stone for the adzes was a contorted vein of basalt that streaked the side of a nearby cliff. This stone had been naturally fractured into prismatic or hexagonal billets a foot or two in length. All that the adze makers had to do was pry loose a billet from its bed to have a handy-sized piece of stock to work with.

Despite the richness of the site, there was nothing there to give us a clue as to how old it was. At that time, we knew very little about the ages of the various distinctive Marquesan adzes, fishhooks, coral files, etc. Naturally, there were some indications of some tools having been made earlier than others, but even these indications were uncertain.

At the bottom of the heavy layer of sharp debris, however, I found some small means of determining the age of the adze factory, for there was a fire bed, crammed with chunks of black charcoal and white ash—a perfect source for samples for carbon-14 age analysis. The charcoal was carefully removed and packed in heavy layers of aluminum foil for protection against contamination from outside influences.

Here, then, I had the potential for establishing the age not only of the adze factory but also of the tuff quarry site for which the adzes had undoubtedly been made. In the collection of broken tools, we had examples of every phase in adze manufacturing, from the initial flakes removed from a natural stone billet to the final product, ready for use—enough to reconstruct the whole process of making an adze and probably even isolate the reasons for many of the failures.

We then loaded the sagging horses with heavy, bulging sacks of adzes and shop debris and moved to the clump of rosewood on the beach of Ha'ata'ive'a.

There, beneath the ruined platforms of coraline slabs, we found unexpected evidence that the site had been occupied for some time. Just below the foundations of the platforms was a house pavement, much like those which had been built in the early phases of construction at Hikoku'a before the megalithic buildings had appeared. The pavement had been built over a very large oven which was surrounded by a number of flat stones. Tiro's sharp eyes spotted faint markings on one, which turned out to be a weird bird figure engraved in the surface of the rock. Bird figures were so far completely unknown in Marquesan rock drawings, and bird representations in any medium were very scarce, even during the days when the culture was still alive. It was, therefore, something of a surprise to see a recognizable portrait of a Marquesan *kuku* parakeet staring up at us from a dark stone slab.

Below this oven was still another, smaller, pit, full of ash, but no artifacts appeared, and we soon found ourselves digging in sterile soil.

Although these ruins did not yield many artifacts, those that we did recover were later proved to be quite distinctive and valuable for dating. The most important thing of all, however, was the evidence that appeared for dating the quarrymen's occupation of the site. There was definite evidence that the workers had lived there, in the form of numerous chunks of red *ke'etu*, but all of it was found either on the surface or in the uppermost layer, indicating that the quarrymen had lived there relatively recently and that the age of Marquesan megalithic architecture with its statues and cut-stone masonry apparently was a good deal more recent than had previously been suspected. It seemed that the evidence uncovered in our digging at Hikoku'a had pointed us in the right direction, and that the supporters and lobbyists for Peruvian Indian sculptors, tiny energetic Melanesians, or inscrutable Orientals from the North China Plain had lost their cause.

There was a lot more evidence to gather and a great deal of careful study to be devoted to the evidence and radiocarbon analyses before any definitive statement could be made.

As we rode out of the parched valley of Ha'ata'ive'a, I felt the heavy lump in my haversack where the charcoal sample destined for bigger things rode safely. The data in my notebooks and the burden of artifacts with which the horses were laden, combined with the evidence discovered at Hikoku'a, had enabled us to move a big step forward in solving the vexing problem of the age of the great florescence in art and architecture that produced the dull red giants and the great stone platforms. The next step would have to be taken some nine thousand miles away in an anthropological laboratory in New York, and it might put us in a position to be even more precise about assigning an age to these monuments. It would rely, to a great extent, on the geochronologist and his radiation laboratory, as well as a detailed restudy of all the evidence. This last step, the final assembling of all the pieces of information from all the disparate sources, was one to which I very much looked forward.

7 / Valley of the Man-Eaters

In November of 1957, our work on northern Nuku Hiva was drawing to a close, and we were preparing for the trip to Taipivai, where we had already arranged to stay with a native family familiar to me: all that remained for us to do was to finish all the "loose ends" of work, pack our equipment, crate the collections of artifacts and skeletons, and wait for the copra schooner so that we could ship the equipment and collections ahead and depart on horseback ourselves.

As usual, we received all sorts of information via the "coconut radio" as to the whereabouts of the copra schooner, which seemed to be something of a latter-day *Flying Dutchman* as it moved mysteriously through the archipelago. Acting on what appeared to be the most reliable of intelligence, we hurriedly packed everything in one day, and had the heavy boxes transported to the locked copra shed for safekeeping, only to find that the schooner was not after all coming. Actually it did not come for two more weeks, but we kept busy examining more of the megalithic sites for which the valley was noted, photographing unusual rock drawings that we had found in our earlier explorations, and finishing up my work on native medicine and plant lore. It was not long, however, until we awoke one morning to the sound of the copra schooner whistle. Looking down the steep hill toward the beach, we saw the rigging of the *Tiare Taporo* looming through the gaps in the coconut palm cover of the valley. Within a few hours we were on our way to Taipivai after sad good-byes to Pauro, Tama and his family, and many other friends from Hatiheu. Tunui, as usual, supervised the proceedings, aided by the silent but genial Corpse Eyes, who had suddenly become interested in joining us in Taipivai. Tiro, unfortunately, had become so much of a problem that he had to be left behind.

Taipivai is cluttered with ruins left by the strongest and most feared of all tribes in the Marquesan archipelago. According to legends, the twelve subtribes of Taipi totaled ten thousand people in the heyday of the native culture. The warriors of this deep valley gained for themselves the epithet *Taipi kaikai'enana*—Taipi man-eaters—in their wars throughout Nuku Hiva and on other islands of the archipelago as well. Not content with constantly stirring the embers of the conflict between themselves and the tribes of Taiohae and Hapa'a, the Taipi men often embarked in their long bird-prowed canoes to fight on Ua Huka and other nearby islands. In the early 1800's a massive "amphibious" assault launched from Taipi was responsible for the complete annihilation of the population of tiny Eïao island, fifty miles north of Nuku Hiva. The island has never since been inhabited.

The slanting rays of the afternoon sun filtered through the leaves of the tall trees along the path as we rode slowly down the great valley of Taipi on the winding trail that led to the main hamlets and the beach. On every side rose the lichen-covered stones of ancient house platforms and temples, some apparently almost intact, others in a terrible state of decay, reduced to almost shapeless weed-covered heaps of stone. At Tunui's direction we paused by a dense hibiscus grove at a bend in the trail, dismounted, and plunged into the thicket. Suddenly, before our feet a huge pit opened in the midst of the decaying branches and weeds. There, plunging thirty feet into the earth, was a tremendous breadfruit storage pit, ten feet square, with neatly squared corners. Now empty, except for a welter of decayed wood and muddy water, the pit had been built by the Taipi warriors after Porter's invasion of 1813, to hold emergency supplies of breadfruit paste in case another invasion should force them into a state of siege in the more easily defended upper reaches of the valley. There were three or four more pits of equal size in the immediate vicinity, clear proof that the Taipi were not only industrious but good war planners and capable gardeners.

Farther down in the valley we began to pass the great ceremonial plazas for which this valley is renowned. No other tribes in the archipelago built such elaborate, extensive *tohua* in such numbers. The missionaries who first arrived among the "man-eaters" were able to list fourteen of the big architectural complexes in use at that time (about 1850), and the ruins of many more than fourteen still exist. One of the main features of our projected work in Taipi was a program of excavations in several more *tohua* to discover whether the information that we had accumulated at Hikoku'a was valid for the region or the result of some unusual situation peculiar to that site alone.

We continued down the rutted, narrow path that dipped in and out of the ravines along the steep north slope of Taipi Valley, with the wide, rapid Taipi River glistening in the valley floor below. Occasionally the silence would be broken by the soft voice of Corpse Eyes, who, speaking with his usual politeness, would indicate some lonely heap of boulders and relate a little story of a bloody deed done there, or point out the temple of a powerful god, whose name, once *tapu*, was now forgotten.

It soon became clear that in the midst of the great natural beauty of Taipivai, and its archaeological wealth, one outstanding bad quality existed: swarms of black, biting *nono* flies. Poor Rae—she had just recovered from her early illness caused by the infernal little pests, and now we were going to a place where they were more numerous than ever.

Near the hamlet, the road widened and the hills and gullies became smooth. We galloped the last few hundred feet to the edge of the hamlet, turning into a broad stone-walled yard before our host's house, a large frame building that had earlier been a trading store. Beneath the palms and fruit trees that shaded the enclosure, chickens, ducks, dogs, and cats erupted in every direction. A couple of tethered sheep raised pitiful cries of fear. Out of the house poured a stream of children, a little afraid of, but very curious about, the two white visitors. They stopped when they came near us, standing pigeon-toed on the outer rims of their feet, shifting their weight from one leg to the other, and shyly sucking thumbs and assorted fingers. One little fellow, oddly enough endowed with blond hair, burst into loud wails and hid his head behind the skirts of a twelve-year-old who looked like his sister. From a bamboo cookhouse nearby a plump, tired-looking woman in faded calico descended toward us, wiping her hands on her skirt, followed by a slender, muscled man. With warm greetings, they shook our hands and held the horses as we began to dismount. Three husky boys came out of the house, followed by a well-constructed, obviously pregnant girl, carrying a beautiful big-eyed baby in her arms. Everyone was talking at once when a deep hoarse voice boomed from the second story of the rickety building, *"Eaha? Te Menike?"*—"What is it? The American?" The familiar figure of our host followed the voice; he was a tall stocky man in his mid-fifties, who bore the improbable name of Charlie Clark, barefoot and in tattered shorts and shirt. Charlie's name and his light skin derived from an American whaler who had put ashore one day in Tahiti, never to return to his native Boston. Charlie, his grandson, had been obliged to migrate to the Marquesas from Tahiti because of a few indiscretions in his youth, and had finally settled in Taipivai.

Descending the unsteady stairs from the second floor, Charlie approached with a huge smile. "Robert! Hello, how you?" he cried in his best English, taught him by his Boston granddad. "Hi, Missus Robert!" Then lapsing into Marquesan, he turned to Tunui, but I interrupted, also in Marquesan, much to his amazement. "Good, good! Now you can talk to us and explain everything. Last year we wanted to hear all about America but you couldn't speak Marquesan and we were ashamed." Someone said, "Hey, listen to him—now he talks Marquesan better than the missionaries!"

We were led into the dark lower floor of the house to a big table, while Charlie's orders began to fly: "Hu'uveu! Grab some bananas . . . and a plate! Do you think the white man eats like us? Ariete, get the baby out of here, it just dirtied the floor! Hina, you thing, shut up! Ma'ati'ae, bring the meat. Titi! Titi? Where are you? Ah, there! Is there any fish left? Look quick! Maha'i, don't stand there and stare! Haven't you ever seen a white man? Here, go down to Haremanu's and buy two loaves of bread. Well, *run!* Before I box your ears!"

While this mob scene took shape Charlie's wife, Heiku'a, galloped up on a big gelding. Apologizing for not having been at home to receive us, she explained that she had been in the copra grove on the slope and had not been able to see the house.

In Heiku'a's speech and that of her family, I noticed immediately the distinctive features of the Taipi dialect: a throatiness and slowness of speech combined with exaggerated intonations and pitch changes. In addition, a phonetic feature, evidently preserved over hundreds of years from the original Marquesan dialect, stood out very clearly. This feature, the "ng" sound in place of the normal Marquesan "k" sound, is found nowhere else in the archipelago.

As the other members of the family trotted around at Charlie's behest he and his wife talked to us, she directing most of her questions to Rae through me. Over a snack, I began to refamiliarize myself with the relationships of the various family members. This was no easy task, for there were sixteen people in the family. Charlie, the patriarch, had come to the islands penniless, but his wife owned approximately half of the good land in the valley through the bounty of her grandfather. Heiku'a allowed Charlie to rule the family, preferring to remain as the power behind the throne.

In addition to the sizable representation of the human species, our company in the house numbered sixteen dogs and seventeen cats, the two sheep in the yard, three ducks and a large number of chickens and chicks which wandered about at will; this entire population was sheltered in only five rooms.

After the meal, we unpacked our baggage in the room that

had been given to us, donning swimsuits for a bath in the river only a hundred feet from the door. A soft bedrock deposit had been worn away at this point by the swift stream, conveniently creating a deep swimming hole.

That evening, as we sat around the little battery radio listening to the news broadcast from Tahiti, the difficulties and animosities of Hatiheu began to fade, and the prospects of several months' residence in this large and happy household made our future seem quite rosy. After a family prayer session, chanted in the typical minor-key Marquesan monotone, we turned in.

The following day, a tropical downpour greeted us after the morning prayer session, which occurred punctually at five thirty and was a repetition of the evening devotions, with Heiku'a taking the lead in spots while the rest of the family intoned the responses, blinking their sleep-swollen eyes and scratching tousled heads in the weak light of the kerosene lamp.

Despite the rain, there was plenty of work to be done. After a little talk with Manuera, the chief, we sent out some feelers for possible workmen in the community, and paid a few calls in the little hamlet along the deeply cut Taipi River, visiting some of the landowners whose permission we might have to solicit for our excavations.

There was a good response to my call to work: in fact, almost every able-bodied male in the valley did his best to appear interested in the anthropological cause. A little consultation with Charlie sufficed to inform us which of the candidates were worth hiring.

In the late morning while the rain still fell from the sky in huge drops, I decided to make a thorough survey of the area before starting any excavation, just in case there might be some outstanding sites that I had missed during the previous year. Some of the Clark clan and I saddled horses and ascended the valley, visiting a number of very remote sites of which the members of our host's family knew.

The following day we descended to the beach of Taipi

to look for possible sites on the sand flats, where the river and its old abandoned channels lead into the bay. The Taipi River is what geologists call an "immature" river, as it is constantly changing its course and eroding away to one side or the other, especially in the seasonal torrents that swell it ten feet above its normal level, carrying livestock, houses, and other assorted private property into the bay. The rapid erosive action of the river had ruined our chances of finding anything in that area, for if any archaeological sites had existed, they had long since been washed away.

If ever there was a likely spot to look for a very old habitation site, it was in the Taipi area, for the Polynesian discoverers of the island could not have refrained from noticing the obvious natural endowments of this beautiful well-watered valley, with its long, well-protected bay with many excellent fishing spots. Therefore, we mounted the ridge on the north side of Taipi and entered the adjacent valley of Ho'oumi, once quite heavily populated by an ally of the Taipi tribes but now sheltering only thirty-five souls, among them Tunui's eighty-five-year-old mother. After visiting a short while with the stooped but active white-haired woman who lived alone in a tiny hut beside the grave of her departed husband, we rode to Ho'oumi beach. There, a deep placid stream entered the bay through a grove of palm trees, beneath which were the remains of many large house platforms. Corpse Eyes, who had been born in Ho'oumi, and knew the area perhaps better than anyone else, identified two of these platforms as having been temples which in his youth had been deeply feared as being inhabited by supernatural beings. I learned that human skeletons had been exposed in the beach sands after the tidal wave of 1946, beneath an old temple floor that had been almost completely destroyed.

Walking on the sand flats behind the beach among the stone ruins, I was delighted by the potential of this site. Wherever we had excavated in or around stone platforms in the past, the sites had been located deep in the valleys on the damp, very acid soil of the valley bottoms. The fragile fishhooks and ornaments of pearl shell that had been so well preserved in the Ha'atuatua sands and the bone-dry caves that we excavated in 1956 could not survive in the humid, corroding soil of the valley bottoms. Therefore, we had recovered practically no shell or coral tools from the stone platform sites, only stone implements surviving in the red earth.

Thus, we had been very much restricted in our ability to associate or disassociate the stone platform sites with the remains found in the dry caves or in Ha'atuatua. Here, however, was a whole hamlet of stone platforms on well-drained, sandy soil. Surely we would find out more about the tools of the platform builders if we were to excavate here.

Permission to excavate was obtained from the landowner, a tall, lanky, loose-skinned fellow, descended from an American whaler who had deserted in the Marquesas. "Yes," he cried, "dig all you want! We Americans must help each other, right?"

There was a good probability that some archaeologically rich cave or rock-shelter sites might be found far down the bay near the open sea, or out along the rocky coastal cliffs between Taipivai and Taiohae, so we decided to take to the sea in the big outrigger canoe which, with a decrepit American jeep that ran only in second gear, was a major source of pride for the whole Clark household. This vessel, twenty-five feet long, was clinker-built, of hand-hewn planks, rising from a dugout keel. The interior, fitted with sturdy seats, ribs, and half-bulkheads, had ample room for as many as six people and supplies. The thick but buoyant outrigger was connected, by means of short struts and lashings, to two long, carefully tapered booms that were in turn lashed across the gunwales of the canoe. The whole outrigger assembly was removed when the canoe was not in use and stored among the rafters of the long shed in which the strong hull rested on log rollers.

Despite the apparent complexity of the assembly, the canoe could be dragged out of its shed and the outrigger lashed in place in a matter of ten minutes. Lashings may seem like a slapdash way of holding together a canoe built for heavy use, but they provide an important degree of flexibility to the whole outrigger assembly, which would be twisted to pieces in a short time if it were more rigid.

The canoe was an impressive piece of carpentry beside the small, light outriggers generally employed by the natives, but its construction was nothing to the unusual way in which it was propelled. Most Marquesans use wide-bladed paddles or sails for their voyages, but the Clark family refused to bow to convention. The funds from their copra lands were carefully set aside for a big Evinrude outboard engine, which was ordered from Tahiti. The canoe was somewhat modified to hold this mechanical symbol of status, but unfortunately the canoe hull had not been designed for propulsion by a fifteen-horsepower motor. As a consequence, the sturdy canoe, instead of riding with the big rollers off the coast, would very often plow through their crests, making constant bailing a necessity; a ride was a rather damp, if often thrilling, proposition.

Early one morning the canoe was assembled and we embarked in the calm river, paddling down to the mouth of the river; there we all hopped out in the waist-deep water to drag the canoe over and around the sandbars that surround the estuary. Charlie and the three elder boys, Tunui, and Corpse Eyes made up the party. Soon we were in mid-bay with the big Evinrude purring along in its housing. Skirting the shore, we traveled for about a mile, carefully watching on both sides of the spacious bay for caves or shelters in the cliffs, or small protected inlets that might harbor valuable sites. The engine tempo slowed considerably and I turned to see Charlie pointing toward a low, wide opening in the vertical cliff face almost hidden by rock slides and gigantic boulders tumbled from the cliff above. "That's Bat Cave," he shouted over the engine, "Want to go ashore for a look?" On an affirmative reply, Poiti, the steersman, cut his wide steering oar into the wake and the canoe wheeled about. The rocks and boulders before the cave entrance made a landing there impossible, so the canoe was brought up along the rocky shelf a hundred yards down and we stood up gingerly waiting for a surge in the sea to lift us even with the shelf, as the boys held the canoe off the rocks with their paddles and feet. When the canoe rose on a swell, we jumped onto the rough tide-pooled surface. Tunui, Corpse Eyes, and two of the boys came along, while Charlie and Poiti drew off into the bay, threw out some fishing lines, and drifted.

Climbing over the rugged rockfall by the cave entrance, we dropped down onto the boulder-heaped beach where the sea washed into the mouth of the cave. Entering, we found ourselves in a humid and very oppressive atmosphere; the atmospheric pressure seemed all at once to have risen considerably above the 14.7 pounds per square inch value that it should be at sea level. The cave floor rose rapidly inside the mouth, leveling off beneath a low, black-splotched ceiling dripping with moisture. Two platforms, from which a white and yellow mineral deposit cascaded down the walls, stood against the back wall of the cave. At the left, against a rock pile, a small terrace had been built. The floor of the cave was a moist compound of earth and bird dung, deposited by the swarms of batlike birds called *kopekapeka* which now wheeled and fluttered outside the entrance. Several circles of stones were laid out on the soft spongy surface, their function not immediately apparent.

The cave swung off sharply to the left, and the floor rose slowly as roof and walls closed in. Here and there, small stalactites had formed in patches on the ceiling, glittering like diamonds in the weak rays of our flashlights. A brown object protruded from the earth near one of the low stone platforms; it was a bone fragment. With my knife I removed the earth from about it carefully, laying bare a large intact human heel bone, or calcaneus. Further examination brought forth more bone fragments, scattered about the floor and on the platforms. Could this be a burial cave? If so, where were the rest of the bones? Corpse Eyes and Tunui compared notes as to their recollections of the cave from childhood; it appeared that the 1946 tidal wave had caused much interior damage, removing without a trace a large platform near the entrance. Perhaps the bones were debris from a burial in this.

Corpse Eyes pointed to the narrow end of the cave where a small passage was now evident to our dark-adapted eyes. "That hole leads to a long cave that goes right underneath the mountain. That is, people *say* it does, but I think everyone who ever went in was too scared to really follow it out." We entered the narrow hole, the seemingly nerveless Tioni, Heiku'a's barrel-chested brother, leading with flashlight. We had gone only a few feet when he stopped and shouted back that there were human bones in there. Crawling up on top of his extended legs, I looked past to see a couple of thigh bones protruding from a pile of rocks. Beneath my stomach small bone fragments were being crushed as I moved. A few feet farther on the light suddenly went out. Tioni fumed curses in Marquesan and French while trying to cajole the temperamental mechanism into working. At length he began to back out, pushing me back against Tunui, who was close on my heels. We finally got untangled and out of the hole, but only Tioni seemed enthusiastic about re-entering. As far as he had gone, he had seen only a few random bones: the cave had evidently been looted.

Neither Tunui nor Corpse Eyes knew any legends about the cave; the miniature platforms on the floor, with enigmatic stone circles and scattered human bones, seemed to indicate that this was a special kind of site, perhaps a shrine of some sort. Interest was further heightened by the discovery of some stone-edged pits on a stalagmitic stone shelf near the ceiling. As these features were also completely unusual, a few days of test excavation seemed to be indicated at this potentially interesting and important site.

The next day we approached the cave by an overland route, descending the cliff with all our equipment, and setting up in the cave to begin excavations.

By the end of three days, however, disappointment had settled over the whole crew, for the Bat Cave turned out to be an archaeologist's folly. Three artifacts, none of which were in any way unique, were uncovered in one of the small platforms. Careful excavation of the stone circles and the stone-edged pits failed to give any satisfactory hint as to their purposes. The only unique find of the whole dig was a hank of knotted human hair, hidden in a cranny of the largest platform. The salt-encrusted hair had probably been hidden by a Marquesan afraid of the witchcraft that might be worked on him if an adversary found his hair clippings.

Our excavations proved one thing, however: the cave had not been inhabited by any group either permanently or periodically. The almost complete absence of tools of any type, the total lack of garbage deposits of discarded shells, fishbones, etc., demonstrated pretty conclusively that this cave had been used only for ceremonies of some kind.

Undisturbed by this stroke of bad luck, we were out the next morning in the canoe, surveying the remaining areas of the bay and the adjacent coast in the hope of finding better sites. I did not realize just how much of a turn for the good our luck would take.

8 / The Cave of the Warrior Band

Venturing out onto the open sea, we cruised down the coast between Taipi and Taiohae, an area once held by the powerful Hapa'a tribe that had long served as a buffer between the tattooed hordes of Taipi and the men of Taiohae.

Our objective was a large cave called Nahotoa—Warrior Band—almost hidden in the curve of a rocky promontory projecting from the Hapa'a coast. I had noticed the cave entrance on an earlier canoe trip, when our route had carried us in close to the coast, the only position from which the opening was even partially visible.

Talking with Tunui and members of the Clark family, I soon found that the cave was "large"; how large seemed very uncertain, as Tunui had visited the place only once, some forty years earlier, and most of the other adults possessed only secondhand knowledge of that region. One thing was certain almost from our first view of the cave—it was impossible for us to reach it overland. Located in the corner of the shallow inlet formed by the curve of the promontory, the cave was surrounded by unscalable granite cliffs rising vertically several hundred feet above the sea. In several spots, the cliffs actually overhung the cave entrance.

On one exciting fact about the cave there was rare unanimous agreement: the cave was inhabited by scores of birds whose droppings had covered the floor with heaps of guano. If any archaeological deposits were in the cave floor, therefore, they would be admirably preserved.

I decided that an exploration was required. Charlie's big canoe was hauled out of its shed, assembled, dragged over the bars, and off we went, with Poiti handling the steering oar.

Approaching the promontory, we observed the height of
the sea's surge against the cliffs and rocks in the inlet. Only
at the south side of the inlet, beneath an overhanging cliff,
would a landing be possible. Across the inlet itself, jumbled
stone blocks descended in a huge pile from the base of the cliff
in which the cave was situated, into the crashing surf, present-
ing a dangerous array of sharp points and edges. With the
engine idling we warily entered the inlet; the swells there
were higher than in the open sea because the force of the rolling
wave action was being deflected off the shallow bottom, projecting the swells higher into the air. The rocky shelf was periodically inundated by a swirl of white which, when it sub-
sided, exposed an expanse of rough granite splotched with
pink and yellow marine algae and bristling with the black
pincushion forms of spiny sea urchins. The closer we got to
this rather formidable "wharf" the more it became obvious
that between waves the rise and fall of the sea against it was
well over the height of a normal man. How were we going to
get out of this? The idling engine suddenly changed pitch as
a sickening surge caught the canoe, hurling it much closer to
the rocks. Tioni, the "engineer," reversed the engine but we
were still drawn closer to the cliffs, bobbing like a cork on
the crests of the swells.

It appeared as though about two more surges would beat
us against the rock walls below the narrow shelf at the base of
the cliff. I was preparing for the shock of collision when
Tunui leaped forward and perched on the bow, and Corpse
Eyes and Tioni took places along the gunwales with their legs
dangling in the water. As we came gliding in to the ledge both
leaped overboard, clinging to the gunwales, and thrust their
legs out against the cliff; Tunui's broad feet and muscular legs
took the shock at the bow, so that when the bow touched the
cliff, it banged resoundingly but lost no more than a few cen-
timeters of wood and paint. Our human ship-fenders had
worked pretty well! Feeling stupidly helpless, I sat in the canoe
as Tioni and Corpse Eyes struggled for good footholds among
the crevices of the rock wall, rising and falling with the power-

ful rollers, but laughing gaily all the while. Charlie had an oar against the cliff and I grabbed a boat hook, while Poiti put an oar in on the outrigger side in case we needed some extra push in making a retreat. Charlie turned to me. "Want to jump for it?" he said, as we rose up level with the shelf and then plummeted down several feet below it in the trough of a swell. The canoe was sliding along the cliff face held off by the legs, oars, and boat hook, but a few feet more and we would be in a narrow box corner of the inlet from which it might well be impossible to escape. I shook my head and jerked my thumb seaward. "*Paó á he'e!*"—"Let's go!" I shouted. "The boat will be smashed now—wait until a calmer day!"

Charlie took over, shouting at the men in the water to push with their feet at his command and then hold tight. At the word, he full-reversed the engine as we all shoved and Poiti dug deep with the oar. Slowly we moved away from the rock walls, pitching as the swells rolled beneath us. Four brown arms appeared over the side; first Corpse Eyes and then Tioni chinned on the gunwales and hauled themselves over. Tioni had his battered pandanus leaf hat pulled down over his ears like a bonnet and a black native stogie still clamped tightly in his lantern jaw. Both appeared to have enjoyed their sojourn between the canoe and the rocks far more than I had enjoyed watching them.

Returning home, we told Heiku'a of the difficult time we had had in making an approach and of the final abandonment of the project to await better seas. She looked hard at the boys, who suddenly wore hangdog countenances. "What! You couldn't put the white man ashore where he wanted to go? Who was steersman? You, Poiti? Hah! Next time you go *I* will steer—it's really very easy, you'll see! I'm surprised at your blundering—the white man might have been hurt."

The next time, we went with a complete archaeological outfit, for I did not doubt for a minute that rough water or not I would be going ashore to see that cave, and I was going to make sure the risk was worth it by testing the cave thoroughly before we left.

The canoe wallowed slightly with its heavy load of men and equipment as we rounded the point of Hanga Ha'a and turned up the coast. This time the sea was fortunately a little calmer; our approach was easier, and the task of holding the canoe close enough to the ledge so that we could unload our supplies was solved by skillful handling of the steering oar with Tioni and Corpse Eyes again holding the canoe off by bracing their legs against the slippery rock wall. After slinging the shovels and earth screens onto the ledge, Tunui leaped from the bow to a foothold in the rock face, gingerly clutching the bag with my cameras and notebooks, after which I followed. Heiku'a, holding the steering oar, kept up a steady stream of terse commands throughout the whole operation, controlling the movements of everyone. When we were all ashore, she and Poiti churned off to fish all day in the deep *toka*, or fishing holes, off the southeast tip of the island, outside of Hanga Ha'a Bay.

Collecting the gear, we climbed over the heaped-up boulders that concealed so much of the cave's mouth from outside view. From closer range, the size of the entrance was large, but it was only when we reached the crest of the rock pile across the cave mouth that its true size was apparent. The entrance was a hundred and fifty feet wide, the walls rising to a vaulted ceiling about ninety feet above the flat cave floor that was exposed below us. In the cave mouth a silence settled over us; the hill of boulders before it and the shape of the cliffs above it combined to produce an unusual acoustical effect, abruptly shutting out the roar of the surf and making one almost wish to walk on tiptoe in the sudden wave of silence.

To reach the cave floor, which seemed to be almost at the level of the sea outside, we had to pass beneath the arch; sound suddenly returned, this time in the form of a shower of soft chirping noises descending from the rough, mottled ceiling where thousands of sacklike birds' nests hung suspended, as their black-feathered occupants fluttered to and fro rapidly in fluid, constantly changing groups.

The floor near the cave mouth was hard-caked and dry with

guano, with scarcely a stone visible on its surface. Farther back were several small platforms in a stone-littered area, and about a hundred yards away, near the rear of the cave, huge conical heaps of guano covered the floor completely.

On the floor around the small stone platforms we found long stone lines, carefully piled heaps of stone, and circular stone arrangements such as those we had seen in Bat Cave. We set up the earth-sifting screens near the front of the cave and had started to test a dark layer under a blanket of solidified guano when suddenly there was a flash of silver. A big, well-finished pearl shell fishhook lay exposed to view in the dry soil beneath the caked guano. In a few minutes, more hooks appeared, then a coral file, some pieces of worked shell, and a few cord fragments. The cord was made of three strands of brown coconut fiber braided together.

A few more test pits were put down in other parts of the deposits; in each we encountered more or less the same artifacts. The layer of earth containing these was only ten inches thick but quite rich in content. Below it lay a black deposit of fine sea-rolled gravel, consisting of rounded grains of basalt, coral, and shell washed in by waves many years before. Evidently the cave had once been much longer and the sea had entered the full length of its corridor. Then, as a result of an earth tremor, or imperceptible changes wrought in the rock of the cave roof by erosion and weathering, the whole front of the cave roof had fallen away, leaving the slightly overhanging cliffs beside it and providing the pile of massive stone blocks that shielded much of the entrance from view.

After our highly successful day of testing, we hailed Heiku'a with great cheerfulness from the rocks that evening as she maneuvered the black-and-white canoe to pick us up. Two days later we were back in Nahotoa again digging in its football-field-sized floor. This time, however, we had come to stay, laden with bedding, clothing, food, fishing gear, and even a small rickety canoe that belonged to Tioni, in case we should have to do any fishing out in the open sea. Our home was a narrow, deep fissure opening onto the rock shelf, reasonably well protected from the waves. To sleep in the cave itself would have been to invite disaster, for the soft rock of the ceiling was constantly coming away in baseball-sized chunks. Although many areas looked reasonably safe, I felt it best not to take a chance. Our rock-walled home was a cozy place, except for the roar of the surf which made it difficult to sleep at night. Outside the fissure on the rock shelf was a deep coral-grown tidal pool in which several black, velvet-finned fish swam languidly and a baby moray appeared occasionally among the urchins and seaweeds. This attraction in our "patio" added a great deal to the habitability of the fissure, providing a source of interest at all times, especially for Corpse Eyes, who was an especially devoted fish watcher at meal times.

After mapping the cave floor, and its complement of man-made structures, we began excavation in earnest, stripping off the heavy layer of guano from the floor of the great echoing cavern to reveal the layer of debris accumulated by the ancient dwellers in the cave. Among the artifacts uncovered at the very start of the digging were numbers of a very unusual kind of fish-hook, one evidently invented by the Marquesans, for it has no counterpart anywhere else in the Pacific. This hook was shaped like any other one-piece hook, but it had an unusual feature in the attachment of a second piece of shell to the shank. This piece, shaped exactly like the hook shank, was fitted closely to it and the two components were tied together for their entire length by fine tough vegetable fiber cords. The double thickness of shell on the shank evidently conferred some extra strength on the hook and at the same time the lashings gave the shank additional flexibility. This device was probably used to land some fierce food fish, which a hook of ordinary strength could not carry.

In the deposits of Nahotoa, as in the dry caves in Ue'a Valley which had been excavated in 1956, we had a good opportunity to see how much an archaeologist normally misses when digging a site that has been exposed to the rain and weather and the normal processes of decay. In Ha'atuatua, for instance, the preservation of artifacts in the well-drained beach sands was good, but no traces of wood or fiber were recovered anywhere in the site; only stone, bone, and shell had survived the weather. In Nahotoa, however, the guano had done its desiccating labor: all that the Marquesans had left was recovered, in a very good state of preservation. Evidently a lot of rope-, cord-, and netmaking had gone on in the cave, for we recovered an amazing quantity of cordage. This included everything from two-strand twisted ropes about three eighths of an inch in diameter to the fine shanks onto which they had been carefully tied so long ago. The majority of cordage was of the three-strand braided variety, made of tough, durable coconut fiber. This material is prepared by a tedious process of removing and shredding the fibers in the husks from the corklike matrix. Once separated, the fibers are cleaned, straightened, and hand-rolled into narrow strands, the cordmaker using his hand and thigh as tool and workbench for this operation. The strands are then braided together to form cordage such as we had found.

An interesting feature of the cordage recovered was the variety of knots that we found. Evidently sailors use approximately the same knots the world over, for we found fisherman's knots, square knots, and hitches.

The inhabitants of Nahotoa had probably derived their water from seepages and springs, one of which was dripping from the cave ceiling and another was draining down the face of the cliff a short distance from the cave mouth. The remains of their water containers—made of large Lagenaria, or bottle gourds, scraped out and dried—were found all over the floor of the cave. Apparently the useful life of a bottle gourd container was very short, for the number of fragments scattered about bore witness to a very rapid turnover. Even today the Marquesans still scrape and sun-cure the gourds for use as water containers or as catch basins for coconut moonshine drippings. Several coconut shell drinking cups appeared, as did fragments of wooden bowls and platters, all broken in use and discarded on the spot. Charring on many of these fragments indicated that any wood objects discarded about the cave were turned into handy sources of kindling, which probably accounts for our not finding more than these fragments of bowls.

The cast-off remains of many a native meal had been trodden into the soft earth of the floor among the stone-lined fire pits that dotted the area. We found many fishbones and the remains of numerous edible shellfish, but here again the dry atmosphere was favorable and we found recognizable remains of vegetables. Wedge-shaped segments of the pandanus fruit appeared; these provide a sort of chewing gum and "filler" in times when other foods are scarce. Also preserved in the dried earth were banana leaves, chestnuts, coconut shells and hanks of coconut fibers, and quantities of the 'ama, or candlenut. This small oily nut provided a source of light for the ancient Marquesans. Strung on heavy coconut leaf ribs, dried 'ama nuts burn with a bright flame and once served as the lamps of Marquesan households and torches for festivals. The oily nuts are also used as a cathartic, the results of which are somewhat awe-inspiring, as I was given to understand. Polynesians in general are rather preoccupied with their digestive processes and seem to be constipated most of the time, probably as a result of the quantities of bulky starches which form the mainstay of their diet. Any laxative that works spectacularly cannot fail to become popular among them and this, I gather, was the case with the highly effective 'ama nuts. Unfortunately, the prestige aspects of European medicine have now eclipsed the dynamic 'ama in favor of brightly packaged but less effective patent medicines from the United States and France.

A large amount of woodworking must also have gone on in the cave, for chips of wood of all varieties composed a large part of the archaeological stratum in the cave floor. Fragments of many finished objects were found, including the bowls and platters described above and some bigger, enigmatic fragments of what might have been canoes. The finish displayed by these objects was interesting evidence of the kind of craftsmanship that could be expected by the use of the stone adzes and coral polishers of the Marquesan master carpenters. Despite the use of the coral abrading tools to smooth the surface of these objects, the adze marks could still be plainly seen. Drill holes in several fragments showed a surprising lack of finesse, seeming to have been partially drilled through and then punched out with a sharp implement.

The number of small, very simple wooden tools that appeared seemed remarkable at first, because archaeologists constantly think in terms of the more elaborate specialized tools of stone, bone, and shell that resist the processes of time. A number of wooden splinters, sharpened into needles of some sort, had cords tied to them. These were probably used in netmaking or in some sort of rigging work. Small hardwood punches appeared to have seen use as marlinspikes in rope splicing.

I uncovered one peculiar bullet-shaped wooden object about two and a half inches long. The boys nearest me looked over my shoulder from their positions by the earth screens and spoke almost simultaneously: *"E niu, hoi!"*—"A top!" I dimly recalled having read that tops were common toys among nineteenth-century Marquesan children, but I had never expected to find one in an archaeological site. This was the first and only time that we ever uncovered any kind of plaything. I wondered whether the child who had left it where we uncovered it had lived in the cave, and merely discarded a tiresome toy, or whether it had been dropped by a captive child from the Taipi tribe, destined for sacrifice on the altars of Hapa'a.

The low stone platforms in the cave gave us some interesting information. The largest of these, built on the surface of the deposits, had been erected somewhere near the end of the time span in which the site was inhabited. In skimming off the guano layers, however, we found small paved house floors, evidently of earlier construction. The earliest inhabitants had either lived in crude shelters on the cave floor, traces of which were obliterated with the passing years, or had not built shelters at all.

One may well ask what the need was for houses within a cave. Two very good reasons are these: first, the requirements of privacy and, second, protection from the rocks which continually dropped from the ceiling. We found during our work that in some areas of the cave rocks fell far more frequently than in others. Testing the deposits in these danger spots, we found that they had been scrupulously avoided by the early inhabitants: no archaeological remains appeared in them at all. All the habitation occurred in a small irregular area near the cave mouth, just back of the caked, hardened, guano area which was a catch basin for rain washing down the slopes into the cave entrance. The periodically soggy drainage area near the rockfall areas farther back in the cave bounded the useful areas of the cave rather sharply for the early inhabitants, but the shelter of the long, vaulted chamber was still enough to offset these major disadvantages and hazards. According to Corpse Eyes, the cave had legendarily been used as a spot where, after the collapse of the native culture in the nineteenth century, circumcisions were held. He believed, as I did, on the basis of the cave's name, that the site had also at one time or another sheltered war parties. The promontory in which the cave was located reached well out into the sea from the Hapa'a coast. From the rocks in front of the cave entrance one therefore had a clear view of the whole coast and the mouth of Taipi Bay. If the men of Taipi sallied forth for a war party, a watcher in front of Nahotoa would see the long canoes in plenty of time to signal his compatriots on the coast of Hapa'a, and alert the valleys that might be endangered.

Although we worked with more than usual diligence at Nahotoa, life was by no means dull. Each evening we would straighten up our work and repair to our temporary home on the rocky shelf. The boys would make a try, with fishing lines and three-pronged fish spears, at getting some fresh fish for supper, rather than face another can of the rather grim bully beef we had brought along. Occasionally Tioni would launch the rickety little canoe and fish in mid-inlet. Once he and Hu'uveu, a twenty-year-old constructed like a football guard, wedged themselves into this homely little craft to chase a big manta ray that was cruising around, close to the rocks. I held my breath as they sailed the nearly swamped outrigger right up over the manta where it lay looping lazily below the surface. Fortunately, the big ray saw them and departed posthaste. Tioni could not get a clear shot with his spear at any of the vital spots on the black-and-white bird of the depths. "How big was he?" I asked when they returned to shore, for I had first spotted the fin tips of the ray as they sliced through the rollers in the inlet. "Oh, he was good-sized," said Hu'uveu matter-of-factly as they hauled their craft up the ledge. "He was nearly twice as wide as the canoe across the fins."

A popular evening dish at the cave was provided by the small soft-shell crabs that skittered along the vertical rock faces. A big bucket of these dainty creatures was gathered every night, after which a can of bully beef was opened, some salt dug out, and a couple of roasted breadfruit peeled and placed on some leaves on the floor of our sleeping cave. After a brief prayer, the prelude to every Marquesan meal, we would dig in—with fingers and occasionally other utensils. Tunui, Corpse Eyes, and the boys always snatched a couple of the squirming crabs and proceeded to dismember and eat them alive. I, for my part, began with resignation on the bully beef, or took a handful of cubed fish if there was any, watching with morbid fascination as twitching claws and feelers disappeared between the men's crunching jaws. After the last crab had met its unhappy end, a pool of reddish liquid—part sea water and part fluid from the bodies of the crabs—remained in the bottom of the bucket, this to be drunk with equal gusto.

After we finished the meal and chatted for a bit, between belches and burps, bathing started. I took a bath in a pool of brackish water draining down from the rock face a short distance from the cave. The minerals in the water made soap almost useless, and I returned each evening feeling almost dirtier than when I had started.

When the last bit of orange afterglow had disappeared from

the cliffs and the ridges, we built a little blaze in the mouth of
the fissure and settled down to the evening's entertainment:
a recitation by Corpse Eyes from his immense repertoire of
legends and stories, bridging the gap between the past and
the present, the supernatural and the concrete, in a wonderful,
plausible way. Sitting beside the fire, Corpse Eyes would lift
his eyes to the winking legions of stars that illuminated the
sky above us. He would pause momentarily, a mere hint of a
smile at the corners of his mouth, and then start to speak, in
a slow, measured voice, at the same time seeming to withdraw
to another plane of consciousness. "There was a warrior in
the valley of Hanamenu on Hiva Oa; his name was Toa
Matakeu . . ." he would begin, and then would follow a
strange tale of warrior heroes and beautiful women, bewitch-
ing priestesses and wicked spirits of the dead, powerful gods
and fish and animals that were possessed of the human faculty
of speech. Often Corpse Eyes' legends would be so evocative
that the boys would become a little afraid, like children at
summer camps, mildly terrified by a counselor's ghost story.

We bedded down on piled branches, the men using burlap
sacks as mattresses and I an old punctured air mattress that
held air just long enough for me to get to sleep. Generally
the surf picked up strength at one or more times throughout
the night, however, and I would wake up after a particularly
loud roar and stay awake for most of the remaining night
hours, gazing at the glow of the tropical heavens.

In the morning, if I got back to sleep, I would be awakened
by the gentle basso voice of Corpse Eyes, chanting a pagan
ru'u as he sat on his pile of sacks rubbing his eyes and yawn-
ing. After a quick breakfast of bread and cheese, topped off
by strong, sugared coffee, we were off to the cave.

As the excavations progressed, it became increasingly apparent that the tools and ornaments of the inhabitants of this
cave were identical with those found in the first sites excavated
in the Marquesas—the dry caves in Ue'a Valley which we
dug in 1956. The artifacts were also almost identical with
those that we had excavated from a small rock shelter called

Moe'ana, or "Sleeping Here," in the valley of Ha'a'au'a'i, after we had finished the work at Hikoku'a and the quarry sites of Ha'ata'ive'a. The shelter was located on a small inlet, beneath an overhanging rock ledge close to the shore. The deposits in the bottom of this shelter turned out to be a startling seven feet in depth and crammed with the remains of human inhabitants. In the lowest layer of this small but productive site the artifacts were exactly like those recovered in Nahotoa and the Ue'a caves.

Our find at Nahotoa, then, added another piece to an ever-growing mosaic of the Marquesan past; I was now sure that these sites, so much alike, were connected with each other in some way.

The similarities were especially apparent in the fishhooks collected at these sites. The unusual two-piece fishhooks of Nahotoa were also very common in the Ue'a sites, and were found in the lowest level of the thick deposits in Moe'ana. Other types of hooks found in Nahotoa were also found in the Ue'a and Moe'ana sites, among them the bonito lures, with their perforated hook points and the simple U-shapes that were so common everywhere. The coral files, the adzes, the knobbed stone net weights, and the oval grooved stones used for weighting down squid lures were also identical.

Finally the simple house pavements, divided longitudinally into two sections, one for sleeping, the other for work, were also similar to one found on the surface of one of the Ue'a caves.

When such striking similarities exist between a number of sites, an archaeologist may safely assume that they are roughly of the same age and can group them as manifestations of the same level of cultural development. Here, then, was a group of related sites on diametrically opposite sides of the island, occupied at approximately the same time. Furthermore, all of the sites were located in caves or well-protected rock shelters in very remote areas, not easily accessible from the main valleys. I had seen house pavements similar to those in the caves, scattered about the rock-strewn plateau of western

Nuku Hiva called *Henua Ataha*—the Deserted Land—by the natives. On the silent island of Eïao, far to the north, similar house pavements could be seen on the rolling hills, clustered here and there near long-dried-up springs and rivulets, surrounded by broken stone tools and the usual accumulation of debris from native culinary activities.

It seemed that this culture appeared frequently in the most remote and less favorable areas of the island of Nuku Hiva and particularly in caves or rock shelters, for we had never found a shelter in which an earlier culture was present. What factors could account for this seemingly irrational selection of the less favorable areas of the island for habitation? The Polynesians were certainly well enough acquainted with their environment to have immediately seen the disadvantages inherent in trying to wrest a living on the dry west coast, which was cut off by the razor-sharp backbone of Nuku Hiva from the southeast wind that brought the moisture necessary for good planting to the southern and eastern parts of the island. Furthermore, there must have been a strong motivating factor to make them move suddenly into caves that had never been previously inhabited.

It is known from legends that many of the uninhabited, barren areas of the Marquesas Islands were occupied as a result of warfare, probably caused by the crowding of subtribes in the bigger valleys, where they were forced to compete for the best tracts of garden land—a limited resource of considerable importance to any islander.

Could these cave dwellings and marginal settlements have been established by migrant groups fleeing from the most crowded valleys where a steady population increase had suddenly exploded in a series of bloody tribal wars? The hypothesis seemed quite plausible and on critical examination appeared to be the most likely explanation of the situation.

Naturally, the earliest inhabitants of the archipelago would have chosen, for their initial settlements, valleys possessing good water supplies, fine garden lands, and other important resources such as basalt quarries which would provide the material for stone tools, beds of pearl shell and coral in the bays for tools and ornaments, and good nearby fishing spots. In the large fertile valleys of Taiohae, Hapa'a, Taipi, Ho'oumi, Hatiheu, and Haka'u'i all these requisites were to be found. If small seedling colonies had been established in these valleys it would have been many years before the population could have reached such proportions as to have made even the most productive areas seem inadequate to provide for everyone. Perhaps the tribes and subtribes had begun to feud over their rights to the vital garden lands and attempted to appropriate each other's. In the resulting conflicts the beaten groups would have had only two choices: to stay and die, or to flee. If they chose to flee, as was apparently invariably the case, they had two further alternatives: they could either take to the sea over which their ancestors had come or they could search for a refuge in the remote unsettled areas of the island—a place where their enemies would have difficulty in reaching them, where they could live in comparative peace despite the poor and unproductive surroundings.

Many subtribes had probably left their homes to ascend to the cool grasslands of the central plateau of Nuku Hiva and push west across the rolling hills and the mountain range that divides the plateau from the west coast. Such was the group that settled Ue'a: according to legends, these migrants were members of a subtribe, called 'Oto Kahe'e, that lived in the head of Haka'u'i Valley, near the great Kahe'e waterfall. The trip through the plateau could not have been without hazards, for the big fortification complexes in the plateau near Taiohae apparently dated from this period and any group of refugees would have been clearly visible from the lofty lookouts on the Mouaka bastion, rising some three thousand feet above the sea at the head of Taiohae Valley.

Still others, such as the groups that inhabited Nahotoa and Moe'ana, moved into barren but protected areas on the margins of the great valleys. Perhaps their strength was such that they had less to fear from their adversaries.

Some may indeed have perished at sea while searching

desperately for uninhabited islands on untried headings, as their supplies dwindled and their bodies grew weaker in the merciless rays of the sea sun, until at last, when their rotting vessels broke up, they resigned themselves to the deep.

For the first time it seemed that we had a firm basis on which to reconstruct Marquesan prehistory. We had been able to define one level of Marquesan cultural development fairly well, and had been fortunate enough to find legendary material to aid us in interpreting our findings.

Thanks to the radiocarbon date from the Ue'a cave, we also knew that this level of developement could be dated at least as far back as A.D. 1560, if not further. Other radiocarbon samples from the bottom of the same cave were also being processed, and we would soon have a better idea of the arrival time of the earliest inhabitants of the caves. With this one bit of evidence tied down to even an approximate date, we could now conjecture that the material from Ha'atuatua was earlier, whereas the ceremonial sites at Hikoku'a and the quarries in Ha'ata'ive'a were probably either about the same age or later. We had begun to make real progress in unraveling the Marquesan past, but there was still much more to be done in the field, excavating additional sites and gathering more data. Dr. Shapiro promised more radiocarbon dates soon, including a set of samples from the enigmatic hamlet in Ha'atuatua. This would aid a great deal in establishing Marquesan chronology. The biggest hurdle of all, however, was still far ahead: the long, careful study and analysis of the collections back in New York, a study that might well lead to a complete revision of these hypotheses and produce some very startling new facts that we could not even guess at present.

Charlie had promised to bring more supplies at the end of a week if we needed them but by that time we had thoroughly tested the habitation area and plumbed the secrets of Nahotoa, so that we were able to leave with him.

We loaded the big canoe with the paper sacks of artifacts, packed carefully in the deep earth sifters. Tunui, the faithful, vaulted into the canoe with the cameras, light meters, and photographic equipment—his special responsibility—I followed, and Corpse Eyes and Tioni pushed us off.

Through a rising gray haze, rain poured down as we buzzed away from Nahotoa, abandoned again to its chirping birds. No downpour could have dampened my spirits, however, for I was glimpsing some pattern in the masses of information we had already collected. After a bowl of Heiku'a's blackest coffee and a good soak in the cold Taipi River with many heavy latherings to remove the layers of guano dust, I was set to start the following day on our next scheduled excavations on the great ceremonial plazas of Taipi.

9 / Masons, Missionaries, and Melville

It was a clear morning when my workmen assembled amid the crumbling walls, tumble-down platforms, and weed-choked terraces of what was once perhaps the finest example of ceremonial architecture in the Marquesas Islands—the *tohua* Vahangeku'a, masterpiece of megalithic architecture in a valley where masterpieces were almost common.

The ceremonial center consisted of an artificial terrace, six hundred and eighty feet long and one hundred feet wide, upon and around which stood the remains of twenty-five separate structures. Along the downhill side, the terrace was supported by a massive stone retaining wall, which rose as much as ten feet above the ground level. At the west end of the plaza, a dark banyan tree reared its imposing mass of aerial roots above a small temple platform.

On the dance floor itself were the remains of a low platform of red tuff slabs, similar in design to the large platform at Hikoku'a. The platform and the concentric rectangles of tuff curbstones that had marked its surface had been despoiled by natives who had used the stone slabs for ovens: there was little left of this interesting building but enough, I hoped, for our purposes.

For this excavation, we needed to expand the work force considerably, and therefore sixteen men had been engaged to begin the project, in addition to my standbys Tunui, Corpse Eyes, and the three boys from Charlie's household. Waiting for stragglers on the long, narrow dance plaza, now rutted by the valley trail which slitheringly crisscrossed its surface, I realized that these impressive ruins occupied the entire range of vision in three directions.

A lot of Marquesan history had occurred around this massive stone heap. The site was probably the one that Captain David Porter called the "capital of the Taipi" in describing his 1813 attack on that valley when he sought and obtained vengeance for his ignominious defeat in the jungles at the mouth of the Taipi Valley. After descending to the floor of Taipi, Porter had advanced toward the valley head, passing through several villages on the way, which his men sacked and burned. Farther up the valley, however, they entered a large village in which the houses were neatly arranged in straight lines; it resembled many European villages both in orderliness and extent. This settlement, in Porter's opinion, was the "capital" of the tribe, and he expressed his regrets at having to put the torch to such a fine example of native architecture.

In the late nineteenth century, after the Taipi tribes had been devastated by warfare, smallpox, and other epidemics, and anarchy had been substituted for the rule of the chiefs and priests, the Catholic missionaries braved the valley of the "Man-Eaters" to establish a foothold among their most stubborn adversaries. A missionary arrived in the long, narrow valley to discuss with the few remaining chiefs the possibility of building a chapel. The chapel, according to legend, was built on the ceremonial plaza of Vahangeku'a but no one knew just where.

One relic of the pagan past, obviously still in use, was a great flat-topped boulder, one of many set about the dance floor of Vahangeku'a for female solo dancers to rest on during special ceremonies. The same boulders were also used in the rites of genital inspection which each Marquesan girl underwent at puberty. The Vahangeku'a stone had a darker significance, however, for it was called a *ke'a heaka*—a "victim stone" literally—and marked the spot where a murder had occurred. According to native belief, the spirit of the victim inhabits the site of his or her demise, lying in wait to inflict illness capriciously on passersby. If a person is suddenly afflicted by a case of boils or some other painful skin condition, he is supposed to visit the site of the nearest victim stones (and there are many) and prepare a medicine made of sweet potato and other ingredients, all ground up on the surface of the rock. This act will solicit the aid of the evil spirit and bring about a speedy recovery. The victim stone on Vahange-ku'a had evidently been very recently used by some practicing "Christian" to solicit the aid of its supernatural dweller, to judge from the remains of decaying vegetable matter on the top.

Just south of the ruins of Vahangeku'a, almost obscured amid the rich vegetation of the fertile valley floor, stood two additional *tohua:* Tepakeho and Te Uhi'atea, both of a much simpler and less impressive kind of construction. Apparently, neither of these subsidiary sites had ever been finished; they might therefore provide good examples of early stages of *tohua* construction that had long been buried beneath the welter of platforms on Vahangeku'a. Our main objective was the big site, of course, but we definitely planned to investigate both of these as soon as possible.

By the time the men had cleaned the site, I had mapped it and selected the locations for our trenches and test pits on Vahangeku'a, and had further inspected the two adjacent sites to see what they might offer in the way of problems or possibilities.

The procedure followed on the Taipi site was nearly identical with that used on Hikoku'a in Hatiheu. The stratification of the huge terrace and some of the major buildings on it was tested by means of strategically placed pits and trenches. As the men labored, the story of the development of this native engineering masterpiece began to emerge: it was a story that differed very little in its broad outlines from that which our earlier excavations on Hikoku'a had uncovered. The long terrace that underlay Vahangeku'a had gone through three stages of development: in each, the terrace had been raised a bit higher, new buildings were added along its peripheries, and in many instances older platforms were torn apart to provide raw materials for the new constructions.

Of the buildings surrounding the dance floor during the first period of construction, no traces were uncovered. From the second period two house platforms remained: low stone-faced terraces built against the sloping hillside with only three sides raised from the ground.

The third and final period of construction seemed to be by far the longest, also, being marked by a great burst of building activity in which were produced all of the spectacular rectangular stone platforms on the site. Some of these buildings rose as much as nine feet above the surface, their façades showing the flat faces of carefully chosen unshaped stones that must have weighed two tons or more. One large platform, designated in my notes as Paepae "M," stood right on the edge of the dance floor. On the top of Paepae "M" was the dais upon which a thatched house had once stood. The step was faced with several massive slabs of carved red tuff, much like that used in such quantity at Hikoku'a. As the workmen excavated pits along the foundations of the massive platform and explored a deep sealed shaft that had been uncovered, I walked about the *paepae* examining it carefully. I had clambered over its crumbling rear walls about half a dozen times when I was arrested by the sight of something in the earth fill of the dais, just behind the quarried stone façade. A rounded knob of red tuff protruded from the earth, a few inches away from the inside face of the slab. I bent down and plucked at the knob, expecting it to be a pebble of the same red stone that formed the slabs of the façade. It did not budge, however, and I began to scrape away the dirt. In a moment I saw that it was part of an extension of the adjacent stone slab itself. A little more scratching and I was able to get a clearer look at the red protuberance: it was the head of a small stone figure. Below it, the figure's shoulders extended out to the sides above a bulging chest and stomach. The figure was that of a rotund *tiki* that had been carved from a large protuberance left on the face of the slab when it was quarried. The back of this little red god was still connected to its parent slab by a thick bridge of rock running from neck to toe. The red slabs that graced Paepae "M" had evidently been removed from an earlier building, in which the little god had been displayed to public view. When Paepae "M" was built, for some unknown reason the grotesquely squatting figure was turned to the inside of the new structure, to remain completely hidden until he had attracted my attention.

Subsequent investigations indicated that the slab and its little *tiki* had been removed from another larger platform that stood behind Paepae "M." Of the earlier building, only the massive walls remained: the pavement and dais had been neatly stripped and reused in Paepae "M."

It was with considerable glee that the workmen carefully chiseled away the rock root that bound the god to the slab, for they had been hoping desperately that our work would be crowned by the finding of a stone figure, and this one, although not impressively large, was still sufficiently so to make them feel that all my digging had not been wasted. As they were quite convinced that our motivation in archaeological research was primarily pecuniary, they were certain that a *tiki* would bring the highest prices in America and therefore would please me most. Corpse Eyes worked away diligently to expose the whole figure for photography first, and then aided in setting it free for its long trip to New York. He said nothing to me but we understood each other in one glance, for only two weeks earlier, during a whispered consultation that took place in our room at Clark's house, behind carefully locked doors and shutters, the tranquil dealer in the supernatural had prophesied from his playing cards that I would find a *tiki* before I left Taipi. I had myself asked him to examine the cards in order to test the quality of his predictions and see if he had anything to say that could possibly be proved. Having long given up hope of finding any kind of monumental figure, his prophecy made little impression on me at the time, but in the future I was to take pains to listen to all that he had to say. As I had long since found out, his observations and understanding of human nature and men's actions were penetrating and even, on occasion, profound.

On the dance floor in front of Paepae "M" were the battered remains of the *tu'u*—the ceremonial platforms upon which the heads and corpses of enemies and sacrifices were exposed for the greater glory of the gods of Taipi's Man-Eaters. To find out in what period this once-beautiful building had been erected, we trenched through and around it, to link up its red slab walls with the clearly defined layers in the dance floor plaza. A few feet from the north wall the workmen's

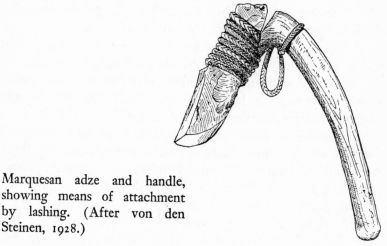

Marquesan adze and handle, showing means of attachment by lashing. (After von den Steinen, 1928.)

spades struck a vertical stone slab below the earth's surface; this turned out to be the north wall of an earlier *tuu* which had been completely obscured by the later duplicate building erected above it. Here again, our finds at Vahangeku'a repeated those made at Hikoku'a, where the builders had also covered a small earlier *tuu* with a much bigger and more elaborate one.

Our trenches showed clearly that the earlier of the two structures was built in the last period of construction on Vahangeku'a—the period when nearly all the megalithic buildings had been erected in a further burst of activity—but we still had no way of estimating how many years ago this had happened.

Few artifacts had turned up so far in the excavations, and

those that had were of little value for dating: nondescript stone flakes, a grindstone, and some bits of crumbling shell. Nearly all of the stone adzes found were of the same type: the long, narrow-blade gougelike adze known to Polynesian anthropologists as the "hogback" type because of the ridge running along the entire length of its top surface. It was the same hogback adzes that had been found in such quantity at the quarrymen's adze factory in Ha'ata'ive'a, and had been identified by the natives as having been used extensively in stone carving and woodworking. The frequent occurrence of these tools around megalithic buildings indicated that many of them had been used in cutting and fitting the red tuff slabs of the platforms. This particular type of adze appeared only on megalithic sites and other open sites that appeared to be relatively young: it had apparently been invented by the Marquesans long after they had arrived in their new home.

Still hopeful of finding evidence that would settle once and for all the question of the age of the quarried stone buildings, we continued excavations around and in the bigger megalithic platforms. On one of these, a long, high *paepae* standing well off the dance platform, two men had been assigned to cut a test pit right through the center of the building. They had gone down about a foot when they called to me: they had found an earlier floor level beneath the surface of the building. Additional excavation showed that the present platform had been built around a smaller *paepae* in which chiseled red slabs had been used in quantity for facing. Digging slowly down through the compact clay fill of the innermost building, they found the dark-stained band of soil that marked the original surface of the earth beneath.

And then came the big surprise: a small piece of an old broken wine bottle and a musket ball lay in the damp band of ancient topsoil where they had been hidden for years by the accumulated tons of earth and stone of the two buildings that had been reared above them. These lovely bits of refuse supplied some of the much-needed evidence for dating the megalithic buildings and the associated quarried stone slabs.

They could not have found their way by accident into the heart of the big platform; they must have been placed on the original ground surface before the platform was built. This demonstrated clearly that when the megalithic platforms were still being built, white men had already visited the island. In fact, the presence of the wine bottle fragment argued that the white men were French and that this structure might have been built after 1840, the date of the French occupation. Naturally, the glass and musket ball did not exclude the possibility of some of the big buildings having been built *before* the coming of the whites, but they made it quite clear that such buildings were not necessarily very old.

As the rest of the history of this monument of an extinct tribe was pieced together bit by bit from the test excavations, we saw that on this site, too, the massive platforms, the culmination of the Marquesan stonemason's art, had been built during an era not long before the arrival of the white men and were still being built when the whites arrived. These structures, formed of colossal stones, carefully fitted and wedged together, were by no means the product of a long-departed race of Melanesians who had reached Polynesia before the present inhabitants, nor were they the handiwork of the Peruvians to whom their construction had also been attributed. These structures had all been built by the Marquesans themselves within the last several centuries at most. The "established" milestones on the route of Marquesan civilization were beginning to become clearer.

Apparently the evidence that we had uncovered at Hikoku'a was by no means misleading, nor were the results of the excavations at the quarrymen's site in Ha'ata'ive'a and the adze factory in the same valley. All evidence pointed to a very late date for the blossoming of Marquesan stoneworking that produced the great *paepae*, the beautiful red stone altars to hold the grisly trophies of war, and the goggled statues of dull red stone.

While the excavations on Vahangeku'a strengthened our knowledge of the timetable of Marquesan civilization, they also taught us much about the techniques used by Marquesan masons in the building of the great terrace and its monumental structures centuries ago, and their use of the irregular-shaped boulders and the rectangular slabs of red tuff. The builders of Vahangeku'a had, for some reason, left many clues scattered about the site: ramps for moving stones, inclined planes, and the remains of structures that had been cannibalized to provide materials for later platforms. On other sites such engineering evidence had generally been removed, but on Vahangeku'a it had been allowed to stay, fortunately for us. The boulders which composed most of the megalithic *paepae* here had evidently been obtained from a field just above the site, where a number of such boulders still stood, just as they had been scattered by natural geological forces. Through experience these primitive engineers had learned to visualize the kinds of contours needed to fit into stones already in position in a structure being built. They knew what kind of general shape they needed for a tight fit, and searched until they had found it, as anyone examining a *paepae* can see: the massive stones are often set so closely together as to appear to have been fitted by chiseling, but the only aids used were small stones that filled in cracks, propped up unstable stones, and wedged the boulders more tightly. From the handy source of raw material near the site, a ramp had been built down to the edge of the dance floor. On this ramp the stones could ride on wooden rollers, restrained from gathering momentum by the combined efforts of many stout ropes and equally stout Marquesans. Once the stone reached the dance floor, it was relatively easy to roll it anywhere on the flat and set it into position in the foundation layer of a platform. However, when it came to placing equally big stones atop the first course, problems arose; since the stones were so heavy, a long, inclined plane was built alongside the platform, its top level with the top of the first course. Then the stone was wheeled up the gradual slope, moved onto the surface of the first course, and set into place. In Paepae "M," stones were not only brought from the field above but from some other area either on or below the dance floor, for there were remains of two inclined planes near that building. The big slabs of red tuff, although heavy and bulky, were still not overly difficult for a group to handle; notches on these slabs indicated where ropes or carrying slings were affixed for hauling the stone rectangles. The Marquesans had no knowledge of the wheel, so anything that could not be rolled on short rollers made of tree trunks, moved by levers and fulcrums, carried, or simply dragged on a route previously prepared by liberal applications of water, could not be used. As there were no beasts of burden in the Marquesas before the coming of the Europeans, all available power was supplied by human sinews.

More evidence of the availability of Marquesan man power came from the excavations in the floor of the great terrace. As in Hikoku'a, the terrace had been built of fill excavated from the face of the hillside upon which the site stood. The Marquesan diggers had cut back into the hill face along the entire six hundred feet of the site's length to obtain the earth needed for fill, leaving many steep banks that had been faced with stone during construction to prevent cave-ins. We estimated that approximately twenty-four thousand cubic feet of earth was contained in the terrace, all of it hand-carried in basketloads from the diggers on the hill to the terrace.

The number of workmen employed at Vahangeku'a must have been quite large, perhaps even larger than the group utilized for the construction of Hikoku'a in Hatiheu. The Taipi "capital" was so much bigger and more elaborate that it appeared that a larger force might have been recruited from among the subtribes to get the project under way. Imagining the size of the work force and the length of time that must have been required for the earth and stones to be obtained, carried, and put into position, one was struck by the obviously sound economic basis of the Marquesan society. From the breadfruit groves, the yam gardens and sweet potato hills, the taro terraces, the ocean depths and the pig sties a steady stream of food supplies had to flow to feed these workers during the weeks of labor when they themselves could not work their own gardens and do their own fishing. Yet the larders of Taipi had evidently been equal to the challenge, as the multitude of ceremonial sites in the valley clearly demonstrated.

My admiration for this dynamic culture soon grew, when we began excavations on the two *tohua* adjacent to Vahange-

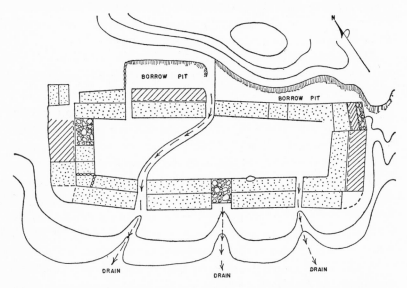

Plan of *tohua* Tepakeho, Taipi Valley, showing house platforms around rectangular dance floor, drains to carry off water from up the slope, and borrow pits where earth for fill was obtained.

ku'a. A study of the stratigraphy and the kinds of buildings around these sites indicated that they had begun at roughly the same time as Vahangeku'a. The tribe, not content with one building project of considerable magnitude, had decided to undertake two more simultaneously. Evidently this ambitious plan soon began to pall, however, for we found that both *tohua* had been more or less abandoned sometime during the second period of construction on Vahangeku'a, and the combined resources of the work groups had been centered on that site. On Tepakeho, the *tohua* slightly upslope from the main site, no further buildings had ever been erected. In fact, parts of the walls of the terrace had been torn down to provide stones for buildings on Vahangeku'a. The *tohua* located just down the hill from Vahangeku'a had been inhabited again, however, but only after the white men came. A few small crude buildings were built on the dance floor of this *tohua* sometime in the nineteenth century. Beneath them we found some broken wine bottles beside fragments of Marquesan stone pestles of a distinctively recent type, beautifully carved and polished.

At the end of our several weeks of work on Vahangeku'a and its two neighboring *tohua* we refilled all the excavations and replaced the stones that had been moved in the course of the work. The site had rightly been listed as a monument of historic and artistic value by the French government: we had no wish to deface it any further than the local inhabitants had already done, with their systematic stripping of the slabs for fireplace-building materials. My only regret was that neither the purpose of the mission nor the time remaining allowed us to restore the great plaza to some semblance of its former condition, as a monument to the departed warriors who had so ably built it and their colorful civilization.

While we were busy at work on Vahangeku'a, Rae was very busy at home. In addition to the work that she did with the artifacts, processing them with chemicals and cataloguing them, she carried on a booming medical practice. Every day she spent both mornings and afternoons looking after the collective ills of the Taipivai and Ho'oumi populations. Most common were skin diseases of various types, boils and infected cuts and insect bites, but she also handled obstetrics, hay fever, allergies, menopausal complaints, burns, and all manner of wounds inflicted by everything from machetes to sting ray barbs.

I got my baptism in midwifery holding two kerosene lamps and carrying on a running translation while Rae delivered Poiti's little son Teiki in the dank storeroom of Charlie's house.

Rae's popularity reached its peak when she saved the life of Corpse Eyes' seventy-year-old sister, who had been refused treatment by the French doctor on the grounds that she was imagining her illness. She had, in fact, a severe kidney infection and was saved only by such massive doses of antibiotics that our supply was almost exhausted.

Rae's work with the children and babies was most enjoyable. The poor things were often visited with respiratory infections that produced startlingly high fevers and convulsions, occasionally resulting in death. During our time in Taipivai, however, no child was lost in this way. The children seemed especially prone to the skin diseases that also afflicted the parents, and Rae dispensed quantities of ointments and powder to protect the little brown-eyed youngsters from the often-dangerous secondary infections.

Dental caries was a constant source of trouble among the Marquesans of all ages; their tooth decay problem was proverbial. Having had more experience with teeth (and bones!), I took over the job of packing medicated cement into cavities so that the patients could make it to the doctor's office in Taiohae for extractions. Once the cement was in place, however, they often did not go, for they feared the doctor's clumsiness more than the recurring tooth pain.

When our supplies were quite low, an epidemic of Asian flu struck and when, after a few weeks, we both came down with the disease, we found ourselves with no drugs left.

Our next objective after Vahangeku'a was a site on land belonging to Heiku'a, far up in the dense, tangled forests at the head of Taipi Valley, not far from the point where the cascade of The Two Big Eels—'Uaku'e'enui—roared over the granite walls of Taipi and into the valley below. Here, in a grove of hibiscus and chestnut beside the cool Taipi River, was the *tohua* of The Descendants of Hou—Te'ivi'ohou—a broad complex of several terraces with a few large house platforms and temples scattered about. The site itself presented little that was remarkable in comparison to Vahangeku'a or Hikoku'a, but we had been given a free hand by Charlie and his wife to dissect any and all of the structures that we wished, and completely disassemble them if necessary. Naturally, an archaeologist is reluctant to destroy, if it can possibly be helped, but we needed to check our conclusions about the construction of the big house platforms and the only way to do it was to do some systematic disassembly of the buildings, with no hope of ever being able to replace the stones in the same way that the Marquesans had done. Therefore Charlie and Heiku'a's co-operative offer was gladly received and we prepared to go to work on Te'ivi'-ohou.

Besides the purely archaeological reasons for working on Te'ivi'ohou I had another reason, based more on curiosity than anything else: according to a legend related to me by Heiku'a it was on Te'ivi that the great novelist-sailor, Herman Melville, had been held prisoner by the Taipi tribe in 1842, an experience he described in his exciting first novel, *Typee*. Heiku'a's story, passed on by her grandfather, was strikingly similar to that told by Melville in his book: Melville and a companion had entered the valley of Taipivai on an old native trail, now unused, that passed down the face of a precipice near the southern waterfall at the valley head. They had been captured by the Taipi men and taken to Te'ivi'ohou, where they were kept more as trophies than as prisoners. The Taipi inhabitants were struck by Melville's fair skin, his eye color, and his reddish hair, according to the story, and treated him as a minor supernatural being. Melville, who had severely injured his leg on the passage over the mountains from Taiohae, where he had deserted from an American whaler, was cared for by his native hosts, being accorded preferential treatment: constantly anointed with native cosmetics that further whitened his skin, and carried often to bathe in a rockbound hole in the river bed. Wherever he went, according to Heiku'a, he was carried in a litter and treated with utmost respect. He was given a wife, Pe'ue by name (Fayaway according to Melville's quaint orthography), who was supposedly an ancestress of Heiku'a on her father's side. He was not given the chance to escape, however, for the Taipi believed his presence to be a good omen. Finally, after much pleading, he was carried to the beach to see an American ship that had stopped there, and managed to reach the visitors' longboat while his native guards were occupied picking up trinkets that the American seamen had scattered in the water to attract their attention. Once in the longboat, he was borne safely to the waiting whaler under a shower of spears and slingstones hurled by his former captors, who were furious at losing their half-god. The story interested me, for it was rather unusual to hear the entire episode passed on by word of mouth in such a faithful fashion, with all the details so well tied in to the local geography. The statements concerning Melville's appearance and their connection with the reasons for his having been held prisoner also had a ring of truth, for white skin and red hair were once highly prized among many Polynesian societies, and if Melville's appearance had actually fitted the description he might well have been suspected of supernatural qualities and been held by the Taipi.

During our stay in Taipi, I had occasion to hear the story a number of times, and was thus able to fill in most of the pertinent details. I pressed Heiku'a about the time of Melville's arrival to see if her information would check with the known dates. "The *ferani* were here," she said, "but they had not taken over yet, when Merivi [Melville] came." This checked precisely with historic fact: when he arrived, Melville had seen the warships of Dupetit-Thouars's fleet in Taiohae. Heiku'a went on, "That was five generations ago, according to Hakata'u [her grandfather]: it was his father's father who saw Merivi come and passed the story on to us."

Old Hakata'u had been a renowned raconteur, as even Corpse Eyes acknowledged. The old fellow, who died in 1943, had evidently built up an incredible store of Marquesan legends in his youth, at the feet of some of the old bards who had lived before the collapse of the native culture. Corpse Eyes said that Hakata'u frequently passed the entire night regaling an excited audience with his legends of heroes, gods, and evil spirits. When I realized, however, that Hakata'u had also been a connoisseur of European stories—*Arati* (Aladdin), *Eihope*

(Aesop)—and knew the tales of *Mo'i* (Moses), *Noa* (Noah), and *Bai'a* (Bayard)—my excitement over Heiku'a's tale abated considerably; was it possible that the old man had picked the story up from a European and simply fitted it into the setting of his own valley and culture, adding interpretations and bits of local color unconsciously as he retold the tale?

A recent study of Melville's life indicates that he may have spent only six weeks in the Marquesas, not six months as he claimed, and may never even have reached Taipivai. His knowledge of the dreaded Taipi Man-Eaters and their valley might easily have been derived from the numerous warriors who had fought in and near Taipi and knew the terrain and details of the valley quite well.

Notwithstanding the impressive scholarship in the Melville biography, the numerous corroborated details of Heiku'a's story that checked so well with history seemed to indicate that it should not be discarded quite yet. It was difficult to see how a story could have been passed on intact, by word of mouth over the years, yet it was as difficult to believe that so many details could check so well if it had been but a recently introduced tale.

Perhaps future research in the field of Melvilleana will produce some facts that will support or disprove the tale of Heiku'a, but for the present, the strangely accurate tale cannot be labeled true or false. Regardless of its veracity, it created a positive atmosphere for me in which to begin work on Te'ivi. Wherever I looked, I unconsciously related the topography and the ruins to Melville's novel, and it often took little imagination to see the ceremonial plaza as it might have appeared with some of the beautiful barbaric ceremonies so ably described by Melville.

As soon as the word had spread that we were going to dig on Te'ivi'ohou, often referred to as "Melville's *paepae*" (*te paepae'o Merivi*), many visitors arrived at the house, proffering advice and relating some utterly fantastic bits of "information" about the great treasure that Melville was supposed to have brought from his ship and buried there. One fellow, a rather loquacious French *colon,* who had grown up in the Marquesas and fancied himself an expert on local lore, described the bars of gold, the diary, and the jewels that Melville had carried with him over the mountains to Taipi. Jean, the Marquesanized *colon,* spouted forth his wishfulness with wild eyes in a peculiar nasalized Marquesan as the whole Clark family sat around with ill-concealed smirks. Known as a prodigious liar, the young fellow posed as an authority until cornered, and then he always sought authority for his argument by reference to his father, a filthy, wizened French peasant type, who posed as the repository of all human knowledge, but who was actually illiterate.

At length I interjected, "How do you know all this stuff you're telling us, Jean? Melville says nothing about any treasure in his book."

"*Ua pe'au papa*—Papa said it," came the retort, which was greeted by gales of laughter. "What, you don't believe me?" shouted Jean. "My papa knows! He has read Melville's book and it's all written there!"

"How can he read Melville's book when he can't read French?" shouted someone. "Or any other language!" yelled another.

"*He knows,* don't worry, *he* knows better than *you!* He's an educated man—why, he even speaks Italian!"

"That's nothing," someone said, "look at the American—he speaks German, American, French, Marquesan, and some Tahitian. Does your papa know more than he?" Jean was trapped: if he admitted that Papa was not a genius he was attacking his idol; if he claimed that he was smarter than I he evidently feared he would offend me and thus lose any hope of being hired as a workman or getting our medicine for his wife and family. He did the only thing he could do—beat a hasty retreat, grumbling about the stupid natives, after ostentatiously apologizing to me for *their* boorishness.

Te'ivi'ohou presented more problems than any other site that we had dug so far: the hibiscus and chestnut trees that covered the site were intertwined so tightly in some spots that they formed a nearly impenetrable wall.

The men soon developed a way of dealing with the tangled trees, however: with their customary agility, they scrambled up the larger trunks, mounting high into the tops to hack off all the branches within reach, freeing the tree from its neighbors' clutches. Their leather-soled brown feet grasping the mossy trunks, they swung their sharp machetes, working down the trunk until no more strong branches remained.

It was at this time that the men began to "play" a typical kind of Marquesan game, which Rae and I labeled "Crush Your Buddy." A workman would be clinging to a swaying treetop, whipping to and fro as he lopped off limbs. Absorbed in his work, he seldom looked down. One of his companions on the ground would make a sign to the others and approach the base of the tree in which the diligent one labored. With careful strokes he would begin to hack at the tree trunk while the others co-operated by making excessive noise, assailing the green wood with vigor and talking loudly to cover the sound of the tree being cut away beneath the hapless man above. All eyes were on the man in his high perch, and as the tree started to bend and crack, it was hardly possible for the audience to control their laughter. I was wondering meanwhile whether I dared intercede. Fortunately, and invariably at what seemed to be the last moment, the man in the tree would realize his predicament and come hurtling down the quivering trunk shouting obscenities and laughing good-naturedly. Next time, after all, someone else would be in the tree and he would do the chopping.

A variation of this fun-packed pastime was something which we called "Cape Canaveral." For this, a tree had to be directed so that it would fall across or at least drag down a tree in which someone was perched. The weight of the falling tree would naturally bend the trunk of the other tree, but if properly aimed (and this took careful planning) it would finally slip off, allowing the uncut tree to lash back into an upright position and catapult its occupant into the air. As the Russian

Sputniks I and II had just become known to the Marquesans, attempts to pull this stunt were always accompanied by shouts of "To the sky, with the Russian star!" "To the Moon!" "Let's see if you can go around the world in an hour and a half!" "Say beep-beep-beep as you go!"

Again, as in "Crush Your Buddy," no injuries resulted from the considerably more exciting "Cape Canaveral," but the number of near-misses was much greater.

Native knowledge of astronautics was a composite obtained from the terse newscasts of Radio Tahiti, amplified by information and clippings that we had received from friends at home. The men had fitted the Russian rocketeers' successes into the only possible niche that their culture provided: the realm of humor. The fact that the United States Vanguard rockets exploded with dismal regularity did not faze them. "America is still better than Russia," one explained. "*We know*, because you never see a Russian yacht with Russian tourists down here, but American yachts come almost every month!"

It was not long before I realized that Te'ivi'ohou was a much more important site than it had first appeared to be, for several reasons.

Te'ivi'ohou consisted not of one big ceremonial plaza built on a great terrace but of three separate terraces, side by side, descending the gentle slope to the stream. We found that each one of these terraces had been built at a different time and represented a distinct stage in the growth of the site. Whereas in Hikoku'a, Vahangeku'a, and the other sites, the Marquesans had buried the early terraces and buildings beneath the heaped earth and stones of the later additions, we had here a clearly visible "fossilized" record of three sequential steps in the evolution of ceremonial plaza architecture. We did not have to probe the depths of the terrace fill on Te'ivi to find the remains of the earlier buildings: they were all on the surface. For some reason, the tribe that had owned Te'ivi had felt it best to build a new terrace rather than enlarge the earlier ones, a decision that helped our work a great deal. I could reconfirm my hypothetical reconstructions of Hikoku'a and Vahangeku'a in their early stages by reference to the two earliest terraces of Te'ivi'ohou.

The terrace closest to the river was a spectacular piece of engineering. The retaining walls, remarkably well preserved, were fifteen feet high in places, built of tightly fitted boulders, and sloped slightly for stability. It was on and around this terrace that most of the house platforms had been built, and the west end of the dance floor was the wide, low platform that was designated as the "*paepae*" of Melville.

Naturally, we excavated this historic structure and in so doing found the remains of an earth oven in the stone-paved veranda floor of the platform. The oven, when cleared, yielded some pig bones, some iron nails, and a piece of an iron strip. The workmen, primed by the constant talk about Melville, were elated: "Melville was truly here! Look, the things that he left! See—the story is true! He left these here, and now another American has found them!"

We began to excavate the largest of the *paepae* on the site, a beautiful specimen of megalithic construction. We had hardly begun our investigations of this building when things started to happen. First, two sealed grave shafts were found in the surface of the platform. Each narrow-mouthed shaft contained a mass of crumbling human bones, the remains of numerous bundle burials that had been placed within. Two more graves were then discovered behind the tuff slabs on the sleeping step. Here more human bones had been stored, evidently in wooden boxes long since decayed in the humid atmosphere of Taipi.

Opening up the shaft graves turned out to be something of a problem: a large number of stones had to be removed to permit a workman to begin removing the remains, which were laid out to dry before being bagged for the trip home. Only a few bones had been removed from the largest shaft when I heard one of the men exclaim. He was holding up a small whale's tooth, in the end of which a hole had been drilled for stringing in a necklace. In a period of ten minutes he had accumulated some twenty similar-sized teeth. Whales' teeth were a sign of rank in the Marquesas; only those of highest rank could wear them in quantity. The natives were able to capture small whales with their bone and wood harpoons, deriving a lot of the teeth needed for ornaments from them. Capture of the huge sperm whales was beyond the ability of the native harpooners, but they were occasionally found dead in the sea near the islands and towed ashore for their teeth, which were of great size and most highly prized. Sperm whale teeth were often split up into sections and small imitation teeth were carved from these to fulfill the pressing demands for ornaments.

One of the Marquesans whose remains reposed in this mass grave must have been of considerable importance, for before all the bones were removed we had recovered one hundred and twenty-eight teeth, all of the same size; some were carved from sperm whale ivory, and others were genuine teeth from smaller whales such as the blackfish.

Then a second astonishing find was made. Half buried in the earth at the bottom of the shaft was a yellowed cylinder about three inches long—a hefty pipe bowl made of a hollowed-out sperm whale tooth, decorated with grooves encircling either end. A wooden stem had evidently been fitted into a hole drilled through one side of the bowl, but the stem had moldered away years before. Here was proof positive of the date of the burial: tobacco was not a native plant to the Marquesans but was introduced sometime after 1790 in Nuku Hiva. Therefore, the grave dated from that period or later. Likewise, the *paepae* in which the grave was located must also have been built at that period, for the burials appeared to have been made while the *paepae* was being built, as the opening of the grave was too small to admit anything as bulky as a bundle burial.

I told the workman who had cleared the grave to remove all the earth in the pit bottom. Suddenly he shouted again, this time loudly, "Something! Something! Look at this glass! Oh, friend, just look!'"

Deep in the earth of the grave floor he had uncovered a

small, perfectly preserved blue glass bowl. When we were able to remove the bowl, we found that it had a ring base with gently outward-sloping sides, somewhat Oriental in appearance. Here was further proof that the structure had been built after the coming of the white men, for such bowls were never made by the Marquesans at any time in their history. An expert subsequently identified this bowl as having been made in the tradition of the well-known Stiegel glass of Pennsylvania, between 1790 and 1840, thus corroborating the evidence offered by the sperm whale tooth pipe. This bit of Americana had probably arrived on one of the early ships, perhaps a whaler, and been traded to the natives for some goods or services. I wondered for what favors the blue bowl had been exchanged; it had evidently been a dear keepsake to the owner, since it had been interred with his or her bones, and not left for the family members.

The other graves in the *paepae* also contained surprises: green glass beads of European origin, a smaller whale's tooth pipe, some stone adzes, and a number of badly decayed pearl shell ornaments. As if to emphasize the date of the building, we found a large pewter spoon beneath the floor, accompanied by a steel chisel. Fragments of bottle glass occurred throughout the earth fill of the platform. Our earlier conjecture, on the basis of all the other fragmentary and sometimes ambiguous evidence, that the megalithic structures were being built when the white men arrived, was now confirmed. Now all that remained was to determine how long before the coming of the whites this type of architecture had developed.

We finished the work at Te'ivi'ohou after excavations at several other platforms, and finding little of note except a beautifully carved small bone figure and some broken stone adzes and pestles.

The men, elated at the spectacular finds, had decided to have some fun with the inhabitants of Taipi and especially with the prevaricating Frenchman, Jean, who had been dubbed "Papa" by virtue of his constant verbal footnotes to his father, the omniscient, unwashed Niçois. Jean and his brothers showed up at the Clark house every evening to see what we had found, and questioned everyone very carefully. One night the boys made a vague reference to the bowl that they had found.

"What bowl?" shrilled Jean.

"Didn't you hear? The big golden bowl the American found in Melville's *paepae*. It's about half an arm's length in diameter, solid gold and just like a mirror."

"What did you say?" Jean was hoarse: his brothers grouped around and all began babbling at once, trying to elicit more information from Hu'uveu, Poiti, and Tioni, who sat looking unconcerned and a bit bored. "The bowl was real gold?"

The boys looked at each other. "That's what the American said, wasn't it?"

"Mmn."

Jean was beside himself, as were the brothers. He demanded to know more: had we found anything else? More gold, jewels, the diary?

"Well, I guess we can tell him," said Tioni casually, looking at his pals for consent. "We found a pile of gold bars, a golden idol, and the diary too. The diary tells where the rest of the treasure is buried and the American is going to get it. We also found some of Melville's things; his spoons, his knife, and his pipe—his name was written on them."

Perhaps prolonged exposure to the tropic sun slows a man's mental faculties, for poor Jean believed this wild fabrication completely. He departed, full of envy for us, but before he left the light dawned—Papa had been right! The gold and the diary were there! He impressed this on all present, making sure that they were properly contrite for their mockery of his brilliant father, and then marched off.

A few days later, while digging near Vahangeku'a in the megalithic temple of Peupeu, in which we had located more shaft graves with interesting burials, we saw an unfamiliar figure on the path far below. Clad in khakis and with a heavy sun helmet on his head, a man rode along the path on a black European horse.

"*Te mutoi ferani hou!*"—"The new French policeman!" whispered one of the men, and we continued work, as I began to wonder what had occasioned this visitation.

That evening we met the pleasant and dedicated new gendarme, a lanky, hawk-nosed fellow from the mountain regions near Switzerland. He inquired about my work over dinner and I showed him some of the artifacts which we had uncovered just that day in the temple excavations. He was especially interested in the beautifully carved whale tooth earplugs that had been found in the shaft graves of the temple—along with a European meat fork and some broken wine bottles.

Finally, he broached the question: "Tell me, what is all this about your finding some gold?" I could not help laughing, for the boys had predicted that Jean would report me to "the law." By the time I finished explaining, all sixteen members of the Clark family knew that the policeman had been summoned by Jean and all were elated that the joke had worked so well. Now they would tell him how they had hoodwinked him and also let him know how stupid Papa really was.

10 / Villages on Villages

Consumed in a seemingly endless procession of brilliant, exhilarating working days, the months slipped by and Christmas was on us before we knew it: a strange Christmas for Rae and me, compared to those spent at home. We managed to make a little tree of the biggest breadfruit leaves that we could find, plus some cardboard, decorated with bits of the aluminum foil that I used for wrapping archaeological carbon samples, and Christmas "balls" cut from cards sent by Stateside friends. One thoughtful couple sent us a massive handmade Christmas candle, encrusted with colored wax drippings and spangles, which graced our table for many days after the holiday. On the day before Christmas the men of Taipi banded together for a yearly hunt, to which I contributed a Winchester 30-06 and a box of soft-nosed cartridges. The hunt, directed by the Ho'oumi Valley native policeman, took place in the plateau between Ho'oumi and Ha'atuatua, where many wild cattle were to be found. Departing in the blackness of predawn, the boys returned tired and bloody late in the afternoon, smiling triumphantly as they nailed up a set of horns on a tree before our house. On the foam-and-mud-flecked horse, dark-stained burlap bags contained our share of the cattle that had fallen before the Winchester—as well as a couple of 22 rifles. After coursing the wild beef through the rolling hills of the plateau, the boys fasted, preparing for midnight Mass at the little chapel. After the Mass, at about 3 A.M. we had a beef feast, and finally turned in, dead-tired, at 5 A.M.

New Year was a bit different from Christmas—for the natives, there was a reason to drink, and every possible effort was concentrated on taking advantage of this opportunity. For weeks before, the five-gallon stills had been bubbling quietly in secluded groves. All work ground to a halt in the morning before New Year's Day, and the drinking began behind closed doors or in secret conclaves, far up in the interior of the valley. New Year's Eve was punctuated by gunfire, mostly coming from the hamlet near the Clark house, where exuberance was running high and the celebrants were blasting holes in the night sky. Charlie and Heiku'a were teetotalers, a very strange phenomenon in eastern Polynesia, and we sat with them on the upstairs porch, talking about New Years in the past, and hoping that the sharpshooters in the village would keep their muzzles turned toward the zenith. They were delighted to see some photographs that had been sent to us of an uproarious New Year's celebration which we had given in Connecticut some years earlier, being especially surprised at the kinds of clothing that were worn, the party hats, the noisemakers, and the balloon-festooned ceiling of our tiny apartment. The big rickety house was rather quiet that evening, as all the males, including Corpse Eyes, had mysteriously disappeared after supper, and only the children, the women, and Charlie remained. About 1 A.M. the sounds of creaking floor boards were heard from downstairs. Heiku'a rose, smiled quietly, and went down to investigate. A few minutes later she returned and whispered in my ear, "It's Corpse Eyes—he's dead drunk and has hidden himself in the storeroom until he sleeps it off. He begged me not to tell you because he's so ashamed."

The erring boys returned somewhat later in a similarly disoriented state, with Titi's husband in tow. This time, however, the reception was far from discreet. Whereas Corpse Eyes was an elder, and highly respected, the boys were family members and young. "*Get out!* Animals! What do you mean coming in like that? Shame for us! Shame for the American! Don't come back till you are sober!" The boys retreated under Heiku'a's tirade and the threats of her broom, not to return until the next day, when they appeared, bright, clean, and a little sheepish, to pass a rigid inspection by Heiku'a before they were admitted to the house and human company again.

With our work in the ceremonial sites of Taipi behind us, we turned to the hamlet site that I had located earlier in the shady palm groves beside the river mouth on Ho'oumi beach. Tunui was happy with this arrangement as he could see his aged mother daily, and Corpse Eyes was equally delighted, as a former passion-flower of his, now a stout, well-married woman, lived next to the site, and he was in hopes of being able to relive some of the days of old.

After a careful re-examination of the ruined *paepae* in the ancient hamlet, I concluded that the big platforms belonged to approximately the same period in time as those on the Vahangeku'a, Hikoku'a, and Te'ivi'ohou ceremonial sites—a period which I was beginning to believe began in the 1500's and continued until the collapse of the native culture in the 1860's. The Spaniards had reported seeing stone house plat-forms and unelaborate *tohua* in 1596, so we knew that these buildings dated back to that time at least, but I did not think that they could be too much older.

The Ho'oumi beach hamlet might therefore have been con-structed as late as the middle 1800's or as early as A.D. 1500, but in any case we now knew that the buildings fell someplace in that span of time. What might be hidden in the sands around and beneath the massive *paepae?* Was this hamlet the first to be built on this supremely beautiful beach with its quiet crys-tal river, flanked by towering peaks and cliffs? Certainly, I thought, it was a good bet that there had been much earlier dwellings on this beach—but there was only one way to find out.

And so, we began to excavate test pits here and there on the site, to investigate the nature of the archaeological deposits and see if any traces of earlier men had been hidden by the ostentatious stone ruins.

The upper fifteen inches of the light-colored sandy soil contained a scattering of pearl shell hooks, coral files, carved whale teeth, some broken stone adzes, iron nails, and bottle glass—pretty much what I had expected. Below fifteen inches, however, the color of the earth changed abruptly to black and many more shell tools began to appear. Then in one test pit the boys found a corner of a stone pavement, a pavement about which tools of all sorts appeared in a profusion similar to that found at Ha'atuatua. Here, then, was evidence of an earlier hamlet occupied before the building of the big stone platforms. Was there still something earlier than that in the dark soil of the Ho'oumi beach? Excavations below the level of the paved floor uncovered no other archaeological strata: at a depth of three feet we reached a consolidated deposit of coral and pebbles that was apparently part of a very ancient beach deposit.

The two superimposed layers in the beach deposits represented two successive occupations. About the later hamlet we already knew a relatively large amount by virtue of excavations on other sites of the same period. The test excavations had corroborated my dating of these ruins, but I had no idea as to the age of the lower black stratum with its paved house floors. It might be only a few years older than the stone platforms; on the other hand, it might be much older, I reflected, for some pavements had been found in the upper level of the Ha'atuatua site, which was still the best bet for the earliest site that we had excavated to date. In places the platform builders had disturbed the layer that contained the remains of this early occupation. They had dug their earth ovens through it and cut into it for the foundations of their *paepae*. I hoped that there was enough of the lower stratum remaining undisturbed to permit us to date it.

Full-scale excavations began, centered in the area where we had found the stone pavements and the heaviest concentrations of artifacts. Soon we had laid bare most of the early house floor, being hindered in our digging by omnipresent and immovable coconut trees and a few unfortunately placed stone boundary walls. The pavement was rectangular, about forty feet long and ten feet wide. After we stripped off the covering mantle of soil the boys carefully cleaned the stones, removing the earth with their deftly wielded trowels and sweeping the pavement with whisk brooms as the moist rocks dried out in the tropical sun. Among the stones of the pavement were big barbed pearl shell fishhooks, stone flake knives, a piece of a bone harpoon point, some broken bone needles, and several stone adzes, some of which appeared to have been left unfinished.

Nearby, in the same stratum, a second stone pavement had been found and traced beneath the basalt boulder heap of a ruined *paepae*, thus removing all doubt that the pavements had been built before the platforms. Just how long before, however, was still a mystery and we were at a loss about the position of the early Ho'oumi beach hamlet in the picture of Marquesan prehistory. Was it older or younger than the hamlet on Ha'atuatua beach? Was it built before, during, or after the period warfare when the Cave of the Warrior Band had been inhabited and refugee settlements had sprung up on the barren west coast of the island?

Unless the remains in the black earth stratum were something completely extraordinary (and that time I didn't know whether I would consider that as a blessing or a curse), a detailed examination of the artifacts would tell us something about the relative age of the site: its position in time, in relation to the other sites of which we already knew. Accordingly, many hours were spent going over the tools from the early layer of the site, comparing these with what we had recovered elsewhere, checking for the presence or absence of the peculiar kinds of fishhooks, stone axes, and other implements that seemed to be characteristic of the stages of Marquesan history of which we already knew.

The house pavements were like those found in the upper level of Ha'atuatua but much bigger, which meant that the site might be later than Ha'atuatua. The Melanesian-type shell ornaments and adzes that had turned up at Ha'atuatua were absent, however. How about the unusual fishhooks found in the cave sites—the hooks with sturdy, double-thick shanks of pearl shell, the like of which were completely unknown on any other Pacific island? These were absent from the black layer, but they were found in the stratum of lighter earth above, where they had been dropped by the builders of the stone platforms. The adzes appeared to be of more advanced types than those found at Ha'atuatua, but the hogback varieties found on the megalithic architecture and in the caves were not present. Gradually, the weight of the evidence seemed to be clustering around one particular period in Marquesan prehistory, but not enough artifacts had been uncovered to permit me to make a firm statement.

The excavations continued, therefore, for I was ever optimistic of getting better criteria for dating, and every additional artifact recovered meant added reliability for any conclusions we might draw.

In clearing around the intact house pavement, we began to push our excavations back farther in all possible directions, and in so doing found a small campfire a few feet away from the south side of the stone floor. With the air of practice, Poiti exposed the campfire neatly, while we plotted its location. He then began to spoon out the charcoal from the fire pit into a sheet of heavy aluminum foil. Suddenly he stopped short. "Hey, Robert! A thing here!" he said, pointing to something in the thin layer of white ash that surrounded the fire pit itself. There, still half buried in the dark soil, was a thick fragment of broken red pottery. Poiti was as elated as I: he had heard about the pottery found at Ha'atuatua and knew that it was important to me, therefore he was happy that his work might prove to be equally important. As a reward for his careful handling of the find, I paid him an extra day's wages that week, which he used for a little gift for his wife and baby daughter.

When the pottery had been removed and examined, it turned out to be quite different from that found at Ha'atuatua. It was thick, of poorly tempered clay, and had been badly baked.

The potsherds that had been uncovered were too few for me to interpret them as being definitely of Marquesan origin. Perhaps the Ha'atuatuans had brought some pottery obtained from trade with nearby Melanesian islands. Or the pottery might have been brought direct to Ha'atuatua by a stray

trading expedition. At any rate, I resolved not to develop any
brash theories concerning Marquesan potterymaking until I
had found pottery at other sites of different periods.

Now I began to realize why we had not found more pottery on other sites—the crude, poorly fired pots such as those
used at Ho'oumi had simply been unable to withstand the
weathering of the tropical soil. It was only in unusually good
conditions, such as the sandy, well-drained Ho'oumi beach,
that potsherds survived.

Now there was also good reason to believe that the potsherds recovered at Ha'atuatua were from locally made pots,
for the pottery found at Ho'oumi was probably of a later
date than that at Ha'atuatua, and it was hard to believe that a
steady or even accidental trade with any of the potterymaking
cultures in western Polynesia or Melanesia could have existed
over a number of years between the times when the two sites
had been inhabited.

Our excavations went on until the archaeological resources
of the Ho'oumi beach seemed to be exhausted. The 1946 tidal
wave had ravaged the area, carrying away large portions of the
site on either side of our work area, which had fortunately
been saved from destruction by a long rise in the sand flats
that channeled the surge of the waves off to either side, where
they dug gullies right down to the semisolid beach deposits.
When the small intact area of the beach had been excavated,
there was nothing left to do but survey the remaining parts of
the beach for material that might be lying on the surface, and
write "finis" to our work in Ho'oumi.

Throughout this time, the few inhabitants of the valley had
observed our work with interest. Initially we had been the
butt of much mockery, for they could not believe that I would
find anything of value on the shore where they had spent their
childhood. Especially scornful of our projected work were
several young toughs in their late teens, representing most of
the subadult population. Sporting long sideburns and scraggly
mustaches, these boys, with an overpowering air of arrogance,

hung around the site, keeping up a stream of verbal obscenity and coarse horseplay.

Their sneers vanished when they saw the artifacts that had been hidden for so long in the sandy soil and contempt was replaced by envy. Soon the owner of the land reported to me that the people of the valley, stirred up by the reports of the boys, had approached him, angrily demanding that he charge us for each relic that we found. The boys had said we were finding too much, and obviously we were going to become wealthy selling the "treasure" back in America. Therefore, a price should be fixed on each artifact and all would profit. The landlord responded by telling the plaintiffs that he had no idea why I wanted these things but if I did and it made me happy, he was happy too, and he sent them on their way with several bluntly phrased, unmentionable suggestions.

Our audience did not thereafter diminish; more adults came around to watch, joining the boys and crowding close to see some more spectacular artifact.

When the last spade of earth had fallen back into our pits and trenches in the palm grove on Ho'oumi beach, I spent hours re-examining the collection. I had all that I was ever going to have from that site; now what could I read from the finds? Where did the ancient Ho'oumi hamlet stand in relation to the other sites?

A strong suspicion had arisen much earlier but I had to check and double-check it several times before I would accept it as a working hypothesis. Comparisons were made with other site collections, hauled out from their careful packings of excelsior and cotton wool. Even some crude statistical methods were tried, much to the amazement of the members of the household, who stood fascinated watching me go through what seemed to them endless calculations. The results of the studies were very encouraging, for they indicated that the site was probably of a very crucial period. The little hamlet on Ho'oumi beach appeared to be a bridge across a great chasm of time, linking our earlier, disconnected archaeological discoveries to some of the later sites such as the Cave of the Warrior Band or Hikoku'a.

The Ho'oumi site apparently formed the link between a very early phase of Marquesan culture (how early I still did not know), represented by Ha'atuatua, and the much later phase in which the Cave of the Warrior Band, the shelter in Ue'a, and Ha'au'a'i had been occupied probably as a result of warfare in the main valleys of the islands. Now we had a reasonably solid picture of Marquesan cultural evolution: an evolution that could be traced in reasonably clear outlines through many years of history. More radiocarbon dates were needed now, to pin this evolutionary sequence down to the yardstick of the years, so that we could measure its ebb and flow.

Not only had the loose ends of the archaeological puzzle suddenly been fitted into place, but the discovery of additional pottery had also cleared up a number of problems. We could be fairly certain that all of the pottery was Marquesan-made, from clay wrested from the thick gray beds frequently found throughout the islands. No foreign migrations had to be invoked to bring this pottery to the Marquesas. Pacific anthropologists of the old school had previously interpreted any unusual find on a Polynesian island as being the result of a special migration, refusing to grant the natives any inventiveness or skills of their own.

The crude pottery of Ho'oumi was much inferior to that found at Ha'atuatua although it was later in time, and theoretically one would suppose that some progress in the art would have taken place in the interim. Later, we knew, no pottery at all had been made by the Marquesans, who did not even possess a special word in their vocabulary for it when the whites arrived. It appeared, then, that the potter's art had simply died a languishing death in the Marquesas. Strange? No. This was precisely what had happened in many other islands in the Pacific.

The natives of islands such as the Banks Islands, Pentecost, and Malekula in Melanesia had no potterymaking tradition, yet the archaeological sites on these islands are loaded with broken pots. In Tonga the earliest sites contain the best-quality pottery, while very poor-quality sherds (or none) appear in the sites that were inhabited at the arrival of the white man. Even in Samoa, pottery had been found on a very early site, and the Samoans themselves were the most surprised of all, for there was no hint in their wealth of legends that pottery had ever been used. The reasons why pottery had been occasionally abandoned were not clear but seemed to be related to the abundance of natural containers provided by Oceanian plants. Coconuts and bottle gourds provided a ready source of durable containers in large quantity, and with a little effort a man could adze out a long-lasting wooden bowl that was of far more value than a clay pot.

Our stay in Taipi was drawing rapidly to a close: to make the proper connections with boats and planes for a return to the States, we were going to have to allow ourselves plenty of leeway. Again, we were forced into the maddening game of trying to double-guess the arrivals of the copra schooners so that we could work up to the last moment and still leave time enough to pack the bulk of material that had been gradually accumulating in the Clark storeroom. We studied all available reports from natives who were supposed to be acquainted with the erratic behavior of the important schooners and tried to correlate these "facts" with what we heard nightly on Radio Tahiti. Often a particular ship would radio to Tahiti and ask the station to broadcast a message to a certain island, informing the inhabitants of its impending arrival there. We soon learned, however, that such messages were often fakes, broadcast to beguile the competing schooners away from choice islands, so that the sender could slip in unhindered. After much deliberation, I decided that we would probably have at least three weeks left before the ship would call at Taipi to pick up all of our collections and another week or ten days before the schooner departed from Taiohae for Tahiti, on the first leg of our voyage home. If this was so, we had enough time to do some more excavating, investigate some local sites of interest, and still pack before the first schooner stop.

There were several sites that appeared to be of equally high potential for excavation, and I quickly selected one located far up the slopes of the southern wall of Taipi Valley, an ancient hamlet site consisting of a number of big megalithic platforms, grouped in a roughly rectangular plan, with old overgrown taro terraces stretching across the slopes between them. Charlie and Heiku'a, who owned the site, had found many artifacts there on the surface, including a stone figure that they had, some years earlier, given to a passing white tourist. As usual, we had permission to dissect these buildings, which were in a reasonably good state of preservation, completely. We had dug in many similar platforms on ceremonial plazas, but the opportunity for intensive exploration of a megalithic hamlet had not so far presented itself.

It seemed that, to be on the safe side, a little extra attention to the spectacular megalithic sites might give me a sounder basis for my interpretations of the age of the massive masonry. This might come in handy later on, for there were many who would not, I knew, accept my conclusions, or even my evidence on this matter.

And so, in the last weeks of our Marquesan explorations we plunged headlong into one final investigation on the lofty site of Ha'i'ie'ia, high above the valley floor, commanding a beautiful view of the narrow bay of Hanga Ha'a on one side and, on the other, of Taipi Valley, spread out before it, and twisting its way into the heart of the Nuku Hiva plateau.

This dig was well worth the effort: the stone platforms of this high-placed hamlet were crammed with artifacts of all descriptions, in contrast to the almost sterile ruins on the great ceremonial sites. The reason for this difference was to be found in the fact that the buildings on the ceremonial sites were mostly temples and used or inhabited only during important ceremonies, while the platforms of Ha'i'ie'ia had been utilized for several generations. These buildings had been the scene for the drama of daily life of a whole family or clan of Marquesans during a period far in excess of the life of one individual, and the archaeological finds in and around the structures showed this prolonged use plainly.

The excavations in the *paepae* themselves brought forth interesting facts on Marquesan housekeeping habits. The small raised dais that ran along the back of the platform had once formed the floor of the wood and thatch house that had stood on the platform. The house had been for no other purpose than to shelter the occupants at night, while they slept, and most of the surface of the *paepae* had been taken up by the wide, paved veranda, open to the elements, that was the center of family life during the day. The dais then had formed a sleeping platform on the surface of the *paepae* itself. In excavating these sleeping platforms, we found that they had also served as convenient disposal areas: they were crammed full of broken tools that the Marquesans wished to get out of the way. Most frequently found in the platforms were vegetable peelers made of cowrie shells, and pearl shell coconut graters. Hidden in the earth as they were, the tools would also have been covered by layers of sleeping mats and leaves that were used in the sleeping platform beds. They were, therefore, very well concealed.

The practice at first seemed inexplicable: why not simply throw the tools away? The stone tools were scattered about on the ground near the *paepae*, without any apparent attempt to hide them; why had these simple shell tools been hidden? Then I thought of the much-feared *nanikaha* witchcraft that was still common among the Marquesans. Objects that had been used by a person could become the vital ingredients in an enemy's spell against that person. Perhaps the broken shell tools, carefully hidden in such quantities, belonged to some special category that made them particularly good for spells, hence the great care expended on burying them in an area where they would be more or less inaccessible to an enemy.

No matter where we dug in the Ha'i'ie'ia hamlet, however, we were confronted by strong evidence of the age of that settlement—evidence in the form of European metal tools of all types. Deep in the community oven pit was an iron paint-scraping tool, probably from some whaling vessel that had once dropped anchor in Hanga Ha'a. Iron axheads and pieces of barrel staves, hammered into the shape of stone adzes, were found in most of the *paepae;* a gunsmith's tool turned up in another structure. Even in the burial of a young girl, an iron triangle used as an ornament was uncovered.

Evidently, the settlement had been inhabited for some time after the coming of the Europeans, in the late 1700's, but the first buildings on the site had perhaps been erected around A.D. 1600. This information supported in every detail that obtained at the big ceremonial sites in Taipivai and Hatiheu, again proving rather conclusively that the megalithic buildings of the ancient Marquesans were not as ancient as many had claimed.

It was with great regret that I saw the excavations at Ha'i'-ie'ia come to a close, for I knew that scarcely any time remained before we would board a copra schooner and weigh anchor for Tahiti, leaving behind the Marquesas and our numerous friends, perhaps never to return. The excavations had been exciting; every minute had been packed with the kind of stimulating problems that an archaeologist loves. Our relations with the Marquesans, so often hostile at first, had become the source of many pleasant hours, and warm friendships had developed that would not fade quickly. Nevertheless, the time had arrived and there could be no backing out. We had to leave the Marquesas then or else risk being caught in Tahiti with no means of return. Thanks to the impossibly complicated and ridiculous schedules for boats and aircraft leaving Tahiti there might, if we failed to return at once, be no other outgoing transportation for weeks. Even leaving when we planned might result in our being stranded, for we had no real assurance that we could board any of the ships or the lone flying boat: reservations were "all tied up," our Tahitian sources informed us. Actually, there was plenty of room on ships and planes alike, and the announcement of lack of room was merely part of a standard policy adopted by the ticket agents in Pape'ete, who could use it as an excuse to refuse passage to one and give it to another, in return for, shall we say, certain small cost-of-living adjustments.

Packing began: the artifacts from our excavations in Taipi-vai and Ho'oumi were wrapped in layers of old newspaper that had been specially brought from Tahiti for that purpose. They were laid away with all our work clothing, reference books, and personal equipment in the heavy cases that had been begged and borrowed and "requisitioned" from various copra schooners and trading stores. As we were finishing our packing, the gendarme arrived with the chief of the valley to oversee the sealing of our cases so that they could pass customs in Tahiti without being reopened. The tall, amiable Frenchman examined the contents of each case and stood by as the lids were nailed in place. Then with heavy twine and sealing wax he sealed each case, stamping the flaming grenade insigne of the Gendarmerie Nationale into the blobs of the red wax at various points along the string. This accomplished, he proceeded to make out a lengthy *procès verbal* attesting to the contents of the cases, stating that they contained no contraband in any shape or form and that my work had not been carried out in violation of any laws relating to antiquities. After having been exposed to a series of gendarmes who had treated us like opium smugglers or white slavers, this co-operative, friendly attitude was most refreshing. Over one of Charlie's prodigious banquets that evening, we found out some of the reason for the co-operation. Our policeman was very fond of Yanks. When on duty in the French sector of Berlin and on the Berlin Corridor checkpoint he had worked con-stantly with the carefully selected American MP's of our sector of that city. During this time he had been taught to play poker and drink Coca-Cola, he said, but he had also developed a healthy respect for the discipline and efficiency of our MP's, a compliment seldom heard in these days of "Yankee go home!" His help to us was merely a repayment for the help that he had received from some of our country-men in his own times of need, in the midst of brawls in the bars and back alleys of ruined Berlin. With his seals on our crates and his documents we should be able to clear Tahiti with no trouble, he said, acknowledging our thanks with the observation that this was, after all, only a part of his service duties that he was particularly happy to perform for us.

The boxes were sealed and carried to the copra warehouse on the wharf where our other boxes from Hatiheu had reposed safely under lock and key awaiting our departure. Charlie was going to see that the boxes were placed aboard the schooner when she called: there was no need for us to tarry longer.

We saddled up the horses one morning, loading our battered valises into sacks tied across the saddles, and said our last good-byes to the Clark family. The little children were nearly in tears, as were Heiku'a and Charlie. Awkwardly we stood for a few moments, trying to make conversation while Tunui took a last look at the saddles and cargo on the horses. One of the children had plaited a garland of flowers for Rae's hat which she presented shyly and sadly. Heiku'a, more expressive than her husband, held our hands and tried to tell us how she felt: "Whenever we sit down to a meal, we will remember the places that you had at our table and how much we enjoyed your company. You were just like our own people and we could talk to you about anything. Rae helped many people in Taipi with her medicine: they will never forget her; many people would not be alive to see you go today if it were not for her, for she healed when the doctor refused even to try. Please don't forget us, as we will always remember you with deepest love."

We walked the horses out of the courtyard for the last time into the rutted trail, and a strange silence prevailed. I looked back to see the whole family on the veranda alternately waving and wiping back their copious tears. As I looked, they turned away; Heiku'a shoved the children into the house and the rest followed quickly. Riding down the trail through the hamlet, we found many people waiting to say good-by, especially to Rae, who had really become the darling of the valley. Family after family dashed out to shake hands for the last time and then retreat with moist eyes. Finally we reached the river ford, crossed it, and started the long climb out of Taipi on the trail that would carry us through the valleys and cool plateau of Hapa'a to Taiohae and a waiting copra schooner.

11 / The Last Round

In mid-May we stepped off a Super-G Constellation at Idle-wild on a chilly, hazy morning—home at last! The trip had not been a pleasant one: the *Tiare Taporo* had been caught in a big weather system a day out of Nuku Hiva and we had ridden out four days of very rough, wet weather huddled on the deckhouse roof. In Tahiti, the local leftist party had taken over the reins of government: all of our collections had been impounded and the French governor had refused any aid for our cause. The radically anti-American faction that ruled Tahiti had decided to put a stop to this "theft of their patri-mony," as they so succinctly described my archaeological excavations. In ten days of bargaining and pleading, I had seen a succession of rather ignorant and arrogant officeholders, all of whom were exceedingly pessimistic, and at times even in-sulting.

The fight appeared to be lost until we encountered a very sympathetic and intelligent member of the ruling faction. With his aid, the collections went through customs and were put aboard a ship before my half-unbelieving eyes.

Besides the trouble with the local government, there was a great deal of difficulty over my expired passport, as no one would issue me a ticket to return to the States without the proper endorsement on this document. Further, there was the tricky problem of getting passage on a ship and co-ordinating the bimonthly flying boat flights from Tahiti with the ship's scheduled stops so that we would arrive in Fiji with barely enough time to catch the boat. Somehow—I am still not sure precisely how—all these problems were solved; we did manage to return, and I plunged into research at the museum while awaiting the arrival of the collections, which had been sent on by another ship.

The weeks flew by as I plowed through the volumes in the museum library, accumulating information from all parts of the Pacific for comparison with the Marquesan archaeological finds.

In the islands of Polynesia and Melanesia, many tools were still in use that had long been obsolete in the Marquesas, according to the reports of anthropologists and archaeologists who had worked in these areas. These reports frequently contained information that helped me to determine the uses of enigmatic tools that had appeared in the Marquesan archaeological sites. Sources of information and exciting reading were the logs and journals of the great explorers who had visited the Polynesian islands and observed the native cultures. The records left by such men as Cook, Porter, Krusenstern, and Marchand proved invaluable for background information that helped me to interpret the meaning of the finds.

In searching for comparative information one could not stop at the limits of Polynesia or Melanesia, for the Polynesians did not evolve in this area but in the regions still farther west, on the coasts of southern and southeast Asia. There was much archaeological literature available from Asia too. I was not only seeking information on the use of tools; I wanted to know whether any of the characteristic Marquesan tools appeared elsewhere in the Pacific, and if so, where. Obviously, one could never know where the Marquesans had come from if one did not know in what other islands archaeological finds similar to those found in the Marquesas had appeared. I was especially interested in determining where else the unusual ornaments, stone adzes, shell knives, and pottery that were uncovered at Ha'atuatua might be found.

Many unusual tools or objects had appeared in the Marquesan excavations: objects that looked like nothing else ever found in the Marquesas or Polynesia. Were these actually made by Marquesans or had they been brought to the islands

by foreign sailors who, either accidentally or purposely, had
ventured into the eastern Polynesian island world? Many
people had claimed that some kind of relationship existed
between the Chinese Bronze Age culture and that of the
Marquesas. I therefore consulted Chinese archaeological reports to see if any Bronze Age artifacts resembled the many
unique finds made on Nuku Hiva. Furthermore, I wanted to
collect comparative information on much more general topics.
How did various kinds of ancient temple architecture in Polynesia fit in with the religious philosophies of the natives? Was
there evidence of warfare on other islands? If so, did the
situations resemble that which had evidently arisen on Nuku
Hiva during the period when so much of the population had
sought shelter in caves in the remote reaches of the island?
How did the village plans in various Polynesian societies fit
with the social organization of these groups? Did population
growth seem to be connected with increases in warfare in
other Polynesian societies? Was the pattern of ancient Marquesan land use—the distribution of villages, temples, garden
plots, etc., in relation to geographical features—the same as
that followed on similar volcanic islands, such as Easter Island,
the Hawaiian archipelago, Samoa, and the Society groups?

This kind of research was necessary, for I was attempting
to reconstruct the entire culture of the Marquesas in as much
detail as I could. In the old days, archaeologists were interested
in the tombs and temples of ancient Egypt, Rome, Greece,
and Mesopotamia. They learned much about the great rulers
of these civilizations and the way of life of the nobles and
upper classes. The upper classes which were so carefully
studied represented, however, only a tiny percentage of the
entire population. In Egypt, for example, the pharaoh, nobles,
and priests were but the apex of the pyramid of society, the
base of which was formed by a huge mass of ordinary working people, who made possible the kind of life that the nobles
led, producing their food, building temples and tombs, serving
in the army, etc. We know next to nothing about the poor
Egyptian commoners whose way of life represented the real

Egypt, and all our images of Egyptian life have been fashioned on the evidence of the lives of the nobles and upper classes.

Suppose that archaeologists, two thousand years from now, decided that they wanted to reconstruct the ancient culture of America in A.D. 1960. How much would they find out about the real America if they spent their time excavating the ruins of the Capitol building, the Washington Monument, the Lincoln and Jefferson Memorials in Washington, D.C., and the remains of the Empire State Building, St. Patrick's Cathedral, and Yankee Stadium in what was once New York? Would they have much information about the kind of life that ordinary citizens lived? The answer is clearly "No."

And so, in recent years, recognizing the shortcomings of the old approach, archaeologists have markedly changed their tactics. To find out about a culture and its past, we must now try to reconstruct every possible detail of the ancient life of the people—not just the aristocrats, but *all* the people. For this purpose every possible bit of archaeological evidence must be obtained. The villages of the commoners, their everyday tools, the remains of their meals, all these must be studied in addition to the tombs and monuments. Objects made of rare stones or shells must be identified, and the sources determined; often these are clues to long-lost trade routes or contacts with exotic cultures important for the subsequent history of the society. Techniques and data from many other sciences such as geology, botany, and zoology are combined with the archaeological information to clarify further the often ambiguous evidence of the past.

The reason that modern archaeologists are no longer content with lists of kings, treasures, and tombs is that we believe today that archaeology must be of great *practical* value to mankind, as completely practical as any historical study. Archaeological, historical, sociological, and ethnological data, taken together, serve as excellent bases for extrapolating future events, and advancing the unified sciences of human behavior, because they add the all-important dimension of time to the view of man's present state; we are enabled to understand what man *is* by seeing what he *was*.

Without total archaeological reconstruction of cultures, our data would be of no value to modern scientists and we would be reduced to the rank of mere souvenir-hunting antiquarians, collecting "old things" because they are pretty.

My Marquesan work had been planned to yield the kind of detailed information that was needed for such reconstruction. The comparative information, abstracted from the ethnographical and archaeological reports and stored in an ever-growing collection of index cards, ensured that I would be able to make the most of all my archaeological information: knowing how other Polynesian cultures had used particular tools or how their social organization had developed would later help me to decide what had occurred in the Marquesas. I hoped that my final report would be much more than a sterile list of milestones in Marquesan technology stating in weary roundelay that, at a certain date A.D., Type X temples were built, to be superseded some years later by Type Y, and that stone adze Types 3, 4, and 5 were made at the same time, while Types 2 and 1 became obsolete.

The library research continued for several weeks; at last the day came when I watched a long train of dollies, loaded with our fourteen crates, come up from the freight elevator. They all looked sound, and without a sign of damage. The seals put on by the gendarme in Taipivai were in many cases still intact. The feeling of relief was overwhelming.

The next few days passed in a whirlwind of activity, as the crates were opened one by one, their contents carefully removed in the wooden storage trays used at the museum, and the trays loaded on handcarts to be laid out for further work in the anthropological laboratories. The artifacts were placed on long tables set up in a side hall, and the skeletons in deep trays which were stacked up to a height of seven feet outside the physical anthropology laboratory.

The skeletons were to be processed and studied by Dr. Shapiro and his assistants, and I turned to the voluminous archaeological collections to begin the final work of analysis. All artifacts that had been prepared during our work on Nuku Hiva were unpacked from their protective wrappings and sorted. Those artifacts which we had not had time to process were treated with chemical preservatives and entered in the field catalogue. Only then could the systematic analysis be begun. The first step was to work out the archaeological artifact sequences and site sequence in detail: that is, to determine which kinds of fishhooks, coral files, stone adzes, etc., were oldest, which kinds were brought to the Marquesas and which had been invented in the Marquesas. This study included not only tools but also temple, house, and ceremonial plaza buildings. All such data had to interlock and be mutually supporting. I had done much analysis in the Marquesas as work was progressing, but a final analysis was necessary to check on the accuracy of the preliminary study.

All the adzes, coral files, fishhooks, and ornaments, from all the sites, were grouped together and studied as a unit. Types of coral files, stone adzes, and hooks were defined and the distribution of each type was traced throughout the various sites that we had excavated. The types were defined and described on the basis of the characteristics of the artifacts: their shape, size, and sometimes the material of which they were made. Statistical analyses of the relative abundance of each of these artifact types in sites of successive periods showed that gradual changes took place in the culture content. Fishhooks and coral files that were very common at the earliest times gradually disappeared as time went on; they were slowly replaced by new types of hooks and files, developed by native workmen the better to fulfill their technical needs. Some types, on the other hand, were very scarce on early sites, but by the time of the whites' arrival had assumed a dominant position in the natives' tool kit.

Just as fashions and styles are born, develop, and ultimately change or die in our own society, so did they centuries ago among the Marquesans.

To know the history of these style changes as precisely as

possible was obviously very important, for we would then be able to know in what periods an archaeological site had been inhabited merely by reference to the various artifact styles and the relative percentages of each that were present.

Soon I was able to define reliably what archaeologists call "cultural assemblages" or "cultural complexes," that is, groups of artifacts that are found in the archaeological sites representing a particular time period in the prehistory of a culture. But these artifact complexes—lists of types of houses, ornaments, fishhooks, coral files, shell scrapers, etc.—represented only the skeleton of the archaeological picture. They were only the bare framework of the history of Marquesan culture, a framework that had to be fleshed out with the mass of interpretative information that had been developed. Future archaeologists, for example, may work up similar sequences for the culture of our era based on beer and milk bottle shapes, automobile models, light bulb types, and lavatory fixtures, but much would have to be added to bring forth a reasonable picture of our culture as it existed.

While these studies were going on, scientists outside the field of anthropology were at work supplying us with other evidence. Geochronologists were processing radiocarbon samples to give us reasonably precise dates for the Marquesan sequence. Samples of earth had been dispatched to pollen analysts to be examined for the remains of microscopic pollen grains from Polynesian food plants. Clay from Marquesan hillsides was being tested by X-ray diffraction techniques for its potterymaking qualities while pottery technologists examined the sherds from Ha'atuatua and Ho'oumi. Animal bones from ancient Marquesan garbage heaps were being examined, and I personally went through the samples of mollusk shells whose contents had been eaten by the Marquesans, as well as the plant and fruit remains found in the dry caves of Hapa'a and Ue'a.

The final phase of analysis began—that of interpreting and synthesizing all the data that had been accumulated through the many months of excavations, study, and research. This is

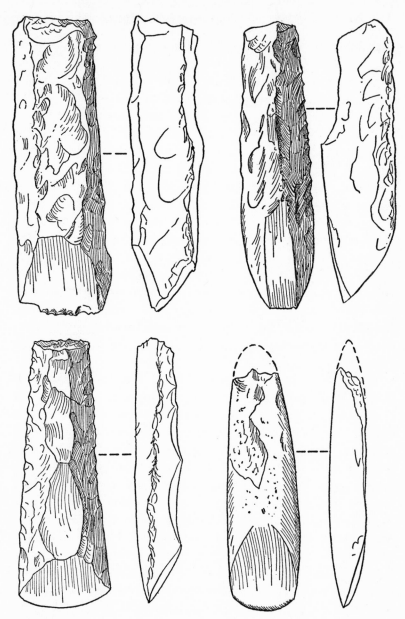

Marquesan adzes. Top, left: heavy adze used for plank finishing; right: narrow-bitted adze used for wood and stone carving. Bottom, left: quadrangular adze, common in early sites; right: adze of Melanesian type, found in earliest sites.

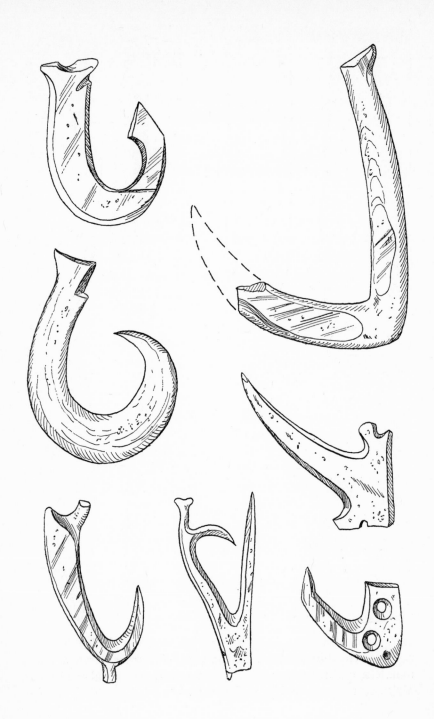

the phase that is most challenging to the archaeologist, calling for the greatest amount of conceptualization and rigorousness of thought, in the same fashion that the clues of a crime confront a detective, demanding that he make something out of them or allow the crime to go unsolved. Any scientist worth his salt loves a challenge, the more formidable the better, and the problems presented by my wealth of data on the Marquesan past were at once a joy and a source of considerable awe.

After several months of effort the data were well in my control: I could see the outlines of the development of prehistoric Marquesan society in the heterogeneous objects and bits of information that had been brought together. Radiocarbon dates had finally been obtained: they were astonishing to us, demonstrating an age for Marquesan culture far greater than had previously been supposed. With these dates we were at last able to chart the dynamics of the native culture across the span of the centuries. Marquesan history could be divided into several successive periods, each of which was characterized by features of social organization, population size and distribution, art style and technology. To each of these periods I attached a name that would serve as a handy label, a shorthand device that would also indicate the major broad characteristics of the period. At long last it was possible to sit down and describe the prehistory of this once flourishing culture of eastern Polynesia, a culture whose past had been completely buried in the dust and mist of the past, before Dr. Shapiro and I first reached the surface of a Marquesan ar-

---

Marquesan pearl shell fishhooks. Top, left: barbed hook found in Ho'oumi village; right: large hook from early village at Ha'atuatua. Middle, left: "rotating" hook, also common on Easter Island, in Hawaii, and elsewhere in Pacific; right: unusual hook point, probably made for attachment to wooden shaft. Bottom, left: hook invented by Expansion Period Marquesans; center: strange hook with barb to hold bait, from early village at Ha'atuatua; right: bonitohook point.

chaeological site in 1956. Where there had previously been
only conflicting theories based on much conjecture and little
fact, now solid, concrete evidence and a mass of facts had
been added to the sum total of man's knowledge of the past
of his own kind.

And here is the story of the "men" as we found it inscribed
in the ancient villages and temples of Nuku Hiva, spelled
out in the tallies of burials and stone adzes, shining pearl shell
fishing equipment and bleached snowy coral files that they
had left behind in their now silent valleys, beaches, and caves.

It is the history of a group of Polynesians who ventured
across unknown seas in their fleet, low-lying canoes and found
a new land, never before seen by human eyes. There, they
founded a settlement that grew into one of the most fascinating stars in the Polynesian firmament. The story spans more
than two thousand years and several thousand miles of island-
dotted sea. This story is a subplot, as it were, of one of the
greatest dramas of human history—the migration of the Polynesians. Until now, little has been known of this great achieve-
ment, but gradually we are beginning to see the ability, the
knowledge, and the courage that drove these brown navigators across the broad Pacific at a time when the great civilizations of the Mediterranean world were afraid to venture
beyond sight of land.

The hamlet of Ha'atuatua with its temple and burial ground
represents the earliest period of Marquesan culture: radiocarbon dates completed in the fall of 1958 show that this
settlement was inhabited as long ago as 120 B.C. and possibly
earlier. (Radiocarbon dates for the earliest levels of Ha'atuatua
are 2080 ± 120 years before the present and 1910 ± 120 years
before the present.) These dates place Ha'atuatua as not only
the earliest known settlement in the Marquesas, but the earliest discovered in any part of Polynesia to date.

The Ha'atuatua site has increased our time perspective in
Polynesia tremendously, demonstrating the short view of the
earlier theorists who often claimed that no island had been

inhabited for more than a thousand years at most, and that few had been inhabited as long as that.

Thanks to the ancient campfires of Ha'atuatua and their rich black charcoal, we know that the Marquesas were occupied by the second century B.C., and that therefore the western Polynesian islands must have been inhabited even earlier.

Was Ha'atuatua one of the earliest settlements in the Marquesas? We found some unusual types of stone in the site that could not have been found in the Marquesas or on any nearby island. It therefore seems fairly certain that Ha'atuatua was settled by some of the *Mayflower* Marquesans, members of the actual discovery party.

The discoverers of Nuku Hiva were no small, poorly equipped party carried to their new home by a fortuitous storm or a series of bad winds. The discovery expedition was well outfitted: prepared to establish a fully independent colony on a new island, they brought pigs and dogs in their long, sleek double canoes along with coconuts, sweet potato sets, breadfruit tree cuttings, and yam plantings for the gardens that they cleared on the grass- and shrub-covered slopes of the Nuku Hiva valleys. They also brought other kinds of plant cuttings and roots for various useful trees such as the banyan and the terminalia, as well as the pandanus and many flowering plants. There is evidence that the number of people involved was quite large, say two or three hundred at least.

This well-equipped fleet of explorers did not come from islands nearby, but all the way from western Polynesia, a distance of about fifteen hundred miles, bypassing many of the major land groups on the way. They probably followed the equatorial counter-current or the counter-trades that blow periodically through the Pacific from the northwest.

The unusual ornaments, stone adzes, pottery, and shell knives found at Ha'atuatua, when considered with the houses and other tools, indicate that the homeland of the Marquesan settlers was probably a volcanic island in western Polynesia where the culture was very similar to that in the neighboring Melanesian islands. At present, it seems that the Tonga Islands

may have been the home of our *Mayflower* Marquesans, supporting a very ancient legend that claims that the archipelago
was settled from islands with names exactly like those in the
Tonga group.

The discovery that the Marquesans arrived from the far
west upsets two theories, the first of which might be called
the "Tahitian dispersal theory." In the past, it was believed
that Tahiti, a strategically placed island, had probably been
the center from which all the islands of eastern Polynesia had
been settled by successive migrations outward in all directions. This was partially because there is good evidence that
islands closest to Tahiti have apparently been settled by expeditions from that island, as have been far-off New Zealand
and Hawaii.

The adherents of this theory had supposed that the occupation of the central band of Polynesian islands had taken
place in an orderly fashion from west to east, with Tahiti
being the last of a series of dispersion points across Polynesia.

Now, we could see that at least one archipelago had been
settled not from Tahiti but directly from western Polynesia
in a giant-step migration. Could it be possible that the Marquesas, in conjunction with Tahiti, had served as dispersion
points for the occupations of the smaller islands?

Certainly, the earliest archaeological remains from both
Hawaii and New Zealand resembled those found in Ha'atuatua
beach in very general forms only. It was clear that the Polynesian discoverers of these islands had neither come from the
Marquesas nor from the original home of the Marquesans in
western Polynesia.

The second theory that was overturned by our Marquesan
discoveries was one that was in any case not worthy of serious
attention—the *Kon-Tiki* theory. According to the well-known
adventure author Thor Heyerdahl, the highly verbal father
and proponent of the theory, all Polynesians are Peruvian Indians who drifted into the Pacific on big clumsy balsa rafts,
and there met Indians from the Canadian Northwest coast who
had paddled down in their canoes. The theory is based on a

few unconvincing and completely accidental similarities between Peruvian and Northwest coast cultures and those of the
Polynesians. Heyerdahl has never explained why no Peruvian
pottery or tools have ever appeared on Polynesian islands, how
his Peruvians managed to change their physical appearance so
radically, or how the Peruvian Indian language was replaced by
the Polynesian tongue, which is related to the languages of the
Philippines and Indonesia.

There was not a single artifact in the Ha'atuatua site that
showed even the faintest relation to any of the remarkable
prehistoric Indian cultures on the coast of Peru. Heyerdahl,
intent upon seeing "Made in Peru, by Injuns" written on
every bit of Polynesian *archaeologica*, had completely lost the
battle. Actually, there was so much in that sun-drenched site
that was completely non-Indian that by no stretch of the
imagination could it be called Peruvian-influenced. In an
earlier book, *The Island Civilizations of Polynesia*, I have
taken the trouble to dissect in detail the *Kon-Tiki* theory in
all its devious byways.

The early Marquesans probably established a series of
small colonies in the major valleys of the big islands such as
Nuku Hiva and Hiva Oa, selecting the well-watered eastern
and southern coasts for their settlement sites. In these valleys
good land was plentiful, and much room was available for
expansion of the population.

After settlement, reconnaissance of the whole archipelago
probably occurred rather quickly, while the all-important
gardens were begun and the colonists prepared to wrest a
living from the soil. This period, which I call the Settlement
Period, probably lasted from about 120 B.C. to A.D. 100, and
was a period in which the inhabitants were getting accustomed
to the peculiarities of their new environment.

Gradually the little seedling colonies took hold, and the
tenuous existence of the first decades, when gardens and
tender young trees might have been ruined by drought or
blight, was well behind the colonists. It was in this period,
called the Developmental Period, that the Marquesan society

began to build a strong economic foundation upon which the later cultural elaboration and growth was to rise.

The hamlet site of Ha'atuatua was still in use during the early part of this period, and the changes that occurred in the culture during these centuries are reflected sharply in the archaeological deposits there. (The latest occupation of the Ha'atuatua site was dated by the radiocarbon technique as being between 1090 ± 180 and 1270 ± 150 years before the present.) House style began to change, from houses with oval plans to larger rectangular houses with paved floors. Ceremonial centers began to be built—crudely, to be sure, but still ceremonial centers foreshadowing the later mammoth dance plazas built during the megalithic period. Potterymaking techniques began to degenerate: the good pottery found in the lower levels of Ha'atuatua was replaced by the crude, thick ware exemplified by the sherd recovered in the Ho'oumi beach site. A few fishhook types dropped out of use, as did some of the stone adzes, to be replaced by new varieties.

It was during the early part of this period that a group of Marquesans may have decided to wander from their homeland (which had already been inhabited for several centuries) and seek new lands, ever pushing into the rising sun. Such migrations were common in all Polynesian islands: for one reason or another, a group would decide to depart, never to be heard of again. Many found the new lands they sought, but many more did not, perishing beneath the lonely sky when their supplies ran out and their ships began to break up.

This particular migration of which we speak, however, may have resulted in the occupation of Easter Island around A.D. 350 to 400. According to legends, Easter Island was settled by a chief fleeing a defeat in war on a volcanic island to the west of Easter. The culture of the Easter Islanders up to contact period resembled that of the historic culture of the Marquesas so closely that Dr. Alfred Métraux, the French ethnologist who studied the Easter Islanders, felt that Marquesan explorers had settled the tiny volcanic island far to the southeast that subsequently came to be known as Easter Island. This opinion was reinforced by the 1957 fieldwork of a German ethnologist, Dr. Thomas Barthel, who also believes the Marquesans to have been the source of the Easter Island culture.

The culture of the Marquesan Developmental Period indicates that Easter Island was probably settled by Marquesans, for the similarities between the Ha'atuatua finds and those made on Easter Island are much closer than those evident when the two islands are compared on the basis of their nineteenth-century cultures.

The old hamlet on the Ho'oumi beach was inhabited during the latter part of this period, when houses were all being built on rectangular stone pavements and were increasing in size above that of the earlier houses of the Ha'atuatua site.

The settlements of this period were still limited to the fertile eastern and southern coasts of the main islands, where population was building up rapidly as a result of the fertility of the soil. Late in the Developmental Period, the Marquesans began to rely heavily on breadfruit as a major staple—more so than other Polynesian societies did. The cultural remains found in the old Ho'oumi beach hamlet included many breadfruit preparation implements, made of cowrie shells.

At approximately A.D. 1100 the quiet development of Marquesan culture was disrupted by what appears to have been a population explosion in the good valleys of the southern and eastern regions of the islands.

This marks the beginning of what I have called the Expansion Period, which lasted until A.D. 1400, during which nearly all of Nuku Hiva and many smaller marginal islands were probably inhabited. The best lands in the fertile valleys were evidently too small to support the rapidly growing population, and war was the result: tribes and subtribes locked in bloody conflict over the rights to garden lands and water sources. Fortresses were built in the high central plateau of Nuku Hiva at this time as the fighting became general. The marginal areas of the island—the small inaccessible valley of the west coast and the infertile regions of the east coast— were occupied by refugee groups. Caves suddenly became very popular habitations as groups sought escape from the victorious enemies who followed their flight into the hinterlands, harassing them from time to time with small raiding parties.

It was in this period that the caves of Ue'a, Ha'a'au'a'i, and Nahotoa were occupied, and probably the little island of Eïao, fifty miles north of Nuku Hiva. In the stone-littered plateau of the west coast a few small hamlets were built at approximately the same time.

Although we had originally thought the caves were inhabited for only some four hundred years, subsequent radiocarbon dates from the bottom of the Ue'a sites showed that they had first been used seven hundred or more years ago.

The beach site in Ha'ata'ive'a Valley where the quarrymen made their homes had been inhabited during this period, but only by fishermen, for the stone deposits of that lonely valley were not yet being used for statues and building.

During this period, about A.D. 1200 to 1300, more migrations may have taken place from the Marquesan archipelago. The refugee groups certainly did not all find shelter in the fastness of the interior or in secluded valleys. Some obviously took to the sea to search for new uninhabited islands, following the time-honored pattern that finally resulted in the settlement of much of Polynesia.

Legends from the island of Raroia, four hundred and fifty miles away from the Marquesas, indicate that it was inhabited about A.D. 1250 by a chieftain called Taneariki, fleeing defeat on an island to the east called Hiva Nui. Could this have been Nuku Hiva's original name? The archaeological evidence of warfare in the Marquesas certainly ties in well with the legend and its date.

Another legend, this time from the island of Mangareva, indicated that Marquesan navigators may have reached that area by A.D. 1275 and settled the island. It is very interesting that the Mangarevan archaeological remains, as uncovered in recent excavations by Dr. Roger Green of Harvard, resemble those of the Developmental Period in the Marquesas.

Houses began to become more elaborate during this period in the Marquesas, and the first hints of the later megalithic platform house design are seen in rectangular stone pavements with very slightly raised sleeping steps across the back.

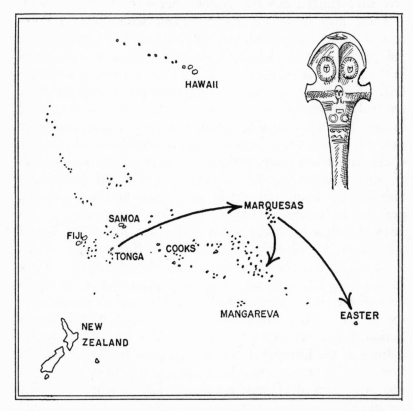

Marquesan travels. Originally from Tonga or Samoa, Marquesans settled their present islands, then sent out colonization parties that discovered and settled Easter Island and Mangareva.

Ceremonial plazas were growing in size and number as the population continued to increase to the limits of the arable land. It was during this period that the early phases of construction had been completed on Hikoku'a, Vahangeku'a, Te'ivi'ohou, Tepakeho, and Te'uhi'atea. These early plazas had been small dance plazas, often merely outlined on uneven ground by rows of stones, later laid out on small terraces, with a few houses built around a small dance plaza.

On the cool plateaus, trenches and breastworks were cut into lofty ridges and peaks, while stout log palisades were erected: fortifications were becoming necessary.

There may have been some contact with Tahitian Polynesians during this period, but it is very uncertain. Some stone poi pestles that display Tahitian characteristics were found in the Marquesas on sites of this period, but as we know very little of Tahitian archaeology we cannot say whether these are truly imports from Tahiti or whether the style originated in the Marquesas and was exported to Tahiti. It seems highly probable that contact between the Tahitians and Marquesans could have taken place, perhaps on the sparkling white sands of some Tuamotu atoll, for both Tahitians and Marquesans visited these islands to obtain pearl shell in the prehistoric period. The Tahitians were aware of the existence and approximate location of Nuku Hiva and other Marquesas islands when Captain Cook arrived in Tahiti on the *Endeavour*.

At the end of the Expansion Period the Marquesan culture bloomed rapidly into the colorful pageant that greeted the eyes of the first European explorers. This period, lasting until the arrival of the whites in 1790, is known as the Classic Period, for it represents the full development of Marquesan culture as the Europeans saw it. Within a few centuries, the low house pavements had been replaced by towering *paepae* platforms formed of huge rocks carefully matched and piled together.

Huge ceremonial plazas such as those represented by the final construction periods of Vahangeku'a, Te'ivi'ohou, and Hikoku'a were built through the combined efforts of entire tribes, working for months under the watchful eyes of chiefs and priests, carrying earth and dragging huge stones.

Other megalithic architecture sites of this period which we had investigated were the later hamlet on the Ho'oumi beach and the temple in Taipivai.

Megalithic architecture was the hallmark of this period, as

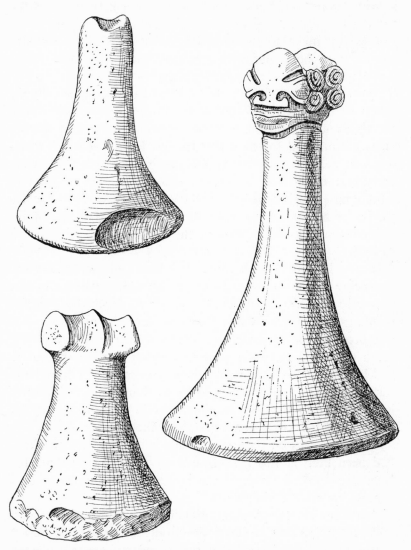

Marquesan stone poi pounders. Upper left: phallic variety found in early Classic sites. Lower left: possible prehistoric Tahitian trade item. Right: Classic *tiki*-head poi pounder.

massive stone buildings sprang up everywhere, throughout the deep valleys. New kinds of religious structures were developed by the Marquesans at this time, such as the red slab platforms to hold sacrificial buildings and other, less important platforms around the ceremonial plazas.

A mania for rebuilding also appeared at this time, for the massive stone structures seem to have been undergoing continual remodeling and renovating or being torn down to provide raw material for bigger platforms. Even the *tohua* themselves appear to have been frequently remodeled, at what great cost of labor it is impossible to guess. These spurts of rebuilding probably marked the accession of a new chief to the leadership of a tribe and were carried on as a part of the tribal ceremonies leading up to the formal recognition of his authority.

It was late in the Classic Period that stone sculpture and quarrying came to be developed. All the evidence of the relatively late dating of the stone statues and the cut slab buildings on Hikoku'a and Vahangeku'a had not been misinterpreted. The radiocarbon date from the campfire beneath the adze quarry site gave final proof of that: the quarry had been used less than two hundred years ago! The red tuff statues and the great oblong slabs used in building appeared in this light as the last developments in Marquesan art and architecture before the coming of the whites.

The platforms on the quarrymen's house site in Ha'ata'ive'a had been built at this period also, for until then the site had been used only by fishing parties that used the bay's good fishing grounds occasionally.

The peculiar, goggle-faced *tiki* figure with its open mouth and protruding tongue also appears only in the Classic Period. Those who have claimed that the figure represents a connection between the Marquesan culture and the Chinese Bronze Age are mistaken, for this kind of statue evolved in the Marquesas by a gradual process of elaboration from some of the motifs that the Marquesan settlers had so thoughtfully scratched in the rocks of the Ha'atuatua river bed for us to see two thousand years later. The little stick-figure men, the pigs, dogs, and fishes that we saw graven on the rocks in Ha'atuatua, along with a simple face or skull motif, made up the major features in the early Marquesan design vocabulary. Later, these motifs were elaborated, altered, worked into new combinations. From this process of evolution came the grinning *tiki* of the Classic Period carved in the living red stone of the Marquesas.

It was clear that the Marquesan art style which was so popular with primitive art collectors had developed during the last century or so before the arrival of the Europeans.

The highly polished and beautifully carved war clubs, bowls, and ornaments of the nineteenth century bore very distinctive designs, but these designs appeared only on the very latest of megalithic sites, on petroglyphs and in statuary: earlier sites show no such elaborate art. In the dry caves of Nahotoa and Ue'a Valley there was not one scrap of decoratively carved wood, indicating that much of the elaborate woodcarving had also been produced very close to the time of European contact.

It seemed certain that the nineteenth-century art of the Marquesas Islanders had developed in those islands and had not been carried from the Bronze Age cultures of China long ago, for it appeared on Nuku Hiva when the Chinese Bronze Age had been dead for two thousand years.

The warfare of the Expansion Period had not ceased by any means: if anything, it itensified itself during the Classic Period. The population had by now reached a maximum of between 100,000 and 150,000, on seven islands, with 30,000 to 35,000 on Nuku Hiva alone. All habitable land was taken, and fights were necessary to hold off one's competitors from choice garden spots. Warfare was also undertaken as a means of gaining personal prestige for men, as the culture allowed this line of manly endeavor to remain open to all comers.

Settlements were seldom built on the beaches during this period. They were more frequently clustered deep in the interior of valleys where enemy raiding parties could not

easily penetrate. Houses on the beach only invited the raiding
parties that slipped in and out of the bays at night in hopes
of catching fishermen or shellfish-collecting parties and carrying them off for sacrifice.

It was onto this stage that the Europeans intruded first in
the sixteenth century for a brief time and then in 1790, to
remain more or less permanently. From 1790 on, the broken
wine bottles and rusting iron tools mix with the pearl shell
fishhooks and the stone adzes and coral files around the
megalithic sites, presaging the frightening end that was just
over the horizon for the Marquesans and their culture.

In the years that followed, the Europeans, as I have described in an earlier chapter, lost no time in planting the seeds
of destruction that were to bring about the collapse of the
native culture within one short century, and the virtual death
of a way of life that had been followed for two thousand
years and more—a way of life that had sustained the Marquesans in their search for their present island home, and had helped
them found one of the most fascinating cultures of Polynesia. This way of life was adequate for all their needs but,
alas, was anathema to their Christian conquerors, and was
therefore doomed to die.

And so we were able to pierce the veil of years, and reach
back into the past to lay bare the record of an interesting
people. In doing so, human knowledge has been advanced,
but as usual, for every problem solved, several new ones
arise, to face the present and future archaeologists who will
delve into the Polynesian past. For example, now that we have
worked out the archaeology of the Marquesan group in broad
detail, on the basis of excavations on Nuku Hiva and survey
on the other islands, it remains for others to investigate the
archaeological picture of each island in the Marquesan archipelago to trace the development of the regional variations
in culture that were evident at the time of the coming of the
whites.

Furthermore, an intensive search must be carried on for

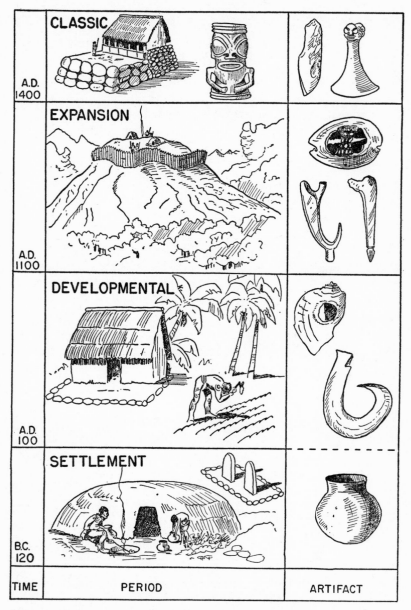

Schematic chart of Marquesan prehistory, showing characteristic kinds of artifacts and structures for each period.

additional evidence of contact with Tahiti, of which we found such ambiguous traces. More sites of the Developmental Period, still the most incompletely known, must be excavated in order to trace the cultural evolution that occurred in that important period of Marquesan history.

Now that the characteristic artifacts, houses, and art styles of each of the Marquesan periods have been identified it will be possible to carry on very informative surface surveys charting the location of all sites of each major period on topographical maps, thus obtaining a three-dimensional picture of the Marquesan pattern of land use from earliest to latest times, a task that would be most exhausting but extremely rewarding.

Before 1956, very little archaeology had been done in any of the Polynesian islands, the exceptions being Hawaii and New Zealand, where very extensive archaeological investigations have provided a wealth of ancient artifacts.

Now, however, Polynesian archaeology has received a new impetus: when we were working in the Marquesas the Norwegian Expedition was winding up a year in the Pacific in which archaeological excavations had been made on Easter Island, Rapa Iti, and Pitcairn, even touching at the Marquesas briefly, after our arrival.

In 1957, John Golson of Auckland University conducted excavations in Tonga and Samoa with outstanding results, uncovering an early site with pottery in Samoa and exciting Melanesian pottery in Tonga. Last year Roger Green of Harvard excavated on Mangareva, that supposed splinter off the Marquesan trunk, and then went on to excavate in Tahiti and Moeréa. Recently Drs. Kenneth Emory and Yoshiko Sinoto of the Bishop Museum have also investigated the archaeology of the Society Islands.

With the publication of the reports of these expeditons, we will see our Marquesan work in a new light and problems now hidden from view will mushroom up beneath our noses, indicating new untried avenues of approach in the fascinating archaeological detective game of tracking the migrations of the sturdy mariners of thousands of years past—the Polynesians. This constant opening of new vistas for scientific research and exploration is perhaps the most exciting part of science in general, for the quest is always on and no sooner is a goal attained than another looms from afar.

12 / A Backward Glance

It is three years now since I watched the shores of Nuku Hiva recede in the gloom of a midnight tropical squall, but despite the distance, the Marquesas and their people are by no means out of reach. The mailman frequently brings light blue air-mail envelopes marked with the colorful stamps of French Polynesia, bearing our address in a quaint scrawl. Inside, on a sheet of cheap ruled paper, are the greetings of our distant friends, written in their own language, bringing me the *tekao hou*, literally the "new talk," from Nuku Hiva and environs.

To Robert and Rae: Greetings to the two of you with your baby. Your letter came and we read it. We miss you very much and want to see you once more. Here is the news from Taipivai: the tidal wave was strong when it hit us here. The sea rose very close to our house and carried off our copra shed, our canoe and launch . . . we heard by the radio that the war between America and Russia is very near and we felt great pity for you. Perhaps we will never meet again. The end of our discourse to you has come. We kiss you and the baby and send our love on this, our meeting by letter . . . may God watch over you—

Written by Hu'uveu and Heiku'a

Each month a few such letters arrive, from Taniha, Tunui, Pauro, and the others who are able to write their language. Corpse Eyes, master of the spoken word, is paradoxically enough illiterate and sends his regards through the media of his neighbors' pens.

The news is sometimes good: So-and-so was blessed with twins; a young girl gets a scholarship to Tahiti; a new and capable doctor arrives, and so on. On other occasions the news has been bad: In November, 1959, our dear friend Charlie died in the arms of his beloved Heiku'a, a victim of throat cancer that had slowly eaten into his robust form.

But still life goes on in Nuku Hiva, and the processes of culture change are constantly at work as the new advancements of the Western world gradually filter into the Pacific and are adopted by the natives. The Marquesas would not be exactly the same today as when I left it in 1958, nor was it unchanged when I returned in 1957 after only a year's absence. Gradually, from the wreckage of a pagan civilization, a new Marquesas is taking form, and sometime, not this year or perhaps not even for fifty years, the men of Nuku Hiva will walk again with their heads held high.